JEAN
RENOIR
INTERVIEWS

EDITED BY BERT CARDULLO

UNIVERSITY PRESS OF MISSISSIPPI / JACKSON

www.upress.state.ms.us

The University Press of Mississippi is a member of
the Association of American University Presses.

Manufactured in the United States of America

First edition 2005

∞

Library of Congress Cataloging-in-Publication Data

Jean Renoir: interviews / edited by Bert Cardullo.— 1st ed.
   p. cm. — (Conversations with filmmakers series)
   Includes filmography and index.
   ISBN 1-57806-730-8 (cloth : alk. paper) — ISBN 1-57806-731-6
(pbk. : alk. paper)
   1. Renoir, Jean, 1894– —Interviews. 2. Motion picture producers
and directors—France—Interviews. I. Cardullo, Bert. II. Series.

PN1998.3.R46A3   2005
791.4302′33′092—dc22   2004061169

British Library Cataloging-in-Publication Data available

CONTENTS

INTRODUCTION

Jean Renoir (1894–1979) completed his thirty-ninth motion picture, *The Little Theatre of Jean Renoir*, in 1970. His first film, *The Water Girl*, was made in 1924 during the silent era. What comes between is perhaps the most impressive body of filmmaking ever directed by one person. But, before any consideration of the length or quality of Renoir's career, one must first consider the length of his life—of *his* life, not just anyone who happens to survive for eighty-four years—because it gave him a unique place that would affect his art.

Jean Renoir connected *La Belle Époque*—from his equally famous father, the painter Auguste—to the last quarter of the twentieth century. And this made him an exponent of a view of art that doesn't promise to be generated again, and that the director amply elucidates in his 1960 interview with Gideon Bachmann: art as community, from which one can make every bitter expedition into blackness, as Renoir certainly did, but whose communal nature supports the expedition and strengthens its unsentimental insistence. Renoir, then, was the film world's first, and perhaps last, great embracer: a loving man who saw clearly what it was that he was loving. This characterization of him is made manifest throughout *Jean Renoir: Interviews*, which assembles a number of (but by no means all) the interviews he gave from 1954 to 1975.

No one knows better than Renoir did, for example, that films cost money and that it would be foolish to think that movies are produced for purely artistic reasons. The cinema, after all, is a business that has to sell, so considerations other than the aesthetic must come into play. Yet with outsized geniality Renoir found a way to co-opt this condition, as he would tell Charles Thomas Samuels in *Encountering Directors* in 1972: "Noncommercial films are rarely good. When you make a film just for yourself, the chances are high that it won't be a good one. . . . My ambition was to belong even more than I did to the world of commercial films. I believe in professionalism. I may sometimes have been stopped from making a film by a producer, but once shooting started, I was always free." His only objection to producers is that they want to make what they call good films, while he wants to "bring in a little piece of humanity."

Any director who could reach such a formulation in the face of experience (for instance, he couldn't raise the money for *Grand Illusion* [1937] until Jean Gabin agreed to be in it) has arranged a pleasant state of mind for himself—in fact, one through which that "little piece of humanity" is more likely to be permitted. Whatever the blandishments Renoir had to practice on others and himself, the results of his tactics lie before us: a body of films that range widely in subject (more widely than is generally assumed) and in quality (more widely than is generally assumed), but are in the main informed with the spirit coursing through these interviews—broad and high, generous and compassionate, always humanistically concerned. Of course he repeats himself, and some pronouncements that he delivers from a throne to which others had elevated him are not free of airy affectation. Still, the current of his talk is so full, knowing, and free-flowing that perhaps these interviews, plus all the others he gave elsewhere, explain why his autobiography, *My Life and My Films* (1974), is meager: he had already said most of it before.

How, indeed, Renoir loved to talk! And that talk brings us riches of more than one kind. As when he speaks—to Jacques Rivette and François Truffaut in *Cahiers du cinéma* in 1954—about how he depends on collaboration as part of creation, how he folds it into his work: "It's difficult to be sincere when you're all alone. Some people manage to do it, and they are gifted writers. I'm much less gifted, and I can only really find my own expression when I'm in contact with others." This is a compact description of the perfect filmmaking temperament—one that, in Renoir's case, usually led to his collaboration on screenplays, for which he usually originated the ideas himself. Such a remark, like many others in the interviews to follow, typifies an artist's purposely transparent practicality as proof of his profound suitability for his art, in which, like a judo expert, he would frequently be called upon to turn the pressures of brute filmmaking against themselves.

Here are other samples of this director's aesthetic wisdom, on subjects that recur throughout *Jean Renoir: Interviews*. On the technical ease versus difficulty of filmmaking, he had this to say to Rui Nogueira and François Truchaud in *Sight and Sound* in 1968:

> When I started to make films we really had to know what a camera is; we had constantly to know what was going on. The technical dangers are bigger today because technique is perfect, and perfection is terribly dangerous in this world. . . . With the perfection of technique, all the solutions are brought to you, anything you want. . . . The danger is that of finding yourself confronted with answers which are not your own, answers you didn't have to work, to use your imagination, to find. Now that technique is perfect, you must become a great technician and then forget about technique. But first you must become a great technician.

Renoir spoke further on the deification—and subversion—of technique in a 1958 interview with André Bazin in *France Observateur*:

> In the cinema at present the camera has become a sort of god. You have a camera, fixed on its tripod or crane, which is just like a heathen altar; around it are the high priests—the director, cameraman, assistants—who bring victims before the camera, like burnt offerings, then cast them into the flames. And the camera is there, immobile—or almost so—and when it does move, it follows patterns ordained by the high priests, not by the victims.
>
> Now . . . the camera finally has only one right—that of recording what happens. That's all. I don't want the movements of the actors to be determined by the camera, but the movements of the camera to be determined by the actor. . . . It is the cameraman's duty to make it possible for us to see the spectacle, rather than the duty of the spectacle to take place for the benefit of the camera.

Renoir acted in some of his "spectacles" and, truth be told, one negative feature common to all his pictures (aside from straggling or muddling storylines that lose themselves in a wealth of incident, as in the case of *The Lower Depths* [1936]) is the maddeningly erratic level of their acting. The director gave a possible reason for this unevenness of performance in his 1970, American Film Institute interview with James Blue: "I am very bad at casting. I am very bad, and sometimes to be bad helps me. In the way that I am attracted by a certain innocence. I am afraid of clichés, tricks. I am afraid of repeating situations we already saw on the screen. People with not too much skill sometimes help me to keep a kind of—I use a very ambitious word, excuse me—to keep a kind of innocence."

Flawed or not, the actor's expression distinguishes the style of a Renoir film. Structured improvisation, allowing the performers *to be themselves as others*, determines how the other elements of the picture will be created. For this is a man who believed that one discovers the content of a film only in the process of making it, and who insisted that his completed pictures have often turned out to be something quite different from what he had originally intended. So much so that it is difficult to associate with Jean Renoir a particular narrative style or tone. Unlike Marcel Carné, who threw over anything he touched a fog of atmospheric fatalism (*Bizarre Bizarre* [1937] honorably excepted), unlike René Clair, whose *Italian Straw Hat* (1927) is discernible in *The Grand Maneuver* (1955), and whose *Le Million* (1931) occasionally breaks through the more ponderous *Beauties of the Night* (1952), Renoir speaks in many voices.

And the fact that his "voice," whatever it may be, is finally translated, interpreted, or expressed by the actor, is made clear in the following analysis of realism, which the director supplied during his extended conversation with Charles Thomas Samuels:

> The word "neorealism" implies a certain style that may not have anything to do with reality. Consider an eighteenth-century play in the style of *commedia dell'arte* and then a modern play or picture about a railroad. In the latter, the actors will wear real grease on their faces, and their hands will be dirty; but if they are hams, they will be hams. If the actor who plays the eighteenth-century shepherd is good and has been helped by a good director, however, he will be convincing and real, even though he is not a shepherd and isn't even authentically dressed like one.

That theater actor, in an eighteenth-century play, would be helped not only by a good director (Renoir preferred the term *"meneur du jeu,"* which might be translated as "master of revels" and has fewer connotations of rigid control). This performer would also be helped by the theater itself, as Renoir explained to Louis Marcorelles in *Sight and Sound* in 1962:

> In the theatre there is greater freedom because there is discipline. The awful thing about the cinema is the possibility of moving about exactly as one wants. You say, "Well, I must explain this emotion, and I'll do it by going into flashback and showing you what happened to this man when he was two years old." It's very convenient, of course, but it's also enfeebling. If you have to make the emotion understood simply through his behavior, then the discipline brings a kind of freedom with it. There's really no freedom without discipline, because without it one falls back on the disciplines one constructs for oneself, and they are really formidable. It's much better if the restraints are imposed from the outside.

On a related subject, the one for which he is aesthetically most noted, the use of theatrical ideas of space in motion pictures—of nearly abolishing the border between the screen and the stage through full shots, deep focus, long takes, and camera movement within a scene in place of cutting—Renoir makes clear in these collected interviews that the day sound was ushered into the cinema, film artists were forced to accept certain rules of the theater. "Certain" is the operative term here, however, not "all," for, as Renoir pointed out to Charles Thomas Samuels, there is something in particular that renders spoken dialogue in a film "cinematic" rather than "theatrical": "The accompaniment of a close-up. People underestimate the importance of close-ups in film. It brings the actor closer to the audience, and it makes each spectator feel that the performance is directed at him alone. It makes you forget the crowd, as you do not forget it in a theater."

That "crowd" nonetheless consists of any number of ideal viewers, would-be filmmakers, as it were, who make their own movies—in their minds—even as they watch other people's. Thus, Renoir explained to Joan and Robert Franklin of the Columbia University Oral History Project in 1960,

> A picture must not be the work only of an author or of actors and technicians; it must be also the work of the audience. The audience makes the

picture, as well as the authors; and it seems to be strange, because you could ask me how the audience can make a picture which is already shot, done, printed. Well, a picture is different with every type of audience, and if you have a good audience, the picture is better. It is a mystery, but we are surrounded by mysteries. . . . I have nothing against that. I believe in it.

Still, this audience, according to Renoir in his 1954 conversation with Jacques Rivette and François Truffaut, has lost the use of its senses in the almost sixty years since the invention of cinema. "This is due," he declared, "to what we call progress. Note that it's normal for them to have lost the use of their senses: We turn a button and we have light, we push another button, and we have a flame on a gas range. Our contact with nature takes place through so many intermediaries that we have almost completely forgotten how to feel natural things directly. We can therefore say that people don't see very much now." Renoir here is discussing visual perception in terms of color versus black-and-white film, and he argues for a color cinematography that "sees things clearly" where the spectator cannot.

He even seems to argue for a cinematography that sees things for the very first time, as in this passage from the 1960 interview with Gideon Bachmann in *Contact*: "You know my old theory of nature—that it follows the artist. I believe that nature is something vague, almost nonexistent. I am not sure that the sky is blue and the trees are green. Probably the sky and the trees have no color, just a kind of indefinite gray, and I believe that God gave man the ability to finish the job. In other words, if man truly wants to exist, he must collaborate with God in the shaping of nature." Such comments as these, it should be clear by now, are a long way from the pretentious or banal mutterings of most film-journal interviews, let alone the silence of many filmmakers, who as a group aren't particularly disposed to speak for the record about their work, preferring instead to let the movies themselves communicate method, philosophy, and intention to the audience.

Jean Renoir was one of the exceptions to the above rule. He had what seemed to be total recall of the conditions of production for all his films, and he could be quite specific about his aims and strategies. The interviews in *Jean Renoir: Interviews* as a whole disclose a candid, cultivated, and unselfish man, genuinely and also slyly self-critical, imaginative yet sometimes merely fanciful, at all times a source of beaming warmth. Soon the suspicion grows that Renoir saw these interviews—*all* his interviews—as components of his career. He was not greatly guileful, but neither was he too naïve to know the sort of persona he had; and he knew that to make that persona as present as possible would only make his films more resonant. As André S. Labarthe wrote in the *Cahiers du cinéma* of January 1967, "Renoir doesn't *converse* at all. He doesn't try to convince his interlocutor, but rather, he tries to *overwhelm* him—not only with an argument, but also, even largely, with his personality."

The interviews with Renoir in this volume span several decades, during which one can sense his ideas evolving and ripening. He had a love for paradox as well as a strong Cartesian streak. Hence the text is full of his playing with ideas, developing them, putting them into conjunction and counterpoint, even ordering his replies in such a way that, frequently, they provoke as well as inform. From time to time, in fact, Renoir will reply to the interviewer with a response not to the question that was asked, but rather to the question that *should* have been asked. All this he does, to be sure, with grace, good will, wit, immense style, and intrinsic passion.

Renoir kept up this process for so long that, by now, those who knew him feel that the man reflected the films and vice versa. This is not true of other book-length interviews with first-rank directors—Alfred Hitchcock interviewed by Truffaut (one of Renoir's interlocutors in the present volume), for example, or Ingmar Bergman interviewed by Björkman, Manns, and Sima. Hitchcock's interview provides fascinating information about the making of his movies, but no one except a specialist need read it in order to enjoy those pictures. Bergman's book, intellectually the superior of the three, can be read with profit by any cultivated person who never saw, or never cares to see, his films. But these conversations with Renoir seem almost synergistic with his work. Obviously, they need not be read in order to enjoy the films; obviously, too, once read, they seem essential.

This is dangerous. A persona has been adduced from Renoir's films; then its re-enforcement by these and other interviews makes the persona so seductive that it can blur judgment of the films themselves. I have no intent in the emperor's-new-clothes vein with these remarks: Jean Renoir is inarguably one of the great figures in film history. Still, not all his movies are of equal interest (despite some books about his work that maintain the opposite). But seeing many of them again, as I did recently, abundantly confirms his directorial distinction and personal flavor. That incorrigible charmer, Renoir himself, will, rightly, have the last word on his life and work: because of the length and variety of his career, the huge influence he has had on other filmmakers, and because his persona, preserved in these interviews and inferable anyway from his films, is like a guardian angel against even sympathetic criticism.

The man or the persona and his longevity-cum-loquaciousness aside for the moment, Renoir's career, it must be remarked, encompasses a history of change in film style. His most celebrated stylistic hallmark, as I noted earlier, was the ingestion into cinematic syntax of theatrical "place," composition, and—as possible—duration: the combination, that is, of the flow of cinema with the relationships within a frame that are standard practice in the theater. The basis of this style is deep-focus shooting combined with the "sequence shot"—i.e., the shot that contains a sequence of action. In the deep-focus approach, the reliance is on the content of any one shot, rather than on a succession of shots as in montage. The shot is held and people may come in or leave; the camera itself may move (as Renoir's often adroitly does): it's the absence of cutting that makes the difference, the exploitation of different planes of depth within one shot to make the film progress, rather than the addition of new views.

Renoir didn't invent this idea—you can see the conscious, deliberate use of it in Edwin S. Porter's *The Great Train Robbery* (1903) in the scene where the posse captures the bandits—but he used it as a principle, a reaction against the principle of montage that had been dominant since D. W. Griffith (who was quickly followed in this approach by Eisenstein and Pudovkin). To many, the idea of composition in depth was a philosophical position. André Bazin, who *mutatis mutandis* was Aristotle to Renoir's Sophocles, said that such a cinematic style was capable of expressing everything without fragmenting the world, of revealing the hidden meaning in people, places, and things without disturbing the unity natural to them. (Montage, by contrast, relies on joining bits and pieces of film together in rhythmic and pictorial relationships so that an effect is created out of the very way the pieces are joined, an effect additional to the effects of the separate bits unto themselves.)

Renoir's own rationale for his camera style was his belief in the primacy of the actor as focus of cinematic interest and source of inspiration. My own view is that Renoir was at least partially motivated by sheer confidence, in himself and in film. He felt that the (still-young) film medium no longer needed to prove its selfhood by relying so heavily on a technique that no other art could employ. The cinema could now be sure enough of itself to translate into its own language a lexicon from another art, the theater. Indeed, Renoir went on to include literal theatrical imagery in his films, from *La Chienne* (1931) to his last one, which was actually titled *The Little Theatre of Jean Renoir*. And, in the 1950s, he directed three plays, Shakespeare's *Julius Caesar*, a comedy of his own, and Odets's *The Big Knife*. (*Jean Renoir: Interviews* includes Virginia Maynard's account of Renoir's rehearsal, in 1960, for the world première of his play *Carola* at the University of California, Berkeley.)

It is mainly because of his theater-in-film style (though there are other reasons) that Renoir had such an enormous influence on subsequent filmmakers: the Italian neorealists (perhaps above all Luchino Visconti, who had worked as Renoir's assistant on *Toni* [1935] and several other pictures), Orson Welles, Satyajit Ray, and François Truffaut, to name a few outstanding examples. As for Renoir's own films, along with the theater, nature (often in the form of water, "nature's bloodstream") is a primary motif. At what I consider his height—*Grand Illusion*, which acolytes rank lower apparently because it's widely admired, and *The Rules of the Game* (1939), in which Renoir himself plays a leading role as Octave—he added first-magnitude stars to the cinema sky: unshakable, time-proof masterpieces on the collective subjects of class, war, friendship, and societal structure. Other films of his have beauties that only he could have given them: for instances, *Boudu Saved from Drowning* (1932), *The Crime of Monsieur Lange* (1935), *The River* (1950), and *The Human Beast* (1938).

Underlying all his work, however, there is a complex of conflicting emotions—of ambiguities, tensions, and uncertainties—which makes every Renoir picture rewarding on re-viewing. From the innate contradictions within his own psyche, he created movies that, whatever the individual weaknesses of some of them, seem to breathe life. Not that

Renoir himself ever made such a claim. As he says more than once in *Jean Renoir: Interviews*, it is presumptuous of any director to suggest that he is presenting real life on the screen, for reality is always bigger, more amusing, and more audacious than any artistic invention. Nonetheless, few other directors have succeeded in conveying so intensely a sense of messy, turbulent, unstructured reality in the cinema.

Perhaps this is because of still another paradox or tension in Renoir's aesthetic self: for he was the prime exponent on film of unanism, the poetic movement in early twentieth-century France that reacted against art for art's sake and sought its sources in the lived life around it—yet without returning to pseudo-scientific naturalism and without any attempt at overt "social significance." Six hundred years of Renaissance humanism, predictably ripening to decline, found a film elegist, then, in this Frenchman born and nourished at its center, the son of a painter who had given *La Belle Époque* some of its sensual loveliness. Yet Renoir himself did not paint with large canvases. His pictures have a modesty or lack of pretension, not to speak of their fluctuating subject matter, which is disarming and occasionally conceals the true depth of his work.

From the extraordinary diversity of his material, in fact, one might jump to the conclusion that Renoir worked, John Huston–like, as an adaptor, occasionally revealing by chance glimpses of himself but choosing his subjects without system from whatever happened to be offered at the time. But such a hastily formed judgment does great injustice to his stature as an artist in his own right. For, while frequently drawing upon other people's work for the bases of his films, Renoir always interpreted their art through his own feeling. As he told Gideon Bachmann, "Shakespeare took his themes in some cases from the cheapest Italian fiction—stories that were quite banal, nothing really. But he made them great because of his own constant communion with the world of which he was a part."

Like Renoir himself. Through his acceptance and even admiration of what is and not what ought to be, in his consistent understanding of the importance of the continuity of life and tradition, in his steadfast refusal to compromise humility with sentimentality, Jean Renoir became one of the few persons of the cinema to attain the status of artist. His imagination was his intelligence: subtle, immensely complex, prophetic, transparently stylish, astonishingly lucid, and always eager to engage, to converse. The world view of this artist, as well as the ethos behind his art, can best be summed up in this complex yet transparent remark by Octave from that filmic combination of comedy, tragedy, realism, impressionism, melodrama, and farce known as *The Rules of the Game* (itself derived from Musset's *The Follies of Marianne*, inspired by Marivaux's *The Game of Love and Chance*, and prefaced by a quotation from Beaumarchais's *The Marriage of Figaro*): "You know, in this world there's one thing that is terrible, and that is that everyone has his reasons."

BC

CHRONOLOGY

1894	Born 15 September in Montmartre, Paris, the second of three sons of the Impressionist painter Auguste Renoir and his wife, Aline (née Charigot).
1902	Education, Collège de Saint-Croix, Neuilly-sur-Seine.
1903	Education, École Sainte-Marie de Monceau.
1904–1912	Education, École Masséna, Nice.
1913	Baccalauréat in mathematics and philosophy at the University of Aix-en-Provence.
1914–1915	Serves as a second lieutenant with the French Alpine cavalry during World War I. Wounded twice; a bullet in the thighbone leaves him with a permanent slight limp.
1916	Transferred to the French Flying Corps.
1918	Demobilized at the rank of full lieutenant.
1919	Death of his father, Auguste Renoir, on 3 December.
1920	On 24 January marries his father's model Andrée Madeleine Heuschling (Dédée, who took the name Catherine Hessling following her 1924 appearance in the first film written and produced by Renoir, *Catherine*).
1920–1923	Works as a potter and ceramicist.
1921	Only child, a son (Alain), born to Catherine Hessling and Jean Renoir.
1924	Directs first film, *La Fille de l'eau*.
1930	Divorced from Catherine Hessling.
1931	Makes his first sound film, *On purge bébé*.

1935–1940	Lives with Marguerite Mathieu, a film editor, who becomes known as Marguerite Renoir even though the director never married her.
1936	Prix Louis Delluc, for *Les Bas-Fonds*. Contributes regularly to the French Communist Party journal *Ce Soir* and the antifascist *Commune;* also acts as artistic advisor to the left-wing theater organization known as Théâtre de la Liberté.
1937	International Jury Cup, Venice Biennale, for *La Grande illusion*.
1939	Joins Service Cinématographique de l'Armée. *La Règle du jeu* banned by the French government. Spends much of 1939 teaching in Rome at the Centro Sperimentale di Cinematografia.
1940	Robert Flaherty arranges Renoir's passage to the United States in December.
1941	Signs with Twentieth Century-Fox in January. New York Film Critics' Award for *Swamp Water*.
1942	Signs with Universal, then terminates his contract.
1944	Marries Dido Freire, his script girl and the niece of director Alberto Cavalcanti.
1946	Becomes a citizen of the United States, but retains his French citizenship. Best Film, Venice Festival, for *The Southerner*.
1951	Reestablishes residence in Paris, though retains home in Beverly Hills. *The River* wins the International Critics' Prize at the Venice Biennale. Active in theater, as a director and playwright, through the 1950s.
1956	Grand Prix de l'Académie du Cinéma, for *French Cancan*.
1958	Compagnie Jean Renoir formed with Anna de Saint Phalle.
1960	Teaches theater at the University of California, Berkeley, where his son, Alain, had become a professor of English literature.
1962	Publishes biography of his father, *Renoir Mon Père*.
1963	Prix Charles Blanc, Académie Française, for *Renoir Mon Père*. Honorary Doctorate in Fine Arts, University of California, Berkeley.

1964	Elected Fellow of the American Academy of Arts and Sciences.
1966	Publishes a novel, *Les Cahiers du Capitaine Georges*.
1968	Osella d'Oro, Venice Film Festival.
1969	Directs his final film, *Le Petit Théâtre de Jean Renoir*.
1971	Honorary Doctorate in Fine Arts, Royal College of Art, London.
1974	Publishes autobiography, *Ma Vie et mes Films*.
1975	Special Oscar from the Academy of Motion Picture Arts and Sciences for Career Accomplishment in April.
1977	Becomes a Knight of the French Legion of Honor.
1978–1979	Publishes three more novels: *Le Coeur à l'aise* (1978), *Le Crime de l'anglais* (1979), and *Geneviève* (1979).
1979	Dies in Beverly Hills, California, on 12 February 1979, at the age of eighty-four. Orson Welles writes his obituary—in fact a moving eulogy—under the heading "The Greatest of All Directors," in the *Los Angeles Times* of 18 February 1979.

FILMOGRAPHY

1924
CATHERINE (UNE VIE SANS JOIE)
France
Films **Jean Renoir**
Producer: **Jean Renoir**
Director: Albert Dieudonné
Screenplay: **Jean Renoir**
Cinematography: Jean Bachelet, Alphonse Gibory
Cast: Catherine Hessling (Catherine Ferrand), Louis Gauthier (Georges Mallet), Maud Richard (Mme. Mallet), Eugénie Naud (Mme. Laisné), Albert Dieudonné (Maurice Laisné), Pierre Lestringuez, as Pierre Philippe (Adolphe), Pierre Champagne (the Mallets' son), **Jean Renoir** (sub-prefect)
B&W
82 minutes

1924
LA FILLE DE L'EAU (WHIRLPOOL OF FATE)
France
Films **Jean Renoir**/Maurice Touzé/Studio Films
Producer: **Jean Renoir**
Director: **Jean Renoir**
Screenplay: Pierre Lestringuez, **Jean Renoir**
Cinematography: Jean Bachelet, Alphonse Gibory
Production Design: **Jean Renoir**
Cast: Catherine Hessling (Virginie), Pierre Lestringuez, as Pierre Philippe (Uncle Jef), Pierre Champagne (Justin Crépoix), Harold Levingston

(Georges Raynal), Maurice Touzé (Ferret), Pierre Renoir (peasant with
pitchfork)
B&W
89 minutes

1926
NANA
France/Germany
Films **Jean Renoir**
Producer: **Jean Renoir**
Director: **Jean Renoir**
Screenplay: Pierre Lestringuez, from the novel by Émile Zola
Cinematography: Edmund Corwin, Jean Bachelet
Production Design: Claude Autant-Lara
Original Music: Maurice Jaubert
Editor: **Jean Renoir**
Cast: Catherine Hessling (Nana), Werner Krauss (Count Muffat), Jean
Angelo (Count de Vandeuvres), Valeska Gert (Zoé), Pierre Lestringuez,
as Pierre Philippe (Bordenave), Pierre Champagne (La Faloise),
Raymond Guérin-Catelain (Georges Hugon), Claude Autant-Lara, as
Claude Moore (Fauchery), André Cerf (Le Tigre), Pierre Braunberger
(spectator at the theatre)
B&W
150 minutes

1927
CHARLESTON (SUR UN AIR DE CHARLESTON; CHARLESTON PARADE)
France
Films **Jean Renoir**
Producer: **Jean Renoir**
Director: **Jean Renoir**
Screenplay: Pierre Lestringuez, from an idea by André Cerf
Cinematography: Jean Bachelet
Cast: Catherine Hessling (The Dancer), Johnny Huggins (The Explorer),
André Cerf (The Monkey), Pierre Braunberger, **Jean Renoir**, Pierre
Lestringuez, André Cerf (Four Angels)
B&W
17 minutes

1927
MARQUITTA
France
La Société des Artistes Réunis
Director: **Jean Renoir**
Screenplay: Pierre Lestringuez, **Jean Renoir**
Cinematography Jean Bachelet, Raymond Agnel
Production Manager: M. Gargour
Production Design: Robert-Jules Garnier
Cast: Marie-Louise Iribe (Marquitta), Jean Angelo (Prince Vlasco), Henri
Debain (Count Dimitrieff), Lucien Mancini (stepfather), Pierre
Lestringuez, as Pierre Philippe (casino owner), Pierre Champagne
(taxi driver)
B&W
120 minutes

1928
LA PETITE MARCHANDE D'ALLUMETTES (THE LITTLE MATCH GIRL)
France
Producers: **Jean Renoir**, Jean Tedesco
Director: **Jean Renoir**, Jean Tedesco
Screenplay: **Jean Renoir**, from stories by Hans Christian Andersen
Cinematography: Jean Bachelet
Production Design: Erik Aaes
Music: Arranged by Manuel Rosenthal, Michael Grant
Cast: Catherine Hessling (Karen), Jean Storm (young man/wooden
soldier), Manuel Raaby (policeman/death), Aimée Tedesco, as Amy
Wells (mechanical doll)
B&W
40 minutes

1928
TIRE-AU-FLANC (THE SAD SACK)
France
Néo-Film
Producer: Pierre Braunberger
Director: **Jean Renoir**

Screenplay: **Jean Renoir**, André Cerf, Claude Heymann, from the play
by André Mouézy-Eon, André Sylvane
Cinematography: Jean Bachelet
Production Design: Erik Aaes
Cast: Georges Pomiès (Jean Dubois d'Ombelles), Michel Simon (Joseph),
Fridette Fatton (Georgette), Félix Oudart (Colonel Brochard), Jean
Storm (Lieutenant Daumel), Manuel Rabinovitch, as Manuel Raaby
(adjutant), Kinny Dorlay (Lily), Maryanne (Madame Blandin), Zellas
(Muflot), Jeanne Helbling (Solange), Catherine Hessling (girl), André
Cerf (soldier), Max Dalban (soldier)
B&W
120 minutes

1928
LE TOURNOI (LE TOURNOI DANS LA CITÉ; THE TOURNAMENT)
France
Société des Films Historiques
Producer: Henry Dupuy-Mazuel
Director: **Jean Renoir**
Screenplay: Henry Dupuy-Mazuel, André Jaeger-Schmidt, after the
novel by Henry Dupuy-Mazuel
Cinematography: Marcel Lucien, Maurice Desfassiaux
Production Design: Robert Mallet-Stevens
Editor: André Cerf
Cast: Aldo Nadi (François de Baynes), Jackie Monnier (Isabelle Ginori),
Enrique Rivero (Henri de Rogier), Blanche Bernis (Catherine de
Médicis), Suzanne Desprès (Countess de Baynes), Manuel Rabinovitch,
as Manuel Raaby (Count Ginori), Max Dalban (captain of the
watch)
B&W
90 minutes

1929
LE BLED
France
Société des Films Historiques
Producer: Henry Dupuy-Mazuel

Director: **Jean Renoir**
Screenplay: Henry Dupuy-Mazuel, André Jaeger-Schmidt
Cinematography: Marcel Lucien, Léon Morizet
Production Design: William Aguet
Editor: Marguerite Houlé
Cast: Jackie Monnier (Claude Duvernet), Enrique Rivero (Pierre Hoffer), Diana Hart (Diane Duvernet), Manuel Rabinovitch, as Manuel Raaby (Manuel Duvernet), Alexandre Arquillière (Christian Hoffer), Jacques Becker (a Hoffer farmhand)
B&W
102 minutes

1929
LE PETIT CHAPERON ROUGE (LITTLE RED RIDING HOOD)
France
Société Française de gestion cinématographique
Producer: **Jean Renoir**
Director: Alberto Cavalcanti
Screenplay: **Jean Renoir**, Alberto Cavalcanti, from the story by Charles Perrault
Cinematography: Marcel Lucien, René Ribault
Original Music: Maurice Jaubert
Editor: Marguerite Houlé
Cast: Catherine Hessling (Little Red Riding Hood), **Jean Renoir** (the wolf), André (notary), Pierre Prévert (a little girl and other parts), Pablo Quevado (young man), Marcel la Montagne (farmer), Odette Talazac (farmer's wife), William Aguet (old Englishwoman), Aimée Tedesco, as Amy Wells (newspaper seller)
B&W
26 minutes

1931
ON PURGE BÉBÉ
France
Les Établissements Braunberger-Richebé
Producers: Pierre Braunberger, Roger Richebé
Director: **Jean Renoir**

Screenplay: **Jean Renoir**, Pierre Prévert, from the play by Georges Feydeau
Cinematography: Théodore Sparkhul, Roger Hubert
Production Design: Gabriel Scognamillo
Original Music: Paul Misraki
Sound: D. F. Scanlon, Bugnon
Editor: Jean Mamy
Cast: Jacques Louvigny (Bastien Follavoine), Marguerite Pierry (Julie Follavoine), Sacha Tarride (Toto), Michel Simon (Chouilloux), Olga Valéry (Madame Chouilloux), Fernandel (Horace Truchet)
B&W
62 minutes

1931
LA CHIENNE (THE BITCH; ISN'T LIFE A BITCH)
France
Les Établissements Braunberger-Richebé
Producers: Charles David, Roger Richebé
Director: **Jean Renoir**
Screenplay: **Jean Renoir**, André Girard, from the novel by Georges de la Fouchardière and the play adapted from it by André Mouézy-Eon
Cinematography: Théodore Sparkuhl
Production Design: Gabriel Scognamillo
Sound: Joseph de Bretagne, Marcel Courme
Original Music: Eugénie Buffet
Cast: Michel Simon (Maurice Legrand), Janie Marèze (Lulu), Georges Flamant (Dédé), Magdeleine Berubet (Adèle Legrand), Gaillard (Alexis Godard), Jean Gehret (M. Dagodet), Alexandre Rignault (Langelard, the art critic), Lucien Mancini (Walstein, the art dealer), Max Dalban (Bonnard), Marcel Courme (colonel), Sylvain Itkine (lawyer), Jane Pierson (concierge)
B&W
100 minutes

1932
LA NUIT DU CARREFOUR (NIGHT AT THE CROSSROADS)
France
Europa Films

Director: **Jean Renoir**
Screenplay: **Jean Renoir**, from the novel by Georges Simenon
Cinematography: Marcel Lucien, Georges Asselin
Production Design: William Aguet
Sound: Joseph de Bretagne, Bugnon
Editor: Marguerite Renoir
Cast: Pierre Renoir (Inspector Maigret), Georges Térof (Lucas), Winna
Winfried (Else Andersen), Georges Koudria (Carl Andersen), Jean Gehret
(Emile Michonnet), Jane Pierson (Madame Michonnet), Michel Duran
(Jojo), Jean Mitry (Arsène), Max Dalban (doctor), Gaillard (the butcher),
Manuel Rabinovitch, as Manuel Raaby (Guido)
B&W
75 minutes

1932
BOUDU SAUVÉ DES EAUX (BOUDU SAVED FROM DROWNING)
France
Société Sirius
Producers: Michel Simon, Jean Gehret, Marc le Pelletier
Director: **Jean Renoir**
Screenplay: **Jean Renoir**, Albert Valentin, from the play by René Fauchois
Cinematography: Marcel Lucien
Production Design: Jean Castanier, Hugues Laurent
Sound: Igor B. Kalinowski
Original Music: Raphael, Léo Daniderff
Editor: Marguerite Renoir
Cast: Michel Simon (Boudu), Charles Granval (Edouard Lestingois),
Marcelle Hainia (Madame Lestingois), Séverine Lerczinska (Anne-Marie),
Max Dalban (Gadin), Jean Gehret (Vigour), Jean Dasté (student), Jacques
Becker (poet in park), Jane Pierson (Rose), Georges Darnoux (oarsman)
B&W
81 minutes

1933
CHOTARD ET CIE (CHOTARD & CO.)
France
Société des Films Roger Ferdinand

Producer: Roger Ferdinand
Director: **Jean Renoir**
Screenplay: **Jean Renoir**, from the play by Roger Ferdinand
Cinematography: Joseph-Louis Mundwiller
Production Design: Jean Castanier
Sound: Igor B. Kalinowski
Editors: Marguerite Renoir, Suzanne de Troye
Cast: Fernand Charpin (Français Chotard), Jeanne Lory (Madame Chotard), Georges Pomiès (Julien Collinet), Jeanne Boitel (Reine Chotard Collinet), Max Dalban (Émile)
B&W
83 minutes

1933
MADAME BOVARY
France
La Nouvelle Société de Film
Producer: Gaston Gallimard, Robert Aron
Director: **Jean Renoir**
Screenplay: **Jean Renoir**, from the novel by Gustave Flaubert
Cinematography: Jean Bachelet
Production Design: Robert Gys, Eugène Lourié, Georges Wakhevitch
Sound: Marcel Courme, Joseph de Bretagne
Original Music: Darium Milhuad
Editor: Marguerite Renoir
Cast: Valentine Tessier (Emma Bovary), Pierre Renoir (Charles Bovary), Alice Tissot (Old Madame Bovary), Max Dearly (M. Homais), Daniel Lecourtois (Léon Dupuis), Fernand Fabre (Rudolphe Boulanger), Pierre Larquey (Hippolyte Tautin), Robert Le Vigan (Lhuereux), Romain Bouquet (Maître Guillaumin), André Fouché (Justin)
B&W
101 minutes

1934
TONI
France
Films d'Aujourd'hui

Producer: Pierre Gaut
Director: **Jean Renoir**
Screenplay: **Jean Renoir**, Carl Einstein, from a true story found by Jacques Mortier
Cinematography: Claude Renoir, Jr.
Production Design: Marius Braquier, Léon Bourrely
Sound: Barbishanian
Original Music: Paul Bozzi
Editors: Marguerite Renoir, Suzanne de Troye
Cast: Charles Blavette (Toni), Jenny Hélia (Marie), Celia Montalvan (Josefa), Max Dalban (Albert), Edouard Delmont (Fernand), Andrex (Gabi), André Kovachevitch (Sebastien), Paul Bozzi (Jacques, the guitarist)
B&W
100 minutes

1936
LE CRIME DE MONSIEUR LANGE (THE CRIME OF MR. LANGE)
France
Obéron
Producer: André Halley des Fontaines
Director: **Jean Renoir**
Production Manager: Geneviève Blondeau
Screenplay: Jacques Prévert, **Jean Renoir**, from a story by Jean Castanier
Cinematography: Jean Bachelet
Production Design: Jean Castanier, Robert Gys
Sound: Guy Moreau, Louis Bogé, Roger Loisel, Robert Tesseire
Original Music: Jean Wiener
Editor: Marguerite Renoir, Marthe Huguet
Cast: Jules Berry (Batala), René Lefèvre (Amédée Lange), Florelle (Valentine), Nadia Sibirskaïa (Estelle), Sylvia Bataille (Edith), Marcel Levesque (le concierge), Maurice Baquet (Charles), Jacques Brunius (Baigneur), Henri Guisol (Meunier fils) Marcel Duhamel (Louis), Paul Grimault (typesetter), Jean Dasté (illustrator), Sylvain Itkine (Inspector Juliani), Odette Talazac (la concierge)
B&W
80 minutes

1936
LA VIE EST À NOUS (LIFE BELONGS TO US; PEOPLE OF FRANCE)
France
Parti Communiste Français
Directors: **Jean Renoir**, Jacques Becker, André Zwoboda, Jean-Paul le
Chanois (as Jean-Paul Dreyfus), Jacques Brunius, Henri Cartier-Bresson,
Pierre Unik, Maurice Lime
Screenplay: **Jean Renoir**, Paul Vaillant-Couturier, Jean-Paul Dreyfus,
Pierre Unik
Cinematography: Louis Page, Jean-Serge Bourgoin, Jean Isnard, Alain
Douarinou, Claude Renoir Jr., Nicholas Hayer
Sound: Robert Tesseire
Original Music: Hanns Eisler, Eugène Pottier
Editor: Marguerite Renoir
Cast: Jean Dasté (teacher), Jacques Brunius (president of the
Administrative Council), Pierre Unik (Marcel Cachin's secretary), Julien
Bertheau (René, a young worker), Nadia Sibirskaïa (Ninette), Emile
Drain (Gustave), Gaston Modot (Philippe), Charles Blavette (Tonin),
Max Dalban (foreman), Madeleine Solange (factory worker), Jacques
Becker (unemployed worker), **Jean Renoir**, Sylvain Itkine, Jean-Paul
Dreyfus, Léon Larive, Roger Blin, Vladimir Sokoloff, and (as themselves)
Marcel Cachin, André Marty, Maurice Thorez, Jacques Duclos, Paul
Vaillant-Couturier
B&W
66 minutes

1936 (final cut 1946)
UNE PARTIE DE CAMPAGNE (A DAY IN THE COUNTRY)
France
Films du Panthéon
Producer: Pierre Braunberger
Director: **Jean Renoir**
Screenplay: **Jean Renoir**, from the story by Guy de Maupassant
Cinematography: Claude Renoir Jr., Bourgoin
Production Design: Robert Gys
Sound: Marcel Courme, Joseph de Bretagne
Original Music: Joseph Kosma

Editor: Marguerite Renoir, Marinette Cadix
Cast: Sylvia Bataille (Henriette Dufour), Georges Darnoux, as Georges
Saint-Saëns (Henri), Gabriello (M. Dufour), Jane Marken (Madame
Dufour), Paul Temps (Anatole), Jacques Brunius, as Jacques Borel
(Rodolphe), **Jean Renoir** (Père Poulain), Marguerite Renoir (servant),
Gabrielle Fontan (grandmother), Pierre Lestringuez (priest), Henri
Cartier-Bresson and Georges Bataille (seminarians), Alain Renoir
(boy fishing)
B&W
50 minutes

1936
LES BAS-FONDS (THE LOWER DEPTHS)
France
Albatross
Producer: Alexandre Kamenka
Director: **Jean Renoir**
Screenplay: Eugene Zamiatine, Jacques Companéez, from the play by
Maxim Gorky; adapted by **Jean Renoir**, Charles Spaak
Cinematography: Jean Bachelet, Fedote Bourgasoff
Production Design: Eugène Lourié, Hugues Laurent
Sound: Robert Ivonnet
Original Music: Jean Wiener
Editor: Marguerite Renoir
Cast: Louis Jouvet (Baron), Jean Gabin (Pepel), Suzy Prim (Vassilissa),
Vladimir Sokoloff (Kostileff), Junie Astor (Natacha), Robert Le Vigan
(actor), Gabriello (inspector), René Genin (Luka), Jany Holt (Nastya),
Maurice Baquet (Aliocha), Léon Larive (Félix), Paul Temps, Sylvain
Itkine, Jacques Becker
B&W
90 minutes

1937
LA GRANDE ILLUSION (THE GRAND ILLUSION)
France
RAC
Producers: Frank Rollmer, Alexandre and Albert Pinkéwitch

Director: **Jean Renoir**
Screenplay: **Jean Renoir**, Charles Spaak
Cinematography: Christian Matras
Production Design: Eugène Lourié
Sound: Joseph de Bretagne
Original Music: Joseph Kosma
Editor: Marguerite Renoir
Cast: Jean Gabin (Lt. Maréchal), Pierre Fresnay (Captain de Boeldieu),
Erich von Stroheim (Captain von Rauffenstein), Marcel Dalio
(Rosenthal), Julien Carette (Traquet), Dita Parlo (Elsa), Gaston Modot
(engineer), Jean Dasté (teacher), Sylvain Itkine (Demolder), Jacques
Becker (English officer)
B&W
114 minutes

1938
LA MARSEILLAISE
France
Conféderation General de Travail, Société de Production et
d'Exploitation du Film *La Marseillaise*
Producer: **Jean Renoir**
Director: **Jean Renoir**
Screenplay: **Jean Renoir**, Carl Koch, M. and Mme. N. Martel Dreyfus
Cinematography: Jean-Serge Bourgoin, Alain Douarinou, Jean-Marie
Maillols
Production Design: Léon Barsacq, Georges Wakhevitch, Jean Périer
Editor: Marguerite Renoir
Shadow Theatre: Lotte Reiniger
Costumes: Coco Chanel, Granier Chanel
Sound: Joseph de Bretagne, Jean-Roger Bertrand, J. Demede
Original Music: Joseph Kosma
Cast: Pierre Renoir (Louis XVI), Lise Delamare (Marie Antoinette), Louis
Jouvet (Roederer), William Aguet (La Rochefoucauld), Georges Spanelly
(La Chesnaye), Andrex (Honoré Arnaud), Ardisson (Bomier), Nadia
Sibirskaïa (Louison), Jenny Hélia (orator in the Assembly), Léon Larive
(Picard), Gaston Modot and Julien Carette (volunteer soldiers), Marthe
Marty (Bomier's mother)

B&W
135 minutes

1938
LA BÊTE HUMAINE (THE HUMAN BEAST)
France
Paris Film Production
Producers: Robert and Raymond Hakim
Director: **Jean Renoir**
Screenplay: **Jean Renoir**, from the novel by Émile Zola
Cinematography: Curt Courant, Claude Renoir Jr.
Production Design: Eugène Lourié
Sound: Robert Tesseire
Original Music: Joseph Kosma
Editor: Marguerite Renoir, Suzanne de Troye
Cast: Jean Gabin (Jacques Lantier), Simone Simon (Séverine Roubaud),
Fernand Ledoux (Roubaud), Julien Carette (Pecqueux), Jenny Hélia
(Pecqueux's girlfriend), Colette Régis (Madame Victoire), Jacques Berlioz
(Grandmorin), **Jean Renoir** (Cabuche), Blanchette Brunoy (Flore)
B&W
100 minutes

1939
LA RÈGLE DU JEU (THE RULES OF THE GAME)
France
Nouvelles Editions Françaises
Producer: Claude Renoir Sr.
Screenplay: **Jean Renoir**, Carl Koch, André Zwoboda
Cinematography: Jean Bachelet
Production Design: Eugène Lourié, Max Douy
Costumes: Coco Chanel
Sound: Joseph de Bretagne
Original Music: Roger Désormières
Editor: Marguerite Renoir
Cast: Marcel Dalio (Robert de la Chesnaye), Nora Grégor (Christine),
Roland Toutain (André Jurieu), **Jean Renoir** (Octave), Paulette Dubost
(Lisette), Mila Parély (Geneviève), Julien Carette (Marceau), Gaston

Modot (Edouard Schumacher), Odette Talazac (Charlotte de la Plante),
Pierre Magnier (the general), Pierre Nay (Saint-Aubin), Richard
Francoeur (M. la Bruyère), Claire Gérard (Mme. la Bruyère), Eddy
Debray (Corneille, the butler), Léon Larive (chef), Anne Mayen (Jackie),
Lise Elina (radio reporter), André Zwoboda (Caudron engineer), Henri
Cartier-Bresson (English servant), Tony Corteggiani (Berthelin), Jenny
Hélia (servant), Camille François (voice of radio announcer)
B&W
110 minutes

1941
SWAMP WATER
USA
Twentieth Century-Fox
Producer: Irving Pichel
Director: **Jean Renoir**
Screenplay: Dudley Nichols, from the story by Vereen Bell
Cinematography: Peverell Marley, Lucien Ballard
Production Design: Thomas Little, Richard Day
Original Music: David Buttolph
Editor: Walter Thompson
Cast: Dana Andrews (Ben Ragan), Walter Huston (Thursday Ragan),
Walter Brennan (Tom Keefer), Anne Baxter (Julie), John Carradine
(Jesse Wick), Mary Howard (Hannah), Ward Bond (Tim Dorson), Guinn
Williams (Bud Dorson), Virginia Gilmore (Mabel), Eugene Pallette
(sheriff), Russell Simpson (Marty McCord)
B&W
88 minutes

1943
THIS LAND IS MINE
USA
RKO
Producers: **Jean Renoir**, Dudley Nichols
Director: **Jean Renoir**
Screenplay: **Jean Renoir**, Dudley Nichols
Cinematography: Frank Redman

Production Design: Eugène Lourié, Albert d'Agostino, Walter F. Keller
Sound: Terry Kellum, James Stewart
Original Music: Lothar Perl
Editor: Frederic Knudtson
Cast: Charles Laughton (Albert Lory), Maureen O'Hara (Louise Martin), Kent Smith (Paul Martin), George Sanders (George Lambert), Walter Slezak (Major von Keller), Una O'Connor (Mrs. Lory), Nancy Gates (Julie Grant), George Coulouris (prosecutor)
B&W
103 minutes

1944
SALUTE TO FRANCE
USA
Office of War Information
Directors: Garson Kanin, **Jean Renoir**
Screenplay: Philip Dunne, **Jean Renoir**, Burgess Meredith
Cinematography: George Webber
Original Music: Kurt Weill
Supervising Editor: Helen van Dongen
Editors: Marcel Cohen, Maria Reyto, Jean Oser
Cast: Burgess Meredith (Tommy), Garson Kanin (Joe and commentary voice), Claude Dauphin (narrator and French soldier)
B&W
34 minutes

1945
THE SOUTHERNER
USA
Producing Artists, Inc.
Producers: Robert Hakim, David L. Loew
Director: **Jean Renoir**
Screenplay: **Jean Renoir**, Hugo Butler, from the novel *Hold Autumn in Your Hand* by George Sessions Perry
Cinematography: Lucien Andriot
Production Design: Eugène Lourié
Sound: Frank Webster

Original Music: Werner Janssen
Editor: Gregg Tallas
Cast: Zachary Scott (Sam Tucker), Betty Field (Nora Tucker), Beulah
Bondi (Grandma), J. Carrol Naish (Devers), Percy Kilbride (Harmie
Jenkins), Norman Lloyd (Finlay), Charles Kemper (Tim)
B&W
92 minutes

1946
THE DIARY OF A CHAMBERMAID
USA
Camden Productions, Inc.
Producers: Benedict Bogeaus, Burgess Meredith
Director: **Jean Renoir**
Screenplay: **Jean Renoir**, Burgess Meredith, from the play by André
Heuzé, André de Lorde, Thielly Norès, based on the novel by Octave
Mirbeau
Cinematography: Lucien Andriot
Production Design: Eugène Lourié
Costumes: Barbara Karinska
Sound: William H. Lynch
Original Music: Michel Michelet
Editor: James Smith
Cast: Paulette Goddard (Célestine), Burgess Meredith (Captain Mauger),
Hurd Hatfield (Georges Lanlaire), Reginald Owen (M. Lanlaire), Judith
Anderson (Mme. Lanlaire), Francis Lederer (Joseph), Florence Bates (Rose)
B&W
86 minutes

1947
THE WOMAN ON THE BEACH
USA
RKO
Producer: Jack J. Gross
Director: **Jean Renoir**
Screenplay: **Jean Renoir**, Frank Davis, J. R. Michael Hogan, from the
novel *None So Blind* by Mitchell Wilson

Cinematography: Harry Wild, Leo Tover
Production Design: Albert d'Agostino, Walter E. Keller
Sound: Jean L. Speak, Clem Portman
Original Music: Hanns Eisler
Editors: Roland Gross, Lyle Boyer
Cast: Joan Bennett (Peggy Butler), Robert Ryan (Scott Burnett),
Charles Bickford (Tod Butler), Nan Leslie (Eve), Walter Sande
(Vernecke)
B&W
71 minutes

1951
THE RIVER
USA
Oriental International Film Inc.
Producers: Kenneth McEldowney, **Jean Renoir**
Director: **Jean Renoir**
Screenplay: **Jean Renoir**, Rumer Godden, from the latter's novel
Cinematography: Claude Renoir Jr., Ramananda Sen Gupta
Production Design: Eugène Lorié, Bansi Chandra Gupta
Sound: Charles Poulton, Charles Knott
Musical Director: M. A. Partha Sarathy
Editor: George Gale
Cast: Nora Swinburne (Mother), Esmond Knight (Father), Arthur
Shields (Mr. John), Thomas E. Breen (Captain John), Radha Sri Ram
(Melanie), Adrienne Corri (Valerie), Patricia Walters (Harriet),
Suprova Mukerjee (Nan), Richard Foster (Bogey), June Hillman
(narrator)
Color
99 minutes

1953
THE GOLDEN COACH (LE CARROSSE D'OR, LA CARROZZO D'ORO)
France/Italy
Panaria Films, Delphinus & Hoche Productions
Producer: Francesco Alliata
Director: **Jean Renoir**

Screenplay: **Jean Renoir**, Renzo Avenzo, Giulio Macchi, Jack Kirkland, Ginette Doynel, from the play *Le Carrosse du Saint-Sacrement* by Prosper Merimée
Cinematography: Claude Renoir Jr.
Production Design: Mario Chiari
Costume Design: Maria de Mattéis
Sound: Joseph de Bretagne, Ovidio del Grande
Editors: Mario Serandrei, David Hawkins
Cast: Anna Magnani (Camilla), Duncan Lamont (Viceroy), Odoardo Spadaro (Don Antonio), Riccardo Rioli (Ramon), Paul Campbell (Felipe), Nada Fiorelli (Isabelle), Dante (Harlequin), Ralph Truman (the duke), Jean Debucourt (the bishop), George Higgins (Martinez), Gisella Mathews (Marquisa Altamirano), Raf de la Torre (Chief Justice), Medini Brothers (child acrobats)
Color
103 minutes

1955
FRENCH CANCAN
France
Franco London Films, Jolly Films
Producer: Louis Wipf
Director: **Jean Renoir**
Screenplay: **Jean Renoir**, from an idea by André-Paul Antoine
Cinematography: Michel Kelber
Production Design: Max Douy
Sound: Antoine Petitjean
Original Music: Georges van Parys
Choreography: Claude Grandjean
Editor: Borys Lewin
Cast: Jean Gabin (Danglard), Maria Félix (La Belle Abbesse), Françoise Arnoul (Nini), Jean-Roger Caussimon (Baron Walter), Gianni Esposito (Prince Alexandre), Philippe Clay (Casimir), Michel Piccoli (Valorgueil), Jean Parédès (Coudrier), Lydia Johnson (Guibole), Max Dalban (owner of La Reine Blanche), Jacques Jouanneau (Bidon), Valentine Tessier (Mme. Olympe), Franco Pastorino (Paulo), Pierre Olaf (Pierrot the whistler), Patachou (Yvette Guilbert), Edith Piaf (Eugénie Buffet),

Gaston Modot (Danglard's servant), Cora Vaucaire (Esther Georges),
Paquerette (Prunelle)
Color
102 minutes

1956
ELÉNA ET LES HOMMES (ELÉNA AND HER MEN; PARIS DOES
STRANGE THINGS)
France
Franco London Films, Les Films Gibé, Electra Compagnia
Cinematografica
Producer: Louis Wipf
Director: **Jean Renoir**
Screenplay: **Jean Renoir**, Jean Serge, Cy Howard
Cinematography: Claude Renoir Jr.
Production Design: Jean André
Costume Design: Rosine Delamare, Monique Plotin
Sound: William Sivel
Original Music: Joseph Kosma
Editor: Borys Lewin
Cast: Ingrid Bergman (Princess Eléna Sorokovska), Jean Marais (General
François Rollan), Mel Ferrer (Henri de Chevincourt), Pierre Bertin
(Martin-Michaud), Jean Richard (Hector), Magali Noel (Lolotte), Elina
Labourdette (Paulette Escoffier), Juliette Greco (Miarka), Jean Castanier
(Isnard), Gaston Modot (Gypsy chief), Léo Marjane (street singer)
Color
95 minutes

1959
LE TESTAMENT DU DOCTEUR CORDELIER (THE TESTAMENT OF
DOCTOR CORDELIER)
France
ORTF, Sofirad, Compagnie **Jean Renoir**
Made for television and not distributed until 1961
Director: **Jean Renoir**
Screenplay: **Jean Renoir**, from the novel *The Strange Case of Dr. Jekyll
and Mr. Hyde* by Robert Louis Stevenson

Cinematography: Georges Leclerc
Production Design: Marcel-Louis Dieulot
Sound: Joseph Richard
Original Music: Joseph Kosma
Editor: Renée Lichtig
Cast: Jean-Louis Barrault (Dr. Cordelier/Opale), Teddy Billis (Maître Joly), Michel Vitold (Dr. Lucien Séverin), Jean Topant (Désiré), Micheline Gary (Marguerite), André Certes (Inspector Salbris), **Jean Renoir** (as himself, the narrator), Gaston Modot (Blaise, the gardener)
B&W
95 minutes

1959
LA DÉJEUNER SUR L'HERBE (LUNCH ON THE GRASS; PICNIC ON THE GRASS)
France
Compagnie **Jean Renoir**
Producer: Ginette Doynel
Director: **Jean Renoir**
Screenplay: **Jean Renoir**
Cinematography: Georges Leclerc
Production Design: Marcel-Louis Dieulot
Sound: Joseph de Bretagne
Original Music: Joseph Kosma
Editor: Renée Lichtig
Cast: Paul Meurisse (Professor Etienne Alexis), Catherine Rouvel (Nénette), Fernand Sardou (Nino), Ingrid Nordine (Marie-Charlotte), Charles Blavette (Gaspard), Jean Claudio (Rosseau)
Color
91 minutes

1962
LE CAPORAL ÉPINGLÉ (THE VANISHING CORPORAL; THE ELUSIVE CORPORAL)
France
Films du Cyclope
Producers: Adry de Carbuccia, Roland Girard

Directors: **Jean Renoir**, Guy Lefranc
Screenplay: **Jean Renoir**, Guy Lefranc, from the novel by Jacques Perret
Cinematography: Georges Leclerc
Production Design: Wolf Witzemann, Eugene Herrly
Sound: Antoine Petitjean
Original Music: Joseph Kosma
Editor: Renée Lichtig
Cast: Jean-Pierre Cassel (Corporal), Claude Brasseur (Pater), Claude Rich (Ballochet), Jean Carmet (Guillaume), Jacques Jouanneau (Penche-à-gauche), Cornelia Froboess (Erika), Mario David (Caruso), O. E. Hasse (drunken passenger), Guy Bedos (the stutterer)
B&W
90 minutes

1969
LE PETIT THÉÂTRE DE **JEAN RENOIR**
France
Son et Lumière, RAI, Bavaria, ORTF
Producer: Pierre Long
Director: **Jean Renoir**
Screenplay: **Jean Renoir**
Production Design: Gilbert Margerie
Cinematography: Georges Leclerc
Sound: Guy Rolphe
Original Music: Jean Wiener, Joseph Kosma
Editor: Geneviève Winding
Cast: *Le Dernier Réveillon:* Nino Formicola and Milly Monti (tramps), Roland Bertin (Gontran), Robert Lombard (maître d'); *La Cireuse électrique:* Marguerite Cassan (Emilie), Pierre Olaf (Gustave), Jacques Dynam (Jules), Jean Louis Tristan (salesman); *Quand l'amour meurt:* Jeanne Moreau (singer); *Le Roi d'Yvetot:* Fernand Sardou (Duvallier), Françoise Arnoul (Isabelle), Jean Carmet (Feraud), Dominique Labourier (Paulette)
Color
100 minutes

JEAN RENOIR

INTERVIEWS

Interview with Jean Renoir

JACQUES RIVETTE AND FRANÇOIS
TRUFFAUT/1954

Part One: Renoir in America

The work of Jean Renoir is too extensive to attempt to address all of it in this interview. We therefore decided to question him on the most recent period of his life, which is also, paradoxically, the least well known. The most conflicting comments have circulated about his stay in America, and we are aware that our interview contradicts many of those that have been published. Allow us simply to point out that we had the benefit of an impartial tape recorder and also that we had no desire to make Jean Renoir disavow any of his films.

In short, we had no greater goal than to continue the famous article that appeared in *Point* in December 1938, in which Renoir summarized the first part of his life. It was therefore only natural that our first question touched on *The Rules of the Game* (*La Règle du jeu*).

JEAN RENOIR: I had wanted to do *The Rules of the Game* for a long time, but this desire became clearer while I was shooting *La Bête humaine*. This film, as you know, was taken from a novel by Zola and is essentially a naturalist work. I remained as faithful as I could to the spirit of the book.

Originally published in *Cahiers du cinéma*, 6.34 (April 1954), pp. 3–22, and 6.35 (May 1954), pp. 14–30. Part I, translated by C.-G. Marsac, was reprinted in *Sight and Sound*, 24.1 (August 1954), pp. 12–17. Part II, translated by C.-G. Marsac, was reprinted in *Art and Artist* (Berkeley: University of California Press, 1956), pp. 125–48. Reprinted by permission.

I didn't follow the plot, but I have always thought that it was better to be faithful to the spirit of an original work than to its exterior form. Besides, I had some long conversations with Madame Leblond-Zola, and I did not do anything that I was not certain would have pleased Zola. Yet I didn't feel obliged to follow the weave of the novel; I thought of certain works like *L'Histoire du vitrail, La Cathédrale, La Faute de l'Abbé Mouret,* or *La Joie de vivre;* I thought of Zola's poetic side. But in the end, people who like Zola declared themselves satisfied.

Nevertheless, working on this script inspired me to make a break, and perhaps to get away from naturalism completely, to try to touch on a more classical, more poetic genre. The result of these thoughts was *The Rules of the Game.*

Since one is always inspired by something (after all, you have to start somewhere, even if there is nothing left of that somewhere in the final work), I reread Marivaux and Musset carefully in order to get ideas for *The Rules of the Game,* but with no intention of even following the spirit of their works. I think that reading them helped me establish a style, halfway between a certain realism—not exterior, but realism all the same—and a certain poetry. At the very least I tried.

CAHIERS: *Rumor has it you started with an adaptation of* Les Caprices de Marianne.

RENOIR: No, I had no intention of doing an adaptation. Let's just say that reading and rereading *Les Caprices de Marianne,* which I consider to be Musset's most beautiful play, helped me a great deal, but it obviously had only an indirect effect. That is, these writers helped me more to conceive of the characters than to develop the form and the plot.

CAHIERS: *You wrote several versions of this script. Jurieu, for example, was an orchestra conductor in one of the first versions.*

RENOIR: Yes, of course, but that's always the case. I am rewriting the same play [*Orvet*] now for the third, even the fourth time. It doesn't even resemble my first draft; the characters even have different identities.

CAHIERS: *Did you also change* The Rules of the Game *during the shooting?*

RENOIR: On the set? Yes, I improvised a great deal. The actors are also the directors of a film, and when you're with them, they have reactions you hadn't foreseen. Their reactions are often very good, and it would be crazy not to take advantage of them.

CAHIERS: *In what way did you change things?*
RENOIR: Well, the changes based on my contact with actors are the same in all my films. I have a tendency to be theoretical when I start working: I say what I would like to say a bit too clearly—a bit like a lecturer—and it's extremely boring. Little by little (and my contact with the actors helps enormously), I try to get closer to the way in which characters can adapt to their theories in real life while being subjected to life's many obstacles, the many minor events, the many little sentiments that keep us from being theoretical and from remaining theoretical. But I always start with theories. I'm a bit like a man who is in love with a woman and who goes to see her with a bouquet of flowers in hand. In the street he goes over the speech he is going to make; he writes a brilliant speech, with many comparisons, talking about her eyes, her voice, her beauty, and he prides himself in all this, of course. And then he arrives at the woman's house, hands her the bouquet of flowers, and says something completely different. But having prepared the speech does help a little.

CAHIERS: *And the last-minute sincerity?*
RENOIR: That's it. There is one other thing: It's difficult to be sincere when you're all alone. Some people manage to do it, and they are gifted writers. I'm much less gifted, and I can only really find my own expressions when I'm in contact with others. And I'm not talking about criticisms so much; I'm mostly talking about the kind of ball game that seems necessary to me. It's exactly the same in all walks of life. For example, in politics, you see politicians go into a meeting having prepared a very "clever" statement. They completely forget that the other side has also prepared a very "clever" statement, and so they never agree. But if the two sides came to this political meeting in the state of mind I try to bring to my work, perhaps they could get along.

CAHIERS: *In short, you prepare your work with the idea of abandoning everything on the set.*
RENOIR: Yes, absolutely. Yet I cannot completely improvise, I can't work like the great pioneers, like the great film pioneers, like Mack

Sennett. . . . I often went to see his little studio, which is still standing in an old neighborhood between Los Angeles and Hollywood. It's no longer a studio, there are offices there now. I spoke to some old stage-hands, some old electricians who were working at that time. I also met a few old cameramen. There's a Frenchman, for example, whose name is Lucien Androit, who is very familiar with that period. You know Lucien, he did *The Southerner* with me. Old Mack Sennett used to tell everyone to be there in the morning, and those who were at least get-ting paid came, and he would say, "What are we going to do this morn-ing?" Someone would say, "We could take a policeman, the seal, a lady dressed as a milkmaid, and we could go to the beach." And they went to the beach: They thought about it on the way, they shot something, and it came out well. I obviously couldn't do that. I have to know what I'm going to shoot, but even when I do, what I wind up shooting may be different. But it's never different as far as the props, the set, and the general feeling of the scene go—only the form changes.

CAHIERS: *To get back to* The Rules of the Game: *Weren't you surprised by the poor reception it got?*
RENOIR: Well, I wasn't expecting it, I never expect it, and for a very simple reason: I always imagine that the film I'm going to make will be an extremely marketable film, which will delight all the distributors and will be considered rather ordinary. I try my hardest to make as marketable films as possible, and when exceptions like *The Rules of the Game* occur, they occur in spite of my efforts. Besides, I'm convinced that this is always the case, that theories follow practice.

I just told you that I begin by being too theoretical and that the prac-tice, the contact with life, changes my writing completely; that's true. So when I say that theory follows practice, I'm not thinking of the the-ories that the characters express on the screen and that disappear little by little from my writing. I'm thinking of general film theories, the con-clusions one can draw from a film, the lesson—the message, as they say—that it may hold. I have the feeling that this message can be truly meaningful only if it hasn't been planned in advance, if it appears, little by little, by itself, just as a certain light effect springs forth from a land-scape: You see the landscape before you see the light effect. You can walk in the country, knowing that you are going to come to a specific

place near a road and that a field with poplar trees will be there. You see
the field and the poplars. Then, little by little, the more subtle details—
the lighting, certain contrasts, certain relationships—appear, which
are the essence of the landscape and are much more important than
the field and the poplars. Sometimes—and this happens with many
artists—one completely forgets the field and the poplars and preserves
only its consequences: That's what we call abstract art. In reality, I
believe that all great art is abstract. Even if a bit of the field and
poplars remains, they must be different enough so as not to remain
mere copies.

CAHIERS: *And so it was later on that you discovered everything in* The
Rules of the Game *that foreshadowed the approaching war?*
RENOIR: Oh, no! I thought about that, but I thought about it only
indirectly. I didn't say to myself, "This film must express this or that,
because we are going to have a war." And yet, even so, knowing that we
were going to have a war, being absolutely convinced of it, my work
was permeated with it. But I didn't establish a relationship between the
impending state of war and my characters' dialogues or words.

CAHIERS: *And your next film was in fact interrupted by the war. . . . But
what were your reasons for going to shoot* La Tosca *in Italy?*
RENOIR: Well, there were several reasons. First, I really wanted to
shoot in Italy; next, I was asked to shoot in Italy. It was before the war,
but people had a sense of what was going to happen, and many French
officials wanted Italy to remain neutral. It so happened that the Italian
government, and even Mussolini's family, wanted me to go to Italy. My
first instinct was to refuse. So I refused, and I was told, "You know, this
is a very special time, and one must forget personal preferences. Do us
the favor of going there," not only to film *La Tosca*, but also to give
a few lessons on stage setting at the Centro Sperimentale di cinematografica in Rome, which is what I did.
    That's the real reason, the practical one. Intellectually, I might say,
I went because of *The Rules of the Game*. You know you can't think of
Marivaux without thinking of Italy. One mustn't forget that Marivaux
started by writing for an Italian troupe, that his mistress was Italian,
and that essentially, he took up the thread of the Italian theater. I think

he can be put in the same category as Goldoni. Working on *The Rules of the Game* brought me fantastically close to Italy, and I wanted to see baroque statues, the angels on bridges, with clothes with too many folds and wings with too many feathers. I wanted to see the kind of complex interplay of Italian baroque. I should add that, later on, I quickly learned that the baroque was not the essence of Italy. I am now much more drawn to previous periods, even those before the Quattrocento. If I were invited to visit one place in Italy, I think I would choose to return to the National Museum in Naples to see the Greek paintings of Pompeii, yes, that would still be my choice. But at the time of *La Tosca*, I didn't know all that. I've learned it since.

CAHIERS: *You shot only the first sequence, I think, in which the taste for the baroque is so apparent?*
RENOIR: Yes, a few gallops at the beginning, a few horses. I don't know if they're in the film, I've never seen it. Koch, my friend and associate and assistant, shot the film for me when Italy entered the war. I've been told that the film followed my script rather closely; Koch told me that himself.

CAHIERS: *It's a very good film, in any case.*
RENOIR: Oh really? That's good. It proves that I can write scripts; that's very flattering.

CAHIERS: *Shouldn't we be sorry that Koch hasn't shot other films?*
RENOIR: We certainly should. He's a remarkable man, one of the most intelligent men I know . . . in the world. He came to film in a strange way: Instead of coming to it from the technical end, as so many people do (which in my opinion creates a whole race of very ordinary directors), he came to film through the study of medieval architecture. He's a man who knows medieval architecture as no one else does. When we started working together, we went to some churches. . . . I remember being surprised the first time. We arrived at a church, Koch looked at the façade, got his bearings, and said, "Let's see, north, south, okay, I've got it." And he told me everything we were going to find in the church, he knew the capital of the least important column—everything—by heart.

CAHIERS: *He was Lotte Reiniger's husband.*

RENOIR: Yes, he still is. I hope to go see them soon in England. He has a hard time working because he wasn't able to get permission from the English unions, I think. It's awful to see a man who has all of film in the palm of his hand—and not like a theoretician but like a very cultivated man with experience—it's really a pity to see that he's not making any films.

CAHIERS: *He was also your associate on* The Rules of the Game.

RENOIR: Yes, we worked together all the time. We were separated by Italy's entry into the war. That's what indirectly sent me to America.

CAHIERS: *Now we're getting to the main part of this interview: your experience in America. We'd like to hear as much as possible about this period.*

RENOIR: Lots of people have probably already told you what it's like to work in an American studio. I would have nothing new to tell you, and my particular case is not very different from the others. Nevertheless, I can divide my American films into two categories: a few attempts with the large studios, and some others with independents. The results with the large studios were not bad, since I shot *Swamp Water*, which isn't a bad film—it's an enjoyable film in any case. The only reason I was able to shoot it, however, is because I was new. My other advantage at that time was that I spoke English very poorly, and so I couldn't understand anything. I wasn't yet able to be influenced.

In fact, everything that is said about the large studios is true, but I think that the main reasons that make it difficult to work there for a man like me, an improviser, have not been touched on: The large studios have enormous expenses; films cost a great deal there; and they cannot risk all that money without having what they call security—the security is the script, it's the work outline. Each detail of a film is decided in advance by a kind of board of directors to which the principal members of the studio belong, as well as the producer and the director. If you're eloquent, you can do just about anything you want as a director, but you have to know in advance, you must be able to convince people beforehand of what you're going to do, and I can't do that. What often happened was that I would convince people that we had to do this or that, and once I was on the set, I found that it was a

stupid idea and wanted to do something else. In other words, what people say about the tyranny of the large studios is sometimes true, but it
depends on the individual. Personally, I could have worked there without being tyrannized at all—if I had known beforehand what I would
want on the set, but I couldn't.

In any case, when I decided to leave Twentieth Century-Fox after
Swamp Water, it all happened in a very friendly way. I explained to
Zanuck what I am explaining to you now, and he said to me, "Of course
we can't; we have to know where we're going; we're very sorry." I said
to him, "Well, do me a favor, break my contract." He said to me, "Of
course." We're the world's best friends. I just don't think my type of
work fits in with a large administration. In any case, I think my type of
work is going to disappear, not just from Hollywood, but from the
whole world, because films cost too much today. The price of a film is
outrageous. That's why I am convinced that people in my category—
and these people have to make films too, after all—may be able in the
future to make only less expensive films, in black and white, less industrial, maybe in 16 mm; it's possible. . . .

CAHIERS: *Was the script for* Swamp Water *your own idea?*
RENOIR: No, not at all. Dudley Nichols wrote it, maybe a year beforehand, and in a different form. At that time Nichols had left Hollywood
and was in the east, in Connecticut, where he was writing other things,
but not for film. When I arrived, Fox gave me many scripts to read and
asked me to choose the one I wanted to shoot. I read piles of them, and
to me, they all were too much like European stories. I'm still convinced
that it is extremely difficult to make films that are not tied in with the
place they are made. I think that the artist's origin is not very important,
but . . . I often use the comparison with the French school of painting,
which was, all in all, as important an event in the world as the Italian
Renaissance. These people were from every possible country, but just the
same, they painted in the French style and were in close contact with
everything that came from French soil. Picasso may be Spanish, but
because he paints in France, he's a French painter. Even if he had been
born in China, he would be a French painter.

That's why, because I was a Frenchman, Fox gave me a lot of films on
France or on Europe, thinking, "He knows France, he knows Europe,

he's going to do fantastic things." But I wanted no part of it. Finally I found this essentially American story, and I was enchanted. In addition, it gave me the opportunity to meet Dudley Nichols, who has remained an extraordinary friend—I could say a brother—with whom I correspond and with whom I planned other films, which were never made.

It was also because of *Swamp Water* that I was able to see America. Here's what happened: The film took place in Georgia, and so I asked the studio, "When are we leaving for Georgia?" They were quite surprised. They said, "Do you think we built a studio worth so many millions, in which we can reproduce anything, so that we would have to go to Georgia? We're going to build Georgia right here." I didn't buy this, and protested mightily. The problem was presented to Zanuck, who squirmed. He said to himself, "Boy, these French people have some crazy ideas." I told him, "I may have some crazy ideas, but I'd rather do nothing than do this film in the studio. It seems to me that in Georgia we'll at least find some exteriors. I'm not saying we shouldn't do the interiors here, or even some atypical exteriors—Why not construct the front of a house in the studio?—but everything that expresses the character of the Georgia countryside, I want to do in Georgia." So we went to Georgia, and I was able to see this swamp, and I must say that it was quite enjoyable and I had a good time.

Another thing happened: The film took longer to shoot than we had estimated. I was supposed to have shot it in—I don't know—forty days, and it was already the forty-fifth day and we were far from finishing it. I had a very slow cameraman, but it wasn't his fault; I was the one who was taking my time to shoot the film. One day they called in the cameraman to complain about his slowness. I protested: "Listen, the cameraman isn't slow, I am, I'm a slow director, and if you don't want a slow director, don't use me." The cameraman [Peverell Marley] became a very good friend of mine, by the way; he was very pleased with my attitude. . . .

Here's what had happened: I had refused a story adapted from a well-known novel, and I had refused to use a star, although I certainly had some very good actors. I had Walter Huston; Dana Andrews, who played a stock boy; Anne Baxter, who played a stock girl; and Walter Brennan, who had received an Academy Award and was very well known. But they were character actors who played supporting roles, and at that time, the star system was very strict in Hollywood: A film that cost a certain amount had to offer audiences a star, a young lead of some importance. Since I had refused, my film automatically fell into the category of films that were to be made with only a limited amount of money. They therefore asked me to stop shooting, and so I stopped shooting the film and went home. That night, I received a phone call from Zanuck, who said to me, "No, no Jean; of course they were kidding, but I'm taking responsibility for it. I explained to the board of directors that despite the added cost, you're going to continue the film." So the next morning I went back to continue shooting, and I received a show of affection that moved me tremendously, that shows that film people are really the same all over the world, and that they understand one another. When I arrived at the studio, at exactly 9 o'clock, which was the starting time of the shooting, I found the entire team in the middle of the set. Instead of being at their lights, the electricians were down below. The cameramen, the actors, the extras— everyone was there standing very formally, almost as if I were arriving at Elysée to visit the president of the republic, and when I opened the door, they all applauded me. There was a great deal of applause, and then we went to work. It was very nice.

I had another cameraman during this same film who was a very interesting young man, Lucien Ballard. He's an American Indian, and like a lot of American Indians, he has a French name, because in the eighteenth century, the French had close contacts with the Indians. Many of them lived with Indian tribes or in Indian territory, or married Indian women. There was a great Indian-French mix. Lucien Ballard was a marvelous person. Because he made a good living, he tried to help other Indians, who often are very unhappy living on the reservations. He brought me with him to a reservation, where we spent several days with the Hopi Indians, in an absolutely charming school, from which I brought back many watercolors done by young Indians, almost all of which had pictures of Santa Claus with a white beard.

CAHIERS: Swamp Water *was very successful in the United States.*
RENOIR: Yes, it was. Later, Zanuck often told me that. Several films came out that year, and five or six were big films with very big stars and had cost millions. But *Swamp Water* made much more money than any

of them, and so they were very happy. Nonetheless, despite this good relationship, I didn't continue working at Fox.

CAHIERS: *Rumor has it you began shooting a film with Deanna Durbin.*
RENOIR: Yes, after leaving Fox, Universal offered me this film. I met Deanna Durbin, and I liked her very much. She's a charming girl, and at that time she was going from being a young girl to being a woman. She had just gotten married, she was particularly ravishing, and I was very excited about it.

The reason I didn't finish the film is that Deanna Durbin was imprisoned by the genre that made her a success. It's a genre that I admire very much, and it was invented by someone whom you know well and who lived for a long time in Paris—Henry Koster. Koster was originally a script writer, and he's the one who had the idea for *Three Smart Girls*. It was a charming film, and he had really discovered an extraordinary genre for Deanna Durbin. Besides, when I started this film, I had asked to see all the Deanna Durbin films—and I must say there were a lot of them—and Koster's films were, of course, much better than the others. But I wasn't good at this genre, and so it was better for the film to be shot by people more familiar with it than I was. Deanna Durbin's success had literally saved Universal Pictures, which was close to bankruptcy when Koster arrived there with his ideas and shot Deanna, who was unknown at the time, in *Three Smart Girls*, which was an immediate success for them. Deanna Durbin had become as good as gold, and this film's script was once again the usual type. . . . Although—I repeat—I could have done things the way I wanted, but in the end, each decision was so important. Even a smile, a wink, was discussed by ten people around a green rug. It was difficult for me to work with so much seriousness.

CAHIERS: *It was a little like changing the laws of the Byzantine mosaics.*
RENOIR: Yes, something like that. After that, I wanted to shoot *Terre des hommes* (*Wind, Sand and Stars*). I still have some recorded conversations with Saint-Exupéry, by the way, mostly about literary subjects. We wanted to do this film, and we had established not really a script but a project, and we had found a style, a formula for making *Terre des hommes*. But I still couldn't interest anyone in the film, despite the book's success in the United States.

I must tell you that since then there has been a great turnabout—Zanuck did a great deal to make it happen: It was the agreement to shoot on location. When I arrived in Hollywood, everyone shot on sets. The idea of shooting on location came about with the war. When I wanted to do *Terre des hommes*, they were still in the intensive-studio stage, but this film had to be shot at the locations described in the book. I think that's the main reason that no one accepted it.

CAHIERS: *That's when you decided to do* This Land Is Mine, *which was an independent production.*
RENOIR: It's an independent production distributed by RKO. But note that the word *independent* is one of the many labels that indicates fifty different ways of making films in Hollywood. This film was independent in the sense that the studio left us in total peace, Nichols and myself, but it was financed by RKO and distributed by RKO, and we had to answer to the studio for the film's budget, its expenditures, and its results.

I must tell you that at that time RKO was directed by Charlie Korner, who was an extraordinary man. Unfortunately, he died, and I was very sorry about that. If Korner hadn't died, I think I would have done twenty films at RKO; I would have worked my whole life at RKO because he was an understanding man, a man who knew the film market, who understood the workings of it very well, but who allowed for experimentation just the same. In addition, the people who preceded him at RKO were also extraordinary people: They enabled experiments like *Citizen Kane*, which would have been impossible at any other studio. RKO was truly the center of the real Hollywood during the final years, until Korner's death, which was in 1946. Korner died while *The Woman on the Beach* was being filmed, and I finished it under the temporary heads of the studio.

CAHIERS: *You produced* This Land Is Mine *in close collaboration with Dudley Nichols?*
RENOIR: Very close, we wrote the script together, completely together; which is to say that we closed ourselves off in a small room—he, my wife who was helping us, and I, and we wrote everything, the three of us. At that time, Nichols didn't think about the stage setting. I was the

one who made him think about it. He has since abandoned it once again, but at that time, he didn't want to get involved in camera angles. I was therefore alone on the set. At the same time, everything concerning the writing of the script, as well as the discussions with the set designers, we did together. By the way, I had brought Lourié from France with me to be the set designer.

CAHIERS: *This film has a style rather different from that of your other American films.*
RENOIR: Maybe with more action-reaction shots, fewer scenes filmed at length? Well, I'll tell you, this is a strange film. In order to talk about it you have to consider the period during which it was shot. It was shot during a period when many Americans allowed themselves to be influenced by a certain propaganda attempting to represent all of France as collaborationist. Therefore I did this film, which was not intended to be shown in France, but only in America, to suggest to Americans that daily life in an occupied country was not as easy as some people may have thought. I must say that the results were extraordinary, and I'm pleased. Not only did the film have a good shelf life, but I also received many letters of approval and many shows of affection and esteem for France. I think the film fulfilled its goal.

Nevertheless, because it was a bit of a propaganda film—I hate the word *propaganda*, but . . . in any case it was meant to persuade people of something. So I thought we'd better be cautious so as to be able to change the editing. Usually I am very certain of my editing on the set, and I take risks. That is another reason for my divorce from the large studios, because their method is not to take any risks, whereas I like to take them. If I know that I have to throw myself in the water and that it's either sink or swim; if I know I can't eventually save myself with editing tricks, I feel that I shoot my scene better. But in the large studios— once again for financial reasons; when a product is expensive, you must be sure it will satisfy the client—the only method is a secure method, and that is why you have to have shots, reaction shots, master shots, medium shots, so that with just a few retakes you can make almost another film if the editing doesn't work. I never did that. I did do it in *This Land Is Mine* because the stakes were too high. It seemed to me that I was somewhat responsible. . . . You know, many French people in the United States during the war indulged in patriotic talk that was totally incomprehensible, completely private and sometimes even a bit hostile, and I had the feeling that this wasn't the right way to represent our country. I therefore had a great responsibility, and so I adopted the mind-set of a large studio that wants to be very cautious, but for different reasons. I composed the film carefully; I wrote a shooting script as if it were a commercial film, so that if need be I could change it during the editing, and with the help of previews, I could find the correct dosage to produce the desired effect on the public I wanted to influence.

CAHIERS: *When seeing* This Land Is Mine, *we couldn't help think of Daudet's "Monday Tales" and especially "The Last Class."*
RENOIR: I thought of that. Listen, my first idea when I left France was to do a film about an exodus of children from Paris to the South. . . . In fact, I was thinking of [François Boyer's] *The Secret Game* [later filmed by Clément as *Forbidden Games*], but without the bit about the cemetery, of course; and then I thought that, with the children we would find to act in it, it wouldn't go over abroad. That is, we would have to use French children speaking French. A film like this therefore had to be done by established actors, who could artistically—which is to say, through their talent—translate certain feelings for the American public. I often talked about it with Charles Laughton, who is one of my good friends—we see each other constantly—and in retelling the tale by Daudet to each other, one day I thought of this story, which I wrote.

CAHIERS: *In any case, that proves Daudet's effectiveness over the years.*
RENOIR: Yes, it's astonishing.

CAHIERS: *You also are said to have fathered a short film entitled* Salute to France, *which we have never seen.*
RENOIR: Listen, I cannot say I was the father of *Salute to France*. I have done many films in my life, which were more or less propaganda films, to help various causes, or very often to help technicians who were my friends and who said to me: "We're doing such and such a film, come help us." As for *Salute to France*, a few friends were working at the Office of War Information in New York: Burgess Meredith, for example, and

Philip Dunne, who is now a well-known writer—he did *The Robe*. They said to me, "You should come to the Office of War Information to help us do a film for American troops, to explain to them that in France people drink wine, that they do this, that they do that, so as to avoid conflicts (which were inevitable, in any case) and to explain what French people are like to the Americans who are going to land there." I then received an official invitation from the Office of War Information. I felt that I couldn't say no and that it was my way of doing my part for the American and French governments. I went there and participated in the film, but I didn't make it. There is a little of me in this film, very little.

CAHIERS: *We've now come to* The Southerner, *which I suppose marks the beginning of the independent producers.*
RENOIR: That's right. *The Southerner* was Robert Hakim's idea. One day he brought me a script that was . . . well, that wasn't very good. It was pretty much the standard script for large studios, and Hakim said to me, "I'd like to shoot this film with a very small budget." I read the script. To shoot it would have required millions. I told him this, and he believed me, but I added, "There are nevertheless some fantastic things in this story, and I would like to read the book" (because it was already an adaptation). So he brought me the book, which is charming. It's a series of short stories that take place in Texas, written by a fellow named Sessions Perry, about characters like those in *The Southerner*. The stories, however, are much more varied—you could make ten films from this book. And after reading it, I said to Hakim, "I'm interested in it, provided I can forget the first script and write another one." It happened that Hakim had proposed *The Southerner* to another producer, David Loew, which enabled me to become friends with this extraordinary character. He's really a wonderful man who was extremely courageous. So I wrote another script, which he liked, and said, "Okay, let's do it." I told him, "I'm warning you, I'm going to change it during the shooting." He said, "OK." I said to him, "Besides, I'd like you to come to the shootings; that way when I change it, we can talk about it together." He said, "I'd love to." He understood my work methods very well.

But when the script was given to the film's two stars, who were used to a very different type, they didn't mince their words. Even though they covered me with flowers, adored me, and said, "Oh, Jean, the greatest director in the world," and so forth, when I showed them my script, the compliments turned into criticisms and they told me, "We don't have to shoot a script like that, and we won't." So David Loew told them, "OK, you refuse. I couldn't care less. Jean and I will find somebody else." And once again, we chose some unknown actors, and we embarked on an adventure.

The film was supposed to be distributed by United Artists, but they told Loew, "We can't distribute it because you promised us a film with stars. Because there aren't any, you can keep it." Loew told them, "OK, I have a rather large share in about thirty films that you distribute, and I'll give them all to Columbia." So United Artists said, "In that case, we'll take *The Southerner.*"

It's a film that I did with complete freedom, and right from the beginning it was a rather ambitious film. Of course it was more ambitious in Hollywood than it would have been here, because we had already told stories like that in France, and we'll continue to tell such stories. But at that time the war was on in America, and there was a kind of tacit understanding that Hollywood had to present a rather glamorous image of the United States to the world. In any case, the film wasn't shown in Europe. It came to France much later, by a bit of a fluke. United Artists hated the film. Because they had been forced to take it, they distributed it with little effort. Even so, it ended up making money. I know, because I had a share in the profits, and I received some money, so there must have been profits. In any case, the film currently belongs to David Loew and me. Right now, we're starting to show it on television.

CAHIERS: *We may be wrong, but it seems to us that* The Southerner *marked the beginning of an evolution in your conception of film.*
RENOIR: That's true—it's an extremely accurate idea—and for one simple reason: It was the end of the war. The liberation took place while I was shooting *Diary of a Chambermaid*, which I started a few weeks after *The Southerner*, and right away, new ideas started coming to me. . . . Many people considered this war to be just a war, but it was much more than a war; it was a veritable revolution, an absolutely uncontrolled reshaping of the world. I think that people will be separated much more by civilization than by nation. I don't mean that

nations will disappear. Nations existed in the Middle Ages; in fact, there were more of them. For example, instead of Italy there was Florence, Pisa, and Ravenna, but the citizens of Ravenna, Pisa, or Florence were first and foremost part of a civilization, the Western Christian civilization. They were Roman Christians and represented certain ideas that were a continuation of Greek ideas altered by the Christian revolution altered by the Roman organization and altered especially by the beginning of the Middle Ages. The divisions among nations were much weaker than the division by interest, by profession, or by intellectual tendency. For example, a medieval clerk—a man whose profession it was to be educated, to try to learn—was not specifically an Italian or a French intellectual but, rather, an intellectual who belonged to the great Western civilization. This clerk was therefore just as much at home at the University of Bologna as at Caen or Oxford. The first great French work known to us—there may have been others that haven't been preserved—the only version known to us of the *Song of Roland* (the one that was translated into modern French by Bédier) was written at Oxford. It could just as well have been written in Milan. In the Western world, there was a kind of international society of intellectuals, and there were also international societies for other interests. For example, a cooper was a cooper belonging to this Western world. He was a cooper in Nuremberg as well as in Bordeaux, and he traveled, by foot, from Nuremberg to Bordeaux and then continued down to Sicily.

I have the feeling that this kind of interpenetration awaits us. I believe this. But it doesn't prevent me from believing even more in local influences than in national ones. I think that it's a mistake, for example, to make a film in Provence that is supposed to take place in Paris. One should make Provençal films in Provence and Parisian films in Paris. To repeat what I said before—and we have proof of this even after the Middle Ages—I think that the origin of the artist is only of secondary importance to the work he creates. Soil is so strong that it naturalizes you, not in a few years, but in a few weeks. Benvenuto Cellini, who worked on Fontainebleau, or Leonardo da Vinci, remained Italian, yet there is something in the works they did for the kings of France that makes them French works. I feel that we are going to return to this kind of international society, in certain professions in any case, and that it was a more arbitrary desire that separated people.

In the meantime, I don't know whether this is good or bad. Personally, I think I'd feel comfortable in a world divided in such a fashion, but I'm probably the only one who thinks this way today, because nationalism has almost never been so strong. Minor details, the most secondary events, are suddenly translated into a waving flag. I believe that these somewhat ridiculous manifestations are precisely the last signs of a dying nationalism and that we will eventually have worldwide categories. That's not to say that there will be only one world, as Mr. [Wendell] Willkie said, but in any case the world we will know will probably be larger, vaster, and wider than our childhood world, which was limited to our borders. I remember when I was a kid (and I assure you the world was much smaller than when you were young yourselves), when I went to my village school in Bourgogne, we didn't think there was anything worth knowing beyond our borders. Besides, we naturalized everything in good faith. For example, I was convinced—until I was at least twelve years old—that Mozart was French, simply because I had seen some prints of engravings that showed him playing the harpsichord for Marie Antoinette, and I had come to the conclusion that because he was playing the harpsichord at Versailles, he must be French.

So I believe that if we think in this way, if we think in terms of being citizens of the motion picture culture before thinking of ourselves as citizens of such and such a nation, it will change our attitude toward film more and more. It will also allow us to create certain kinds of film for a certain public, for specialized audiences. I think that this kind of film will be better and will be possible because it will be shown in several countries. It will therefore be able to pay for the cost of making it— not as a result of large audiences in one place, but because of smaller audiences in many places. I truly hope that this will come about, because I'm convinced that film is a more secret art than the so-called private arts. We think that painting is private, but film is much more so. We think that a film is made for the six thousand moviegoers at the Gaumont-Palace, but that isn't true. Instead, it's made for only three people among those six thousand. I found a word for film lovers; it's *aficionados*. I remember a bullfight that took place a long time ago. I didn't know anything about bullfights, but I was there with people who were all very knowledgeable. They became delirious with excitement when the toreador made a slight movement like that toward the right and then he made another slight movement, also toward the right—which seemed the same to me—and everyone yelled at him. I was the one who was wrong. I was wrong to go to a bullfight without knowing the rules of the game. One must always know the rules of the game.

The same thing happened to me again. I have some cousins in America who come from North Dakota. In North Dakota, everyone ice-skates, because for six months of the year there's so much snow that it falls horizontally instead of vertically. It's cold; everything is frozen; and everyone there skates very well. Every time my cousins meet me, they take me to an ice show. They take me to see some women on ice skates who do lots of tricks. It's always the same thing: From time to time you see a woman who does a very impressive twirl: I applaud, and then I stop, seeing that my cousins are looking at me severely, because it seems that she wasn't good at all, but I had no way of knowing. And film is like that as well. And all professions are for the benefit of—well—not only for aficionados but also for the sympathizers. In reality, there must be sympathizers, there must be a brotherhood.

Besides, you've heard about Barnes. His theory was very simple: The qualities, the gifts, or the education that painters have are the same gifts, education, and qualities that lovers of painting have. In other words, in order to love a painting, one must be a would-be painter, or else you cannot really love it. And to love a film, one must be a would-be filmmaker. You have to be able to say to yourself, "I would have done it this way, I would have done it that way." You have to make films yourself, if only in your mind, but you have to make them. If not, you're not worthy of going to the movies.

This idea of the world about which I've spoken to you inspired me to travel to India. It convinced me that if I can lovingly apply myself to the exploits of a fisherman on the Ganges, then maybe I can also identify with him because I am a man of the cinema, and though a foreigner, I am still the brother of the man of the cinema who works in Calcutta, and there is no reason I can't talk about the Ganges as he does.

CAHIERS: *It seems you are seeking greater conciseness, greater density.*
RENOIR: That's right, a greater density in the location. Right now I am trying to forget ideas, formulas, and theories, but at the same time I am

trying to identify with the only thing that remains truly solid after all these turnabouts, catastrophes, and stupidities that we have witnessed, and this one thing is our civilization. God knows I adore India, and I admire Hinduism; I know a little about the Hindu religion, which is fascinating to study. Yet I think that if I want to work properly, I would be better off reading Aristotle and Plato, and following in the wake of all the people who are in my situation, whether in Washington, Oxford, Palermo, or Lyons. That is, following Greek civilization, by way of Christian civilization.

CAHIERS: *In essence, you seek a certain classicism?*
RENOIR: Exactly.

CAHIERS: *Your next film,* Diary of a Chambermaid, *was rather poorly received in France.*
RENOIR: Very poorly.

CAHIERS: *As far as we're concerned, it's very good, and we might even prefer it to* The Rules of the Game.
RENOIR: I'm very proud of it. Oh, you know what I'll ask you to do? Since you feel this way, some day, if you don't mind, let's get together and send a note to Paulette Goddard; she'll be pleased because she feels the same way; she likes the film very much.

CAHIERS: *It was a rather old project.*
RENOIR: It was a very old project that had been completely changed, because I made it at the beginning of the period when I envisioned scenes in a more concentrated, more theatrical manner, with fewer action-reaction shots. I envisioned the scenes more as small vignettes added one to the other. My first attempt was during the silent era, and I conceived of it, at that time, in a very romantic way, very *Nana*-esque.

CAHIERS: *The scenes in the servants' quarters in* Nana, *in fact . . .*
RENOIR: Well, listen, each person embodies all that he will do later in life, which changes all the time. Obviously, no one knows what one will do tomorrow, but it is likely that a shrewder observer than ourselves would see it in us. The possibility is certainly there. Anyway I

went back to this project because I wanted to make a film with Paulette Goddard. In fact, I was looking for a part for her, and I thought she would be very good in the role of Celestine. That's the only reason.

It was an independent production. Burgess Meredith, a few friends, and I were a small group of associates. Benedict Bogeaus found the money. He was the owner of an independent studio that works like the studios in France. That is, it rents its sites to individual producers and doesn't even have a sound department; you have to rent the sound nearby, at Western Electric. It's a studio like the old ones in Hollywood. In any case, it's a very old, charming studio, called General Service. Bogeaus was the owner, and he had connections that enabled us to find a small down payment and the necessary bank loans to make the film. It's also a film that was shot in total freedom and with a great deal of improvisation.

CAHIERS: *And yet a few years ago, many people in France said, "Jean Renoir wasn't able to do what he wanted, he was bullied."*
RENOIR: No, not at all. This film may be good or bad, but if it's bad, I alone am responsible for it. Notice that I was influenced—I'm the most easily influenced man in the world—because people say, "You may be wrong in doing that; why are you doing it?" And then, well, you tell yourself that maybe they're right, and you're cautious. Obviously, you can be influenced in good ways or bad ways, but that's true of all films. Even if you do films the way Chaplin did, with his own money, without making any concessions to anyone else's interests, you're still influenced. . . . But I repeat, I always did what I wanted to in Hollywood, and if I made mistakes there, I would have made the same ones in Paris.

CAHIERS: *Is it true that the final lynch scene was entirely improvised on the set?*
RENOIR: Naturally it was improvised, it wasn't in the script, but it's not the only improvised scene; there are many of them.

CAHIERS: *It seems as if you're seeking a mounting climax in this film. You're trying, as they say, to go all out.*
RENOIR: Yes, of course, and I was interested in seeing an actress work toward this, an actress who doesn't normally do this in her films and

whom I like very much. She's an extraordinary working companion, a really good associate, and so I wanted to push her in this direction. . . . I also wanted to do scenes that were almost sketches, to leave them undeveloped, to simplify them to an extreme. I wanted them to be like sketches or rough drafts.

CAHIERS: *Finally we come to* The Woman on the Beach, *a film in which you met with a few difficulties, so they say.*

RENOIR: It was quite an adventure. It's a film that one of my friends, Joan Bennett, asked me to do. She said to me, "RKO has asked me to do a film; come do it with me." RKO also asked me. I had been very happy with this studio, and I was pleased to go back. At the beginning, the producer of the film must have been Val Lewton. I'll say a few words about Val Lewton, because he was an extremely interesting person. Unfortunately he died several years ago. He was one of the first, maybe the first, to have had the idea of making inexpensive films, films using the budget allocated to B pictures, but with a certain amount of ambition, with high-quality scripts that tell higher-caliber stories than was typical. Not that I don't like B pictures. In principle I like them better than the grand, pretentious, psychological, big-budget films; they're much more fun. Whenever I go to the movies in America, I go to see B pictures. First, because they demonstrate Hollywood's high technical quality. In order to make a good western in one week, as they do at Monogram—to start it on Monday and finish it on Saturday—believe me, you have to have extraordinary technical capacities. And the adventure films are done just as quickly. I also think that the B pictures are often better than the so-called important films, because they are done so quickly that the director is necessarily free: There's no time to watch over him.

Val Lewton, then, gave RKO a list of films that were inexpensive but that told more ambitious stories. I'll name one, a successful one that was done with Tourneur's son [Jacques] and that starred Simone Simon: *Cat People.* It was a very good story and a very good film. Anyway, Val Lewton very kindly helped me begin *The Woman on the Beach,* and then he had other projects that conformed better to his list and in which he was probably more interested, so I found myself all alone. I was practically my own producer, in association with a friend, named Gross, for the practical side of things. In fact, I was entirely responsible for *The Woman on the Beach*. No one interfered, and I was able to do exactly what I wanted. I have never shot a film for which so little was written, which was so improvised on the set. I took advantage of the situation to try something that I had wanted to do for a long time: a film based on what we call today sex—maybe we called it sex then, but we talked about it less—but envisioned from a purely physical perspective. I wanted to try to tell a love story based purely on physical attraction, a story in which emotions played no part. I did it and I was very pleased with it. It may have been a slow film, but it had some rather strong scenes. It was acted admirably by Robert Ryan, whom you know—you saw him in Wise's *The Set-Up* and in many other films, but this was his first important part—and Joan Bennett, who was wonderful.

The directors of RKO, the actors, and I all were very happy with the film, but we had some doubts about the public's reaction to it, so we all agreed to show some previews. We showed them, mainly in Santa Barbara, to a very young audience, mostly students. They reacted very poorly to the film; they weren't interested in it at all. I felt that my way of presenting these sentimental questions shocked them, or maybe it didn't correspond to what they were used to. In any case, the film was very poorly received, and we returned to the studio very depressed.

You know, a preview is a horrible test. You sit in a theater, and it's as if someone were stabbing you with knives all over your body. I must admit to having been very discouraged after returning from this preview, and I was the first to suggest cutting and changing the film. The film had been rather expensive, because to achieve this somewhat different style, I had to work slowly. Joan Bennett kindly lent herself to what was almost a personality change. I even asked her to change her voice. I worked to lower its tone—she had a rather high pitched voice, and in this film she had a low voice—all that took time, therefore money, and I was the first to fear a financial catastrophe for the film, to feel responsible, and to become a little crazy. The studio graciously offered, "OK, we'll make changes, but you'll make them." I asked for a writer to help me so that I wouldn't be alone, so that we could talk and bounce ideas back and forth. At the same time, Joan Bennett's husband, Walter Wanger, also came to see a screening and to give me his opinion. In sum, it seemed to me at the time that I didn't have the right to take all the responsibility for the film by myself. I think, by the way, that I was wrong and that this fear didn't help the film.

So I went back to a number of scenes very cautiously, that is, to about a third of the film, essentially the scenes between Joan Bennett and Robert Ryan, and I finally released a film that I think was rather middle-of-the-road, which had lost its reason for existing. I think I allowed myself to be influenced too much by the preview at Santa Barbara, which was decisive. All of a sudden I was afraid of losing contact with the public, and I gave in. But once again, the people who criticize this film should not criticize the influences on me. I'm responsible for the changes, just as I was responsible for the film beforehand.

The truth is I think I tried something that would have worked today. If I were to shoot *The Woman on the Beach* now, in America, with the ideas I had in mind when I made it, I think it would work. I'm afraid I was ahead of the public.

CAHIERS: *You were saying that you were looking for a certain style.*
RENOIR: The word *style* is rather ambitious. What I wanted, without using that exact word, was to suggest that my characters were very physically in love, and to express this idea with different words, with very ordinary words, for example, with memories. Thus Joan Bennett recounted her childhood memories and spoke of a certain Italian professor who had taught her music, and these very common memories were told in such a way as to suggest a mutual desire by both Joan Bennett and Bob Ryan. These things, of course, are very difficult to express, and it took time. Another thing is that it's the kind of film that requires facial expressions that the audience can easily grasp, and that calls for many close-ups, and close-ups take time in film and are expensive.

CAHIERS: *There's the cigarette scene, for example. I personally would be unable to pinpoint what makes it so remarkable.*
RENOIR: It's probably because of the quality of the actors in the close-ups. It's also a scene in which the conversation has no relationship to the interior action. The conversation in the scene you mentioned is about deep-sea fishing. God knows no one there could care less about deep-sea fishing, but anyway, they talk about it. In the meantime, the

only question in the mind of the new guest, the man who desires Joan Bennett, is "Is that man blind or not?" That's all, but it isn't said.

Part Two: *The River* and *The Golden Coach*

JEAN RENOIR: After *The Woman on the Beach*, I was confused. I realized that this film hadn't touched the public as I had wanted, and I had many more projects. For instance, I had formed a small company with a few friends, which I called the Film Group, and I wanted to try to shoot classical plays on a small budget. I wanted to create a kind of film revival using young stage actors' groups that had been very successful in Hollywood at the time, not financially successful, but very respected. Moreover, these theatrical enterprises were valuable in America. There were many of them: notably the Circle, which operated out of the first floor of an old house. Because there was no stage, they placed the audience around the actors, as in a miniature circus. These different groups performed all the time, and their actors, their members, were often very interesting. I therefore had the idea—with many rehearsals and working with classics or with good modern texts—of trying to create a kind of classical American film. I must admit that I didn't succeed, and for one simple reason: Bank loans started to become more and more difficult to obtain, and because this was a new enterprise, the American banks were less amenable to taking a risk than they might have been one year earlier when all films were making money. I don't know if I told you what my friend Charles Korner said to me one day, shaking his head, "Jean, all films are making money these days, even good ones." Those days were gone.

Seeing that things weren't going to work out, I started thinking about other things. One day, by chance, in the book section of the *New Yorker*, I read a review of a book by an English author, a woman named Rumer Godden, and the name of the book was *The River*. The review said something like this: In terms of its language, it was probably one of the best books written in English over the past fifty years, and it added that the book would most likely not make a cent. It was encouraging enough for me to go out and buy the book. I went to a bookstore right away, bought it, read it, and I was immediately convinced that it was a top-notch film subject. I wrote to Mrs. Godden through my agents, so that everything would be done by the rules, and she agreed to sell me an option on the book. At the same time, I wrote to her saying that I thought her subject was a tremendous inspiration for a film but was not a film story, and so she would have to rewrite it with me, change the events and maybe even the characters, while keeping the general idea of the story, which, in my opinion, had the makings of a great film. She agreed, and I found myself with an option on *The River*. Then I went to see lots of people, but I wasn't able to interest anyone in my project. . . . Because to many people, a film on India means charging cavalries, tiger hunts, elephants, and maharajas. People said to me, "Now if you could add a few maharajas and a few tiger hunts, it would be a beautiful story, but we think that people who go to see a film on India expect something else. After all, we do have to give the public what it wants."

In the meantime, I didn't get discouraged, and this is what happened: A man who wasn't involved in films wanted to make them and had found a group that could finance him in India. What he lacked was any knowledge of film, a subject, and a director. He knew people in the Indian government, and it happened that one day he had a conversation with, I think, Pandit Nehru's niece, who told him, "You know, making a film in India isn't easy for a Westerner. If you want to shoot an Indian subject, you might fall flat on your face and say things that aren't true. If I were you, I would start by making a film in which there were some Westerners. This would permit a director capable of understanding India to establish a kind of bridge between India and Western audiences." And she added, "As far as I'm concerned, the English author who knows India the best today is Rumer Godden. She wasn't born in India, but she came here when she was a few months old, she grew up here, she speaks some Indian languages, and she knows India as if it were her own country." This gentleman was very impressed and inquired about *The River*, asked if he could buy the rights, and came to me because of my option. He asked me, "Do you want to do *The River* with me?" I told him, "Yes, but on one condition: You have to send me to India so that I can find out whether I can really do something interesting." So I took my first trip to India, and I was convinced. I returned with a great passion for the country. I wrote the script with Rumer Godden—we rewrote it on location, by the way, while we were shooting—and that's how I shot *The River*. Very roughly, this was the practical story of it.

CAHIERS: *So Rumer Godden was with you.*

RENOIR: She was with me during the shooting, and she watched two-thirds of it. She helped me both decide on the script and rewrite a story that is different from the book, and of which she is the author as much as I am. She also helped me with many other things. For example, we used many inexperienced actors, especially for the leading role, the little Harriet, who is an English girl we found at the school in Calcutta. I must say that the professional actors I had in *The River* also helped a great deal with these inexperienced ones. We had to train them. I don't believe in total inexperience, I don't believe in luck, I believe that everything is learned. In the villa that you see in the film, which was our headquarters, our everything, we set up a little acting school and even a dance school, because Rumer Godden was a dance teacher. We had to teach these young actors and actresses a new profession. She helped me give a professional side to these young people's acting.

After the film was shot, the producer and I were, of course, wondering how it would be received. My last experience had been *The Woman on the Beach,* and the poor reception at the previews had been a great surprise to me. So I asked myself if we weren't going to have a problem with a subject that, according to some very intelligent people who know their profession in Hollywood, doesn't give an audience interested in India what it wants. The India that I was supposedly showing in this film was—how can I say—a bit colorless. Because of all this, I wanted to be cautious, and as I worked on the editing, I constantly monitored the audiences' reactions. I screened it in an old studio in Hollywood—now almost entirely used for television—called Hal Roach. Hal Roach was a place for pioneers; the first comical films were shot there. It has a very large screening room with more than a hundred seats—it started to feel like a real audience—and I gathered people in this room quite often, people purposely chosen from certain categories. From time to time, for example, I had people who worked in industry, in the neighboring factories, or sometimes people who worked in business, in the shops in Beverly Hills, or professional people, designers, and, once in a while, very mixed groups. At each step of my editing, I showed the film to small groups like that.

This was all the more dangerous a test because the cutting copy was in black and white, although it was shot in color. I made up for that sometimes by showing certain color samples, either before or after. I had what are called *pilots*, which Technicolor sends to help you imagine what the film will be like while you're editing it. You could print the work print all in color, of course, but it would be very expensive, and you save an enormous amount when you do the editing in black and white. In addition, it's an especially ugly black and white, since it's printed from one of the three color separation negatives. It therefore lacks some of the values, other colors aren't visible at all, it's not even orthochromatic [lacks red]; altogether, it's quite disappointing.

I was very worried about one thing: the music. I was lucky enough to make many friends in India, especially with young film people, technicians, journalists, or actors, who introduced me to the Calcutta art world, and especially to the music world where I was able to meet some very good musicians. In addition, I had a wonderful adviser in *The River* in regard to India: Radha, the dancer who plays the role of the half-Indian, though in reality she's a pure Brahmin. Anyway, she plays the role of a half-caste. And obviously, as a dancer, she was familiar with music, especially that from the South (she's from Madras). So, on the one hand from my friends in Calcutta, and, on the other hand through Radha for the South, I was able to understand something about this music and to hear a good deal of it. And with the help of these friends, I was able to tape some exceptional Indian music, very classic, very pure, and not at all influenced by Western thought. The music in Indian films is often very bad. Indian producers think they will make a hit by adapting European instruments and often by forgetting the old Indian scale. You know that the Indian scale—like that of European music in the Middle Ages, before all the great revolutions brought on by Bach and the seventeenth-century Italians—had between forty and seventy notes, or even more; it was infinite. Indian music is still like that, and many Indian producers don't hesitate to rewrite old songs on the modern scale, with modern instruments, which are, so they say, more vivid, but it's very contrived in my opinion. It winds up sounding like fake Mexican music, and it's not very good. I therefore avoided that. But the music I used is unusual just the same, and I wondered how European and American audiences would react to it. My previews helped me a great deal here, as I tried mixing the dialogue and this music.

I must say that the previews helped me establish a bridge to the public more easily, but right from the beginning I realized that I hadn't been wrong about *The River*. The reactions were good right from the start: People were engrossed in my characters but had varied reactions. From time to time we had them fill out questionnaires, and the responses were very different. Part of the audience was interested in the English people in India and saw in them a picture of themselves had they been there; others, on the contrary, were interested only in the life-style of the natives. It soon became clear that there were different topics of interest in this film and that I could "go ahead"; so I opened the flood gates and asked the producer not to make any musical recordings for the film, following the modern principle that music underlines the images. In any case, I'm against that, I think the music should act to counterbalance the film, I'm against having it repeat the action and sentiments. The producer accepted this, and even the European music was taken from classical pieces, [von Weber's] *Invitation to the Dance,* for example. I also used some piano airs by Schumann, a little air by Mozart somewhere.

Anyway, the question of the music had worried me a great deal, and these previews helped me confirm my opinion. They were very valuable, especially because they gave me the courage to make the film as a whole as I had conceived of it, as I saw it, and as Rumer Godden and I had imagined it. The editing was done in the same way: My first previews were very cautious. In my first cut, I simply tried to follow the film's action. Then, little by little, I understood that it was a film in which I could allow myself to add a few purely poetic morsels that had no relationship with what we call the action, for example, the passage on the stairs, which I liked very much but which I dared to insert only when I had finished the editing. So to a large extent because of the moral support that these audiences gave me, *The River* is a film that fully represents what I had imagined at the beginning.

CAHIERS: *In what way was the adaptation of Rumer Godden's novel different from the novel?*
RENOIR: I can tell you the biggest difference in two words: We decided to make the film much more Indian. In Godden's novel, which is marvelous, India penetrates the walls of the house, though you never

go there. We decided to break down the walls. The part of the Indian half-caste didn't exist in the novel, either; it's an invention of ours that permitted us to bring more of India into the story.

CAHIERS: *This character in a sense symbolizes the main subject of the film, that is, the relationship between two civilizations.*
RENOIR: Absolutely. I symbolize the theme in this character; it exists in the novel, but in a completely different manner. That is, it exists through the thousand little relationships that Harriet, the heroine of the film and the novel, has, and through the different servants in the house, through the people who come to the house, and through many short conversations, but not through a specific fact like that of being a half-caste. India penetrates the walls of the house by means of a thousand minor details and by means of Harriet. But Harriet, like Rumer Godden in real life (because Harriet is Rumer Godden; it's an autobiography, and this shows up in the film), Harriet is very influenced by India, and Rumer is very influenced by India. Her last book is the story of a voyage she took during the last war in Kashmir, and it is fantastic. She has very deep roots in the country. She lives in England now, but I wouldn't be surprised if she were to return to India.

CAHIERS: *Which brings us to a question about another aspect of the film, Westerners' understanding of Indian religion and philosophy.*
RENOIR: That also is in the novel and in other novels by Rumer. It is especially apparent in a magnificent novel called *Breakfast with the Nikolides*. The Nikolides are Greek neighbors—there are many Greeks in the jute industry in Calcutta—and there is a character in the novel who is very influenced by Hindu philosophy. Harriet is almost the only person in *The River* who is influenced by it. Now in real life, the Westerners can be divided into two categories: those who consider anything Hindu, Indian, or Muslim to be extremely inferior, not even worth thinking about, and who manage, while in India, to reconstruct a purely English, or purely French, or purely Greek life, although the Greeks mix in much more easily. On the other hand, there are those who allow themselves to be absorbed, and they are also very numerous. In the film, the English family is neither one nor the other, which also is possible. They obviously remain completely English, but at the same

time they know that the Hindu civilization exists, which is the position of many Englishmen.

CAHIERS: *It is, in a sense, a kind of Western meditation on Asia?*
RENOIR: Exactly, and it would have been very difficult to do anything else during my first contact with India; I would have risked going completely astray. I had to see India through the eyes of a Westerner if I didn't want to make some horrible mistakes.

CAHIERS: *Is it through this contact with India that you became aware of the theme of "acceptance," which has been appearing more and more clearly in your films?*
RENOIR: Not really. This is my own theme, but India could not have helped but develop it. The main idea of the Hindu religion—let's not say religion, because it's not exactly a religion, let's say philosophy or Hindu metaphysics—is that the world is one. We're part of it, we're part of the world just as a tree or your tape recorder is. That doesn't imply an acceptance, as in the Muslim tradition, which is fatalistic. No, it's an empowerment. But nonetheless, you can't go back to what has been done. In other words, for example, there is no remission of sin. For them the remission of sin is just like saying that if you cut off your arm, you can glue it back on. It's obviously very impressive; it's a kind of understanding of the meaning of everything that happens. It's a religion that comprehends the world, but it isn't fatalistic; it's a philosophy.

In any case, I must say that Rumer and I were extremely influenced by Radha. Radha is quite a person, she has a master's degree in Sanskrit, and she reads Sanskrit as easily as she reads English or several Indian languages. She's a very educated girl, and she comes from a good family, which means a lot in India, where studying is a tradition. It doesn't mean that she is morally or physically superior to people of other castes. Besides, the idea of superiority from caste to caste doesn't exist in India. What does exist is the idea of specialization. The truth is that the Hindu caste system is a bit like a hereditary union: You belong to a certain union, but you belong to it for four thousand years. That's the difference: You can escape it only by death or resurrection, since death and resurrection are quite common. Radha, with her knowledge of her country, her religion, and the West, was therefore an extraordinary associate, with incredible perception and intelligence. I would have loved to do other things with her as an actress. Maybe you noticed this: At the beginning, when she comes home from school with a little European outfit, doesn't she remind you of the very good Russian actresses? She makes me think of a young Nazimova. Yes, you could do wonders with her, only this is a difficult profession, everything takes so long. Getting a new project going takes years, times passes. But film-making is not a convenient profession, and circumstances may never allow me to return to India. There is one other problem. Because *The River* worked so well, now everyone is shooting in India. India is full of producers and directors from all countries.

CAHIERS: *Did you plan the script's structure in detail?*

RENOIR: No, we both agreed to leave the structure rather loose during the shooting. I shot it so that I could either create a narration, that is, stay with a booklike tone or else not tell the story and not have any commentary at all. During the little previews, when I saw that the documentary side got good reactions (let's say the poetic side), I decided to go with the seminarrated form, which permitted me to present certain purely poetic parts without having to back them up with dramatic action and dialogue. But the construction of the script was rather loose, rather easy, and allowed for the two solutions. When I shot these poetic passages, I thought I would use them as they were, but I wasn't sure it would work, and if it hadn't worked, I would have had to shorten them enormously and integrate them into the action scenes.

So I shot the film very cautiously, but this caution did not apply to the scenes. I'm never cautious with my scenes. You know that the main system of film production, all over the world, whether in Paris or in Hollywood, is what they call "taking precautions, being covered." It's like in the army, where you have to have an order in writing before sweeping a courtyard, to ensure that it isn't a prank. The way you cover yourself in film is by taking many shots of a scene, so that you can either lengthen it or shorten it. I wasn't any more cautious in this respect in *The River* than I am in other films. Many of my scenes are shot in one single take and must be used as they are; they can't be cut. No, my precaution was having enough material for the editing so that I could use a commented style or a noncommented style for the overall outline of the film.

CAHIERS: *There is still another aspect of* The River: *its metaphorical, or symbolic, side, which I am unable to define clearly, but many images, for example, the recurring one in which three boats come together, make one think of a meaning other than their immediate one.*

RENOIR: It's obvious that not only I but also most of my collaborators, and especially my Hindu collaborators, had our minds off in that direction and that solutions of this type constantly came to mind, so that often it was intentional. Not that it was planned, but it was intended in the sense that we were attracted by this kind of mental exercise, and we were extremely open to such solutions.

CAHIERS: *Thus, the stairway sequence . . .*

RENOIR: That one was entirely intentional, and for a good reason: The sequence is an edited piece, which means I did it at the end, when I was much surer about my principles. Don't forget something that I repeat all the time: You discover the content of a film as you're shooting it. You obviously start with guiding principles that are as firm as possible, but when the subject is worthwhile, each step is a discovery, and this discovery brings others, and so a subject . . . That's perhaps the main thing about film, which is why certain films have become so important to the history of cinema, to the history of culture and modern civilization. It's that the film medium carries technical obstacles that make it a slow means of expression (you can't shoot a film quickly), and this battle with technical obstacles forces you—more than in any other medium—to discover and to rediscover. You benefit from forced pauses that a writer would be obliged to impose on himself. The halts, the delays, are very good for the quality of a film, and this one was greatly strengthened by them. . . . To begin with, I had a lucky break: We were supposed to start on a certain date, but the camera blimp, the sound insulation for the cameras, hadn't arrived, so in order to avoid problems for the producer, I had to start filming certain things without sound, and so the camera noise didn't matter. It was a delay, but this delay helped me, because whatever I filmed in this way was purely documentary. It therefore forced me, before starting the film's real scenes, to get more in touch with the country by means of the documentary, and this did me a great deal of good.

CAHIERS: *After seeing* The River, *one cannot help being struck by something that also appears in many of your other films, but in a less apparent way: the predominance of the number three.*

RENOIR: That's not something I owe to India. I owe it more to my admiration for early films in which the number three was a kind of magic number. I don't know whether you've noticed it, for example, in Mack Sennett's comedies. It's also a very old music-hall and café-concert theory. In Mack Sennett's comedies, the gag generally worked only the third time, and so I guess that film's early directors tended to use this number three. I was brought up on the films from this period, and I still admire them greatly. I obviously must have been influenced by them; they were my film education. But, you know, the slightly ridiculous actors of the great romantic period, at whom everyone laughs today but who carried some weight with the public, believed in the number three. I'll always remember, when my brother was very young and was beginning to think of an acting career, and to get practice in it (it was before he went to the conservatory), he took lessons with an old romantic actor who could no longer take roles, who was crumbling with old age and who, from time to time, came to our house in Montmartre to give lessons to this young man who wanted to pursue a career. I remember the following bit of advice very well: "In the *Tour de Nesle* you have this line: 'It was the noble head of an old man that the assassin often saw in his dreams, because he assassinated him'; here you count: one, two, three, and you say, 'the villain.' "

CAHIERS: *So you use this kind of construction as a springboard, in a sense.*
RENOIR: I don't think I used it intentionally, but I saw so many films from the beginning that it probably became almost automatic. Besides, I think we should use every technical and practical means, but we must be sure of them, and apply them instinctively when they're convenient.

CAHIERS: *We don't want you to tell us your professional secrets.*
RENOIR: I don't have any. That would be very difficult, I couldn't talk about it. No, I think that the only secret—which is very convenient in

our profession, as in others, and which helps a great deal—is to try to see and to fill yourself with good things. If you're a playwright, better to read Shakespeare and Molière than to read . . . an inferior writer. In film, it's the same thing, and I was very lucky to start loving films and to want to make them at a time when they were really good. One can honestly say that the bad films were the exceptions. This was because it was a primitive period and the primitives have an easier time doing good work than do people who have the advantage of better technology.

CAHIERS: The Golden Coach *was also an old project.*
RENOIR: Yes, but the *The Golden Coach* that I filmed has nothing to do with this very, very old project. I had thought of it in the days of silent films, and I saw it as a kind of great adventure story. It no longer corresponded to my ideas at that time, and when I was asked to film it (I wasn't the one who had the idea for *The Golden Coach* at the time, it was also one of the producer's old projects), when I went to shoot it—I was, in any case, convinced that it would be shot in France. I didn't know it was an Italian project—I agreed to do it because I was very interested in Magnani. Having seen her in many films, I was convinced—despite her usual appearance and her reputation as more of a romantic, naturalist actress—I was convinced that I might be able to make a move toward classicism. It was my pilot film. An admiration for classical Italy replaced India for me in *The Golden Coach*, the Italy from before Verdi and romanticism.

CAHIERS: *Which in the film is expressed by Vivaldi's music.*
RENOIR: That's right. My first draft was without Vivaldi; I owe Vivaldi to a friend. . . . You know, when you work in a country, you have to allow yourself to be absorbed by the country, or else you have no chance of doing something correctly; and the character who played the role in *The Golden Coach* that Radha played in India was a director, my assistant for the film, whose name is Giulio Macchi. Macchi is not only very intelligent, he is also a very cultivated man, and he's the one who pushed me to Vivaldi. I hadn't begun the shooting script yet, nor the treatment, and I only had some vague ideas as to how I wanted to handle it. I bought all the Vivaldi records I could find. There was a composer at the Panaria Company who generally took care of the music in

the company's films, and I asked him to help me get to know Vivaldi better. You know, Vivaldi is still unknown, his manuscripts are being discovered every day. It's incredible what he did. Just played on the piano, this music made me hear things I had never known, and Vivaldi's influence obviously had a tremendous influence on the writing of the final shooting script.

CAHIERS: *But in what way did Vivaldi's music influence you?*
RENOIR: It influenced the entire style of the film, a side that isn't drama, that isn't farce, that isn't burlesque. It's a sort of irony that I tried to combine with the light-spiritedness one finds, for example, in Goldoni.

CAHIERS: *That's almost what you had looked for in* The Rules of the Game, *but I suppose in a very different manner, since many admirers of that film were disturbed by* The Golden Coach.
RENOIR: Luckily, we are constantly discovering things in life, and I think that little by little, as I grow older, I rediscover things that I unconsciously knew all along.

CAHIERS: *Because of Italy. . .*
RENOIR: What happened in Italy is extremely important. Italy, in my mind, is perhaps first and foremost the active symbol of a particular civilization. I told you of my interest in, my love for India. Nonetheless, I remain a member of a particular community. Italy happens to have transmitted the elements of the civilization to which we belong. You can go anywhere, to any world capital, but you will notice that although London, for example, is essentially an English city, most of its monuments were built by Italian architects. The Italians influenced our entire civilization. If we eat with forks, it's because the Medicis brought them to France; if our chairs are a certain shape, it's because we imitated the Florentines at a certain period.

That said, I don't think that Italians are important as Italians per se. Rather, I think they are important because of their geographical placement (their country was the center of the Roman Empire, which brought together all the elements of our civilization). They could gather together all the different parts of this civilization and then spread them around.

Therefore, the more time that passes, the more I become convinced of Italy's importance to the history of our civilization's development, and the more I want to assimilate the Italian spirit in order to do things in this vein. In our profession, especially in theater, they were often our masters: Molière was very influenced by Italian comedy; Marivaux started by writing for the Italians; and all our theater, up until romanticism in which the German influence became predominant, all our classical theater was influenced by Italy. So that's the reason for my attraction to Italy. It's because I accept what I consider to be a fact. Whether we like it or not, we belong to a civilization that started in Greece, continued through Rome, spread throughout the West by way of the Christian revolution, or, that is, by way of the Jewish influence.

CAHIERS: *And at first, you wanted to make a "civilized" film.*
RENOIR: Yes, I wanted to make a civilized film. Thank you for thinking of that; I wouldn't have thought of it myself, but you've put your finger on it. . . . We have many ideas in our minds, but we don't know how to find the words to express them; and it's true, this desire for civilization was the driving force that pushed me to make *The Golden Coach.*

CAHIERS: *That explains the relief of each detail, and that an article of clothing, or the design on a chair, can have the same importance to the whole as does each of the plot's shifts in the action.*
RENOIR: Yes, that's true. I think that if one wants to create a classical work, one must do that. The idea of artificially attracting the audience's attention to certain elements, to a star, for example, is a purely romantic idea. Even in painting, in drawings, modern people are used to romantic simplification and get lost when they see classical works such as tapestries; they find them a bit busy. They aren't actually busy, but classicism contains an idea of evenness that no longer exists in romanticism.

CAHIERS: *Despite all the prefaces, in which the romantics proclaimed almost the opposite of what they did.*
RENOIR: As usual, that's why one must avoid having very precise theories, because it seems that fate maliciously enjoys contradicting you,

leading you to goals that are the exact opposite of what you intended. This tremendous contradiction is rather strange. It is, in fact, expressed very clearly in the writings of every religion, notably in the Christian religion. Proverbs like The first will be the last, or the parables on wealth—The poor will be rich, Little children are the most intelligent— aren't paradoxical, they're the truth. This world is made up of contradictions, often comical contradictions. The fact that the powerful will fall, for example. I've witnessed that four or five times during my life, which hasn't been relatively very long.

CAHIERS: *There is a musicality pervading* The Golden Coach: *The scroll of the violins, for example, seems to be present in all the spirals of the decor, and even in certain details of the clothing.*
RENOIR: I will repeat the same thing about *The Golden Coach* that I said about *The River:* I think we try to perfect ourselves, we try to learn, we try to work constantly, we discover things at each stage in a career. But the discoveries and the little we've learned are a bit like a battery, and we are not necessarily conscious of the electricity released from it. So we try to keep all of this inside ourselves, and we use it, hoping that it will come when we need it. It doesn't always come when we need it, however; that's the trauma of creation. Often, all that we've accumulated, all that we've tried to learn, comes too late or too early and not at the moment we need it. On the other hand, if we proceed in too orderly a fashion, that is, with notes, cards, with filed memories, and if we try to apply them mechanically and arbitrarily, I think we become removed from life. One must be very wary of knowledge and theories. One has to have them, but it is best to tackle each subject as if we knew nothing, as if we were completely new to it, and as if the subject were unexplored. If we don't approach a subject with a certain degree of freshness, then we're not alive, we're dead. You also have to have a good time while you make films. It's very important. I had a good time while making *The Golden Coach.* It was very strenuous, it was very hard, but I had a great time.

CAHIERS: *Doing what, exactly?*
RENOIR: Well, constantly discovering a classical Italian spirit in modern Italians. I had fun dealing with the Italians, whom I found to be

exceptional people, people who have maintained a classical freshness, I might say, particularly in their way of approaching life's problems with a kind of simplicity, a very direct side, although it's hidden beneath superficial complications. But these complications are only superficial. When it comes to feelings, their feelings are very straight-forward, very simple.

CAHIERS: *Which is a type of classicism . . .*
RENOIR: It also is classicism, like a piece of lace, whose design—which is really quite distinct—we decipher little by little. There is an American critic who doesn't like my films. He showers me with praise, but he makes one very interesting criticism. This is what he says: "It's a little like those boxes that you open, and there is another box, and you open it, and there is another box." Note that this critic made me very happy by saying this. He considers it to be a defect, however, that a film shouldn't be made in this way, but personally I find this box game rather interesting.

CAHIERS: *There is one question we would like to ask you about each film: What role does improvisation play? Isn't the structure, which seems subtle and complex, already decided in the script?*
RENOIR: Oh yes, the outline is planned. It's the dialogues that are improvised. Or if you like, the scenes and their sequence have been decided in advance, but the way of arriving at the final goal, which is the last shot of a scene, sometimes changes. It takes place on the same set, with the same characters, but often the words or the characters' reactions are different.

CAHIERS: *In the morning, I believe, you rehearse the scenes that are to be shot that afternoon. You decide then on the placement and the shooting, according to the acting?*
RENOIR: Yes, that's right. The so-called French system, which is to start working at noon, is excellent, in my opinion, for the film's quality. First because the actors, the technicians, and the workers like it better; they come to work well rested; they spend the morning at home, with their families; and they eat dinner a bit later, but also at home with their families. From this point of view, it's very good. And it allows the

director to spend the morning on the set, or in any case to concentrate on certain problems before getting caught up in the whirlwind of shooting.

CAHIERS: *And that's how you did* The Golden Coach?
RENOIR: Yes, but I also do that for all my films.

CAHIERS: *You rehearse the actors first, then, without worrying about the camera?*
RENOIR: Oh, I do more than that, you know. I really believe in one method of rehearsal: It's first to ask the actors to recite their lines without acting them out, by allowing them to think, shall we say, only after several readings, so that when they're ready to try out certain theories according to which they will have certain reactions to the lines, they'll have these reactions to lines they know, not to lines that they don't yet understand, because you understand a line only after repeating it several times. And I even think that the method of acting must be discovered by the actors, and when they've discovered it, I ask them to temper it, not to use it right away, but to search, to advance cautiously, and especially not to add gestures until the end, so that they completely understand the meaning of the scene before they move an inch, grab a pencil, or light a cigarette. I don't ask them to try to act naturally, but to act in such a way that the discovery of exterior elements comes after the discovery of interior elements, and not vice versa.

In any case, I am extremely opposed to the method used by many directors, which consists of saying: "Look at me, I'll act out the scene for you. Now, do as I do." I don't think this is a very good method, because the director doesn't act out the scene, the actor does. The actor has to discover the scene himself and has to bring his own personality to it, and not the director's.

CAHIERS: *In this film, you were looking for a dramatic atmosphere that would be that of both film and the theater?*
RENOIR: Yes, because the period and the subject were so theatrical that it seemed to me the best way of expressing the period and portraying the subject was to subordinate my style to a theatrical style.

CAHIERS: *That's why* The Golden Coach *is structured like a three-act play?*
RENOIR: Yes, that's right. . . . To create this intended confusion
between theater and life, I asked my actors, especially those who played
real-life roles, to act with a little bit of exaggeration, so as to give life to
this theatrical side and to allow me to create the confusion.

CAHIERS: *So there is no fourth dimension, everything happens facing front?*
RENOIR: Yes. Note that at first, I gave certain sets a fourth side, but little by little I gave that up, and I shot the film almost entirely as if I were
on stage, with the camera in the place of the audience. Sometimes I
used the fourth side, but not in the same scene. Each scene was conceived of as seen from one side. Moreover, I must say that as time goes
by, I'm starting to use this method in all my films. In *The Rules of the
Game*, it's already extremely clear: There is no fourth side.

CAHIERS: *But in* The Rules of the Game, *the camera constantly pivoted
whereas it seems that more and more, you direct with still shots and panning
shots. Thus in* The Woman on the Beach . . .
RENOIR: Yes, but *The Woman on the Beach,* for the reasons I gave you,
is a film in which the fourth side plays an important role. It's a film that
has reaction shots. Theoretically, *The Golden Coach* has no reaction
shots. Those that it does have are simply to get close to the actors once
in a while so that the audience can understand what's going on in their
heads. But it's simply a practical necessity, not a style. The style consists
of placing the camera in front of the scene and shooting it.

CAHIERS: *You've talked to us about classicism, but another striking thing
in* The Golden Coach *is its modern character. Aren't you looking for a
certain modernism through this classicism?*
RENOIR: Yes, that's obviously true, but if the results I got can be called
modern, I think, once again, that it can't be done deliberately. I believe
a great deal in teachers, in school, in examples. I told you that. I think
that seeing films one admires, good films, helps enormously. I'm very
disciplined in my way of working, and I'm convinced that if you start
by saying "I'm going to destroy everything, I'm going to be modern,"
then you won't be modern. You can be modern, and you must want to
be so, because you must contribute something, but you can be modern

only by humbly following your predecessors. Now, in spite of yourself, if you're good at that, you'll be modern without even trying.

CAHIERS: *So, for example, you try to achieve a juxtaposition of elements rather than a connection?*
RENOIR: Yes, because it's easier for me. You know, in this profession I have almost always been guided by practicality, by convenience. After all, you're trying to tell a story, and you're looking for the most practical ways of doing it.

CAHIERS: *For you it's a springboard, not an end.*
RENOIR: It's not an end. No, absolutely not, but it's a means.

CAHIERS: *And it's the simplest, therefore the most efficient?*
RENOIR: I think so. . . . Of course, each time, after having rehearsed, I find myself faced with the problem of shooting a scene. For example, I never start with an idea of the camera angle, I start with the scene. I rehearse it, and then, with the help of the cameraman, we decide on the angle. We say, "Well, this scene could be shot like this." There is another thing I never do. I never divide up a scene into action and reaction shots, start with a master shot, and then move to closer shots, and then, in the editing, use all of them. It seems to me that each piece of a scene has one angle and not two. In fact, the cutting of my films, except in special cases like *The River*, is extremely simple. It consists of merely putting pieces back to back that were shot back to back.

CAHIERS: *You shoot chronologically?*
RENOIR: The scenes, in any case, yes.

CAHIERS: *And the film? Wasn't* The Rules of the Game *shot . . .*
RENOIR: Yes, almost chronologically. You can't do it completely because there are location shots and also the matter of contracts with the actors, people who are free or not free. But in any case, I like to shoot chronologically as much as possible.

CAHIERS: *And* The Golden Coach?
RENOIR: It was shot almost chronologically, but not entirely.

CAHIERS: *There still is one question we'd like to ask you, the question of color: What, in your opinion, is the best way to use color?*

RENOIR: First of all, it seems to me that color is not important. Certain subjects do have to be in color, and others are better in black and white. But in the end, I think here again, as in everything, that technology is at the service of the story. The goal is to tell a story. If it helps to tell it in color, let's tell it in color. Now, how should this color be used? I think it should be used without much thought to technology. At this point, all the different systems are very good. Technicolor in London is exceptionally good, but that is due mostly to the quality of their laboratories. They have old crews that have been working on color together for years. Here again, it's not the machine or the invention that creates the technical superiority, it's the quality of the manpower.

Therefore, you have to admit that we have a good color system, and if we do have a good system, I think that the only way to proceed is by trying to see things clearly. One thing that has happened over the past fifty years is that people have lost the use of their senses. This is due to what we call progress. Note that it's normal for them to have lost the use of their senses: We turn a button and we have light, we push another button, and we have a flame on a gas range. Our contact with nature takes place through so many intermediaries that we have almost completely forgotten how to feel natural things directly. We can therefore say that people don't see very much now. For example, everyone thinks that the French flag is red, white, and blue, but the French flag is no longer red, white, and blue. I don't know why, but the blue is violet, probably because the manufacturers found that making true-blue material was too expensive. The blue is just about the color of your jacket, it's not blue at all, it is nowhere near blue. Yet everyone is convinced that it's blue. So when you photograph a French flag and you see a kind of violet on the screen, everyone is surprised. It's simply because they haven't looked.

Therefore I think that the way to use color is first of all to open your eyes and look. It's easy to see if things correspond to what you want on the screen. In other words, there is practically no translation of the color onto the screen; there is photography. You simply have to place what you want on the screen in front of the camera, and that's it.

CAHIERS: *You are aware, however, that there are many critical theories of color, one more clever than the next, "When painters get involved . . .," and so on.*
RENOIR: I'm convinced that if a painter, or any gifted artist, decides to make color films, he will do a very good job but will not use his knowledge as a painter to obtain good results in Technicolor. He will surely be helped along by the fact that his profession gave him an educated eye, which is indispensable. It's in this way that painters could perhaps help in color films: They would bring with them the collaboration of someone who has received a visual education. It's not by applying their knowledge as painters but by applying the exercises they've done with their eyes when learning to paint.

CAHIERS: *You don't believe in chemical or optical treatments of color?*
RENOIR: Absolutely not, I'm absolutely against that. It exists of course, and it gives good results sometimes, only right now I'm talking about my own way of working, and personally, I'm too egotistical to rely on a chemist for my film's final results. I prefer to have confidence in my eyes and in the cameraman's eyes, rather than in some chemical solution. It seems more fitting and, once again, more practical.

CAHIERS: *You prefer to stick to the idea of fidelity?*
RENOIR: That's right. Note that there are many special effects in black and white, more than in color. Contrasts, for example, can give unexpected results. There's an element of surprise in black and white that you don't have in color. Black and white also gives the director and the cameraman an infinite number of possibilities for special effects. Suppose you have an actor who can't play a scene well. You have to admit he's a little weak in expressing certain emotions. So you use some unrealistic lighting, with exaggerated lights. On one side you have absolute blackness, and on the other you hide half of his face. He emerges from a kind of vague shadow, and suddenly he becomes very talented, and the scene can be very good. So I think that with color, you have to abandon these special effects; it's a matter of being more and more honest. That's all.

CAHIERS: *You seek purer colors?*
RENOIR: It's a matter of taste. I like simple colors. In Bengal, in India, nature is divided into fewer colors. Compare a tree on the avenue

Frochot with a tropical tree: The second has fewer greens, only two or three, and this works well in color films. Take this room, for example: It wouldn't be bad in color. There's one thing that wouldn't work, the brown tone of the chimney and the table; but the gray of the door and the walls, the white curtains, all that would be very easy to photograph in color. I think that this chair, on the other hand, would be horrible, it would be abominable. But in fact, it's abominable in real life, too. In the end, it's all very simple, it's a matter of putting things that you like in front of the camera.

CAHIERS: *You like to arrange foregrounds full of lively colors in front of rather neutral backgrounds?*
RENOIR: Yes, but I think that one could do the opposite. For example, one could do the opposite with the greens in nature. Use *powerful* backgrounds. I do have a few of them in *The River,* in fact. I shot in a banana field with a small lake just because of the green, which made a wildly powerful background.

CAHIERS: *But for the interiors you kept very soft tones.*
RENOIR: Yes, which is how things are there. The interiors are often shadowy and soft. Although in *The River,* I am far from conveying the impression of the colors of Bengal, far from it, especially those of the houses.

CAHIERS: *And you don't give any thought to the rules of relationships among colors?*
RENOIR: No, I'm convinced that our profession is that of a photographer. If we arrive at a set saying, "I want to be Rubens or Matisse," I am sure that we will wind up making big mistakes. No, we're photographers, nothing more, nothing less. I think that the concerns with plasticity have nothing to do with our profession. I don't think that the dresses in *The River,* for example, have any pictorial value. I think that they have a value on the screen, a photographic value, or, rather, a film value, because it's photography . . . no, it's cinematography; it's a category in itself.

CAHIERS: *And color, a realist method, necessarily limits the filmmaker to realism.*
RENOIR: I'm convinced of it. We live in a period in which we all are more or less intellectual before we are sensual, and our beliefs or our

choices are decided for intellectual reasons. For example, it's the Dubonnet ad opposite the café where you drink your aperitif that makes you instinctively ask the waiter for "A Dubonnet!" Our senses have nothing to do with it, it's a mechanism of the mind and not of the palate. It's the same in everything, and it's extremely dangerous. I think that one of the artist's roles is to try to recreate the direct contact between man and nature.

A Conversation with Jean Renoir

GIDEON BACHMANN/1956

BACHMANN: *This is an interview with Jean Renoir, recorded in New York on August 23, 1956, at the Royalton Hotel. Perhaps the best way to start is to ask you to mention some of the films that you have made.*
RENOIR: Well there are so many that it is difficult to know where to start. But let's say that my first picture—my first important picture—was an adaptation of *Nana*, the novel by Zola. And I made many silent pictures. You know, I even made very expensive ones with plenty of people and battles and big sets. I made such expensive pictures that when sound arrived people didn't trust me. They thought I would be too expensive a director. And it was very difficult for me to start a new career in sound. I did it by suggesting a story that could be shot in a week—a feature film of an hour-and-a-half—that was taken from a stage play by Feydeau. You know Feydeau, a very famous French writer of comedy. He died about fifty years ago. Well, I don't know how to translate the name of this picture in English. It's about a child who needs to be helped a little bit—he needs medicine. Well, it was a very French, or Gallic, picture. I shot it in six days and I did the cutting in six days; and three weeks later the movie was shown in many theaters in Paris, where it made plenty of money and I was considered to be a good director of talking pictures.

BACHMANN: *What was the name of the film in French?*
RENOIR: *On Purge Bébé.* My first important talking picture after *On Purge Bébé* was *La Chienne.* It was remade here in the United States, under the

---

Originally published in *Contact* 2.5 (June 1960), pp. 9–24. © Gideon Bachmann.

title *Scarlet Street,* by Fritz Lang in 1945. *La Chienne* was a very difficult picture. As a matter of fact, *La Chienne* was the first film in this new style people call "realist." I mean, before me Feyder had done *Thérèse Raquin,* but that was silent. And some of my friends among film directors had done a few other, realistic silent pictures. But *La Chienne* was the first talking picture of this sort, and it was very difficult to get it accepted. Number one, the producer who asked me to do the movie—let's say the producer I convinced I could do it because I had done *On Purge Bébé* in six days—thought that I was shooting a comedy again. But it is a very sad story, very gloomy, and when he saw the picture he was very disappointed and wanted to re-cut it—so we had horrible fights. Finally I won. The film was edited in the way I wanted, and it was shown first in a provincial town: Nancy. The result was that the next day this movie was removed from the screen. They had to interrupt the presentation because the audience couldn't accept such a realistic story in a talking picture. Strangely enough, the audience did accept realist narratives in silent cinema, but when the characters in such sad, gloomy situations were *talking* the viewers rejected what they saw.

Well, it was looking very much like a catastrophe when a friend of mine who owned a movie theater in Biarritz came to my aid. And this man let my picture run at his theater. He proposed the idea of a certain kind of unusual poster to be put up all over the town of Biarritz. The poster explained to people that the film was horrible, impossible, and please don't bring your children. Well, the theater was packed for many weeks and then a big theater in Paris decided to run the picture. And it became the first movie to be shown for three or four straight months in the same theater; *La Chienne* had a long first run. It is still one of my favorite pictures.

BACHMANN: *Perhaps your earliest film that American audiences still remember would be* La Grande Illusion. *When was that made?*
RENOIR: 1936. It was a little bit of an answer to growing world nationalism. It was an appeal to peace—let's say a very useless one, since you know what happened shortly afterwards.

BACHMANN: *This film had Erich von Stroheim in its cast.*
RENOIR: Erich von Stroheim, Pierre Fresnay, and Jean Gabin. But Gabin was really the center of the picture.

BACHMANN: *Is he one of your favorite actors?*
RENOIR: Yes, he's wonderful. He was born for the movies.

BACHMANN: *What other films have you made with Gabin?*
RENOIR: *La Bête Humaine—The Human Beast.* And *Les Bas-Fonds*, with
him and Louis Jouvet. And now a comedy, *French Can-Can*, which is
being released all over the United States. When we found ourselves in
front of a camera again after fifteen years, we were very happy to work
together. He was still the same powerful actor.

BACHMANN: *You did make some films in this country, didn't you?*
RENOIR: Oh, yes, I made a number of movies here. I arrived in this
country the last day of the year 1940, December 31. Just coming from a
very dark Europe and arriving on New Year's Eve in New York with the
whole town full of joy and light, I felt wonderful. What a contrast! And
I went to Hollywood. I started with Twentieth Century-Fox, convincing
the company to send me to Georgia to make a picture. They were very
much surprised and asked me why I wanted to go to Georgia, given
that Fox had such big studios in California. "We build studios in which
we can shoot anything, including Georgia!" Well, I insisted. Darryl
Zanuck was very nice. He understood what I wanted and he sent me to
Georgia, where I shot *Swamp Water.* That was my first American picture.

BACHMANN: *Who were the stars in that?*
RENOIR: Well, no stars—which was also a surprise at Twentieth
Century-Fox. I was very firm about this. I insisted on using a young
woman who was a stock girl. And the young man was a stock boy. The
boy was Dana Andrews and the girl was Anne Baxter.
    Then I made a picture called *This Land Is Mine*, with Charles
Laughton, which is still playing. As a matter of fact, it's on television
now. And I was very happy with this film, which was done for RKO. I
started several more, but I didn't finish them. You know: I like to try
things. I did make *The Southerner*, which was a wonderful experience,
with the most wonderful producer I know. Unfortunately, he's not producing any longer. His name is David Loew. Well, it was absolutely
delightful to work with him. We went to a beautiful valley full of cotton fields where we built a camp; we shot outside for weeks and weeks,

and I don't believe the result was too bad. In any case we were happy during the picture and after the picture.

BACHMANN: *What specific difficulties have you experienced that have been caused by "interpretations" of the audience by American producers, distributors, and censors?*

RENOIR: The belief that the American public would require a sentimentalized and romanticized version of my film *Eléna et les Hommes*. This picture is a satiric farce, nothing else. The French version, faithful to this particular genre, has been well received by the public of several European countries. In the United States, the title has been changed and a different beginning and ending have been substituted for those of my original film. I assume further changes were made, but I cannot judge the extent of the massacre myself, having refused to look at a film that is no longer mine. I attribute this mutilation to the publicity and promotion requirements of the American distributor. They were ashamed to present Ingrid Bergman in what they considered to be a "low" kind of comedy. The title of this American version is *Paris Does Strange Things*.

BACHMANN: *Now I would like to ask you for your opinion on the influence of European screen productions on the recent change in the type of film we turn out in this country.*

RENOIR: Well, number one, I believe firmly that the spirit of the whole world is changing slowly but very surely, and that it's no longer just a question of America or France or Europe. I believe human beings are discovering new things around them and are considering life with different eyes. Now the change occurred sooner in Europe because of certain facts: because of the war and the occupation, the occupation and the ordeal—let's say, no food—the postwar period and recovery. Well, the suffering occurred more over there, and probably it helped filmmakers to understand certain problems sooner than they were understood here. But I believe that the spirit manifested on both continents is exactly the same.

Now what we see on the American screen today is very much like what we saw ten years ago on the Italian or French screen. It seems that contemporary pictures all belong to this "neo-realistic" school. I believe that such a school is just a new way for the world to consider life and that's all. Now I don't believe that neo-realism means more reality; let's say, it's the safest approach to reality. Reality has nothing to do with that or any other style. The make-up of an actor has nothing to do with the person's inner reality. It's just a case of giving more importance to external reality; and sometimes giving weight to outer reality can be very handy. By understanding external reality we can understand inner reality a little more perhaps, a little better. But I don't believe that this new style—which is so obvious now in American film and which started, let's say, in Italy around 1945—did anything except help the movie business to get rid of some old routines. Pictures shot in the neo-realistic style aren't necessarily more real or closer to the truth.

BACHMANN: *Well, I suppose it depends on what you call "real" and "realism." I've discussed this matter with Otto Preminger and Stanley Kramer, who have both been identified in a sense with the new type of film being made in America. And the word "truth" always comes up during the conversation. Therefore I was interested in what you said—that style itself does not add a dimension to the truth.*

Your style always showed more "realism," or perhaps it was more directly involved with the small things that go to make up the big ones. Perhaps in that sense you might be able to tell me what it is inside yourself that drives you, or that did *drive you, truly to explore this realism long before the Italians came out with it in such a large way.*

RENOIR: Well, as matter of fact, the reason why I decided to try to capture this outer reality—which we call realism—was that I wanted to react against the conventional movie picture of the world. When I started in the motion-picture business, the most successful films were the American ones, which were absolutely sugarcoated at the time. And I must say that I loved them, I admired them, and I still admire them. For me the Hollywood period before the talkies is maybe the greatest period in the history of cinema. It was absolutely wonderful. And even if they were sugarcoated, I still maintain that Hollywood movies of this time explained to the whole world American life as it really is— more than anything else except perhaps one thing, jazz. Jazz music and motion pictures were probably the two most important artistic realizations of the period.

Now, even if I was extremely impressed by those movies, I knew that as a Frenchman working in Paris I had to do something else if I wanted to be sincere. And I adopted the realistic style only because I was trying to copy what I used to see around me, and to copy it—I should say—almost clumsily, almost childishly. My point of view was that a camera, after all, is a camera; it is photography. If you want to distort reality or, let's say, to *stylize* reality, well, you have to use another way: you can't go through the camera. A camera does just photography, humble photography, nothing else. And photography was created simply to photograph or replicate, nothing else—not to invent. Now I am more ambitious, I must say.

I started to get more ambitious with *The River,* which I shot in India. And India brought me the revelation of a world that by itself encouraged stylization. There is stylization in India in the street, in the movements of women, in the colors, everywhere. India helped me to get rid of a certain external realism, which I still trust, still admire. But I now believe that any style can be used on the screen, and to be quite frank, in every new picture I am trying to adopt a new style in which I forget everything I did before. I am trying to know more about this world. I don't know very much but the little I know, I like to express it, and I like to try not to lie to myself. That's the main thing. I'm no longer interested in the "outer" or surface style of my movies.

BACHMANN: *Do you feel, then, that the realism or, better, naturalism of the Italian cinema was just a very naïve way of presenting an image, which only happened to be accepted because there was misery or poverty portrayed? And that if, with the same naturalism, the Italians had portrayed the idle wealth and luxury of* The Earrings of Madame de . . . , *neo-realism would not have been accepted in the same way?*
RENOIR: I'm convinced that Italian neo-realism was, as you say, just the product of naïveté and, may I say, if it hadn't been, it wouldn't be great, because I don't believe that when things are done on purpose or calculatedly they are good anymore.

BACHMANN: *Well, calling the influence of the Italian style on American film "naïve" will not, I think, be particularly appreciated by all the people over here who are trying to "implement the lessons of the Italians," and who*

*probably think that by introducing the same style into American movies they
have achieved something great. Do you think, then, that this is a negative
development?*

RENOIR: I don't know. Because the American spirit—I mean the spirit
of the nation—is also changing. Let's say that after one hundred years
of romanticism people want to get rid of romanticism—people who
have been living with a certain kind of lie for a hundred years, a lie that
is sugarcoating all the facts of life. I don't say that romanticism is bad;
I just say that it's a style and the style is going to change. For instance,
many people are wondering about existentialism and they ask: why
existentialism now, in the postwar and cold-war period? Well, the
answer is very simple. It has come about because people want to
remove the rosy or pink curtains (if such colors are appropriate in
this instance) of fascist or totalitarian ideology that have been hiding
and may continue to conceal the landscape; they want to see the landscape as it is. And you have such a revolution in the history of art about
every hundred years. New people arrive who tell the audience: "My
dear friends, do you know that what you have seen on the stage up to
now was just a routine, just a style? We are presently going to show
you life as it really is." And they succeed for only a few years because
the new style, the new reality, itself becomes a style and a routine
very quickly.

Take, for instance, the actors. Let's talk about something trivial, like
their make-up. When I first started in the movies, make-up was very
white, and the type of cinematography at the time used to show the
lips and the eyes as very black. Well, for everybody, for the whole audience, that was reality. Then we introduced panchromatic film, with different make-up required, and we convinced the public that the old
method or the previous reality was false and that the new make-up was
the real one. Yet this new reality is as false today as the earlier reality
was then—the reality of pale faces with dark lips. You know, between
the beautiful plume of D'Artagnan and the greasy make-up of an engineer in a modern film about the railroad, there is no difference. The
engineer's grease is a new sort of plume, that's all.

BACHMANN: *What you're really saying is that "style" is a matter of putting
in a can, so to speak, something that was once new and is now old.*

RENOIR: That's it. Now if the author is talented, none of this matters. Let's take, for example, a comedy by Shakespeare. Well, Shakespeare very humbly did follow the style of his time. But let's suppose that today you take *As You Like It*, give it a different name—say, *Two Lovers*—and explain to the audience that it was written by a young, unknown writer born in California. Everybody would say: "Well, that's very nice but absolutely childish, you know. It's unbelievable! False, even. Look at the way they are dressed, the way they walk!" Still, Shakespeare's play is a great thing, an enormous work because its artistic reality has nothing to do with exterior appearances. The reality is inner, it comes from within. Let's say that this outer reality—call it "realism" or "naturalism," anything you want—may be a *help*, but it is not in the end *important*. What is more important is the knowledge of life displayed by the work—this is the essence of aesthetic excellence.

BACHMANN: *Before, when you talked about India, you said that style there is everywhere—in the women on the streets and in everything you see—and that this gave you a new idea or approach as to how to do something better, something different, in your films. But after that, you said that the Americans are trying to emulate the Europeans, and that in a sense this is only following something that was new but that has already become old. Now where does the fine, dividing line lie between what makes something into a work of art that endures—like Shakespeare or like "style" in India—and what makes a similarly created work into something that is only an instance of copying, and which will be forgotten by tomorrow?*

RENOIR: I don't believe that there is any rule or regulation. There is no recipe. It would be too handy if we could buy a book of recipes in which we could find the right, sincere style. Well, unfortunately in our business, the artistic process is more difficult and more mysterious. I think that in Hollywood, where there are some wonderful directors, the wonderful directors are the ones that know something about life. Now maybe they know about life according to their own angle; but each of us is the same in that we know something about life from our own point of view. You know, in our profession, our tools are somewhat like glasses. We have to see through those glasses and we don't see through other people's—only *our* glasses, that's all. Now sometimes, adding to our glasses features that have already been used by people with a different pair—this can help. Fine. I don't see any reason not to adopt some Italian methods in Hollywood. Why not, if it helps? And perhaps it does.

The same is true with any great painter. For instance, when my father was a young man and started to paint, his god—the artist he admired most—was Diaz. Diaz is completely unknown today, and many people would probably be surprised to learn that my father wanted only to become another Diaz. But this ambition helped him to define himself; and, his personality being strong, he did overcome the desire to imitate Diaz. At first he sincerely was sure that he was just an imitator of Diaz when actually he was just Renoir, or would become the Renoir we know.

The greatest forms of art, it follows, are the primitive ones. If we take any civilization—say, modern civilization beginning with the Renaissance, or the civilization of the Middle Ages starting with the end of the Roman Empire—the best works are the first ones, the early ones. For one reason: people had no theories; they were just trying to copy reality, and the stylization came from the fact that they *couldn't* copy reality. So this stylization took place in spite of their best efforts. And that was great.

We need naïveté in art. You know what terrifies me in the movies today? The fact that we know, or have to know, too many things; this kills our naïveté. We can no longer be children. And I believe that to be a great artist you must first of all be a child.

BACHMANN: *There comes the question, then, of who fits your glasses. Your own personal development creates the personal approach, which you call being a child. "Style" is imposed by your background, and its influence makes your work into great art if that art relates to your surroundings in such a way as to create a unity.*

RENOIR: True. On the other hand, if you create with the idea that only your own self-expression is important, you do nothing. You must humbly believe that you have to copy the world as it exists around you, and if your own personality is strong enough, well, the world you paint will disappear and you yourself will appear.

BACHMANN: *And yourself in relationship to the world.*

RENOIR: Absolutely. Let me make a parallel between painting and film-making here. First, artists were busy with long shots—the broad canvas.

With the Renaissance, there emerges more concern for the individual, and the artist behind the camera (so to speak) is getting nearer and nearer. So close, he is even on the other side of the lens. A movie now is a portrait of himself. Perhaps there's no help hiding behind a story anymore.

BACHMANN: *And that would be the quality that makes this work into an enduring piece of art; it would be acceptable to so many other people precisely because of this relationship.*

RENOIR: And also because you help other people who have no time to create art. I don't say that we artists are more intelligent or that we know more than everybody else. Not at all. It's just that we have more time, and we've dedicated our time to the search for truth. All the other people, after all, have to work to make a living as bankers, state employees, or railroad engineers. When we artists discover a little bit of truth, well, we open a new window and show a new landscape, and people are thankful to us for that. They say: "But that's the truth!" And it's even truer, because the landscape we discover, the landscape we show, is one they already *know*. But they never saw it in that way before.

A related point: recently I learned something very interesting about *Man of Aran*. I met a gentleman who knows very well the Island of Aran, since he owns a house there. He told me, "You know, this picture *Man of Aran* has nothing to do with reality. The island is utterly different from its portrayal in the documentary. The people are not at all like the ones shown by Flaherty: they are not so unhappy, they haven't got such a frantic spirit, etc." I was delighted at these remarks because they were proof to me that Robert Flaherty was a great man. Any great man in the movies must be an author, as in any art; he must invent, he must create, and if the island of Aran as shown by Flaherty had been the real island, this would just have shown that he had no imagination.

You know my old theory of nature—that it follows the artist. I believe that nature is something vague, almost non-existent. I am not sure that the sky is blue and the trees are green. Probably the sky and the trees have no color, just a kind of indefinite gray, and I believe that God gave man the ability to finish the job. In other words, if man truly wants to exist, he must collaborate with God in the shaping of nature. Now the only ones with the courage to do this are artists. They invent colors. The first person to paint a tree green was so successful and probably had so much genius, that ever since then we have believed that trees are green; but I'm not sure that they are. A great artist decided that they should be green, that's all. And Flaherty decided that the Island of Aran should appear the way he saw it. We believe that Aran looks like that, or will become like that. And why not?

You know the beautiful line by Oscar Wilde about the painter Turner, who painted so many foggy landscapes of London? Wilde said that before Turner there was no fog in London. And, you know, it's true. Because you take any piece of English literature before Turner, and nobody talks about the fog. You have no fog in Shakespeare, no fog in Ben Jonson. They never talk about it. But the day Turner decided to paint London the way *he* saw it—filled with a heavy fog—well, London had fog from that day forward, that's all. After Turner, in every English novel there is fog. And we are thankful to Turner for having discovered something that was obvious, but that none of us could see: that there is fog in London. Don't you think that's wonderful?

To get back to Flaherty, Bob knew how to penetrate human beings, to find their reality—how to get in touch with the most secret part of them, and how to help them to express what they did not even know they had inside themselves. That was Bob's great quality. It was primarily a human quality, which resulted from his affection for and understanding of human beings. Bob made all those people who are not artists see and understand things they really knew about already.

Ordinary people are blind; they don't see what is around them or inside them all the time. Sometimes a very gifted man—a saint, a scientist, a philosopher, an artist—all of a sudden discovers something none of us has ever seen before, he shows it to us, and it immediately becomes obvious. That is what I mean when I say that artists are shaping the world. They certainly are, but they are shaping the world by comprehending and loving it more than others do. And Bob Flaherty was one of them. This is our big task, and it's what makes our profession wonderful: to discover the obvious reality. That reality is in front of our eyes, but we won't see it unless we dedicate our lives to discovering it in all its obviousness.

I believe very strongly that human beings are related to the country where they live, with all its habits, foods, and prejudices. For instance, the case of India, about which I was talking earlier. There is no doubt that if I found such stylization in the daily living of the Indian people, this is because the country itself is *naturally* stylized. With the camera you have to take what nature gives you. (The painter, by contrast, can choose the shades he wants and can even create a new shade that will help his composition, given that this new shade is the sum of all previously selected shades.) And in India, mostly in Bengal, instead of a thousand shades of color you have maybe five or ten. That makes it very easy to achieve a beautiful color shot because a beautiful shot in color is possible, I think, only if the colors are extremely simplified and few. Let's say that nature in India, being stylized, makes for stylization in the people living there.

Now in a country like America, which is enormous, there is a Southern portion that in summer comes close to having a tropical climate. Still, American civilization for the most part is a Northern civilization. We may say, without exaggeration, that English customs and tradition, along with German and Scandinavian habits, are more important or easier to detect in America than Latin ways. Well, this is eventually going to change because there is a kind of law that has applied throughout the history of humanity. It is that the Northern peoples are always the practical winners in military struggles, but the Southerners are always the spiritual victors in the end. And very slowly in the United States we are going to see the Southern spirit rising up and winning out.

Now distinguishing between a Northern ethos and a Southern one is difficult, but perhaps there is something that can help us to understand what I mean. I believe that in Northern countries people like to hide reality a little more, even much more. I think that in a Northern country a house is painted more, decorated more, than in the South. I also believe that in a Northern country there is more, let's say, formality in human relations. I'm not saying that this is bad or good; it's just a fact, in my view. Let's say, too, that sugarcoated romanticism came from the North: it is basically a German invention that was adopted enthusiastically by the British and then the French, but romanticism was born in a Northern country. In Southern countries people believe more in what they say or see, as it is.

Now let's use a symbolic story as an example. You go to a butcher shop in a Latin country, say Naples in 1700. You want to buy a leg of lamb at this butcher shop, which is small and not too clean. There are flies everywhere. And the butcher is probably killing the animals in the backyard, where you can watch and see his apron full of blood. You feel as if you are a witness to murder, and you buy your leg of lamb knowing that to have this piece of meat an animal had to be killed, had to suffer. In other words, the idea of sacrifice is connected with your pleasure as you eat your leg of lamb, and to me that's very important. It is the basic idea of Christianity, in fact: you get nothing without sacrifice. Without sacrifice you cannot attain greatness.

Now Northern peoples are trying to suppress sacrifice, to remove it from daily life. They are trying to achieve greatness by reading books, in houses with no cold in winter and no heat in summer. They are trying, you know, to make life sugarcoated, easy, and even attempting to remove, figuratively speaking, the literal distances between people. But the Southern spirit is rising up in revenge. And I believe that this revival of almost medieval ideas—which to me are wonderful—is exactly what is influencing Hollywood now. The neo-realism in Hollywood movies is just the acknowledgment of a certain reality that belongs to the Southern mentality, which represents the future.

BACHMANN: *In other words, the sanitary, super-market leg of lamb wrapped in cellophane is on the way out, and we're going to be shooting our movies in the backyard as it were.*
RENOIR: That's it. That's exactly what I mean.

BACHMANN: *Do you feel that this Northern-Southern dichotomy is also apparent in Europe right now, and that this is perhaps one of the reasons why "real" pictures have been made in Italy while "Victorian" movies have come out of England?*
RENOIR: I think the Northern-Southern dichotomy is apparent all over the Western world. Of course, I don't know about the Arab, Indian, or Chinese worlds, which are very different from ours. But let's talk about the civilization that I know: the Western one. I think our civilization is probably going to stage a terrific reaction against all the neat lies of the previous century.

BACHMANN: *Well, that reaction has really been going on for over fifty years—not so much in movies as in painting and the other arts. And sometimes people seem to seize on the lies of the last century as a sort of scapegoat with which they can hide their own shortcomings. Thus, too often you find that young people who are "revolutionaries" or who have a torch-carrying drive, they say: "Well, we have to change the old way of doing things." Whereas, really, in terms of creating something new in the way that you mentioned earlier, creating a new dimension (one that was obvious but hitherto unacknowledged), very little is being done. Very little is being achieved that is creatively new, as opposed to just a reaction—and a destructive one at that—against the old.*

RENOIR: Well, the problem is also economic. But to go back to what you said, that this reactionary movement has been going on for, say, half a century. That is true. But, as you know, it was limited to litera-ture, to painting, to a certain type of art that was a part of the life of only a limited number of persons. When we talk about the movies and public response, this means that the entire world is going to be shaken by the revolution I'm talking about. In any case, no revolution takes place in one day. Many people believe, for example, that the French Revolution is just a matter of Bastille Day. In fact, however, the French Revolution started a hundred years before and has not yet ended—it is still going on. And it's the same thing with any revolution. I believe that the romantic movement, which started in the middle of the eighteenth century, continues to this day, but we are probably very close to the end of romanticism.

BACHMANN: *Do you think there's a consciousness about this reactionary or revolutionary development here in the United States? I personally have a feel-ing that Europeans are conscious of this change, whereas over here we create a lot of good art without really being cognizant ourselves of what we are doing. Do you think that this is good or bad?*

RENOIR: I think it's good. I think this "unconsciousness," which is related to the primitiveness or naïveté of which I spoke earlier, helps the Americans to do great things. I believe that when you start to be conscious of what you're doing, it's a weakness—it's the beginning of the end, in fact. As a result of their unconsciousness, the Americans have given to the world—to me—the two most important recent forms

of art, which I've already cited and shall repeat. One was jazz, a great
revolution in music, and the other was early Hollywood cinema, which
to me is still the pinnacle of moviemaking.

BACHMANN: *I'd like to ask you one question about moviemaking itself. Since
you are an individual film creator who has worked in so many different styles
and has created so many new things on film, I would be interested to hear
your ideas about the relative importance of such matters as style versus
theme, the actor's role versus the role of the director, and the like.*
RENOIR: Well, all these matters are extremely important, of course.
But my point of view has changed very much since I first began making
motion pictures more than thirty years ago. In the beginning I was
absolutely convinced that filmmaking was, for me, the only form of
artistic expression. This notion of mine was probably the result of the
importance of technique at the time. Technique being very uncertain,
we had to pay a great deal of attention to it. We had to know all about
the camera, scene painting, cutting or editing—I don't say sound
because pictures were silent when I began, but we certainly had to consider the music that was going to accompany a movie. Filmmaking was
thus more of an individual job rather than a committee assignment. I
could compare the making of a picture in the early days to the writing
of a book, during which the writer is alone with his typewriter and a
blank sheet of paper. Because of the situation back then, the idea of
expressing myself by any other means than a camera was very far
from my mind.

Today it's very different. Today technique has been perfected to such
an extent that we no longer have to worry about all the technical
details. And I myself am sorry about that. Maybe it's more difficult to
make a good picture today because the technical side has become so
easy. I'll give you one example, that of the "lap dissolve." Today when
we want to dissolve from one scene to another, we just cut. The director
yells "Cut!," the camera stops, and the actors stop acting; then we start
the next scene—maybe on another day or even in another month—and
in the lab they manage to create a lap dissolve between the end of the
first scene and the beginning of that next one. When I started in the
movies, though, it was impossible to achieve such an effect in the lab.
That means we had to know exactly where to start the dissolve and end

the first scene, and when to start the next scene on the same piece of film with the same camera. We didn't dare make a mistake. In a sense we were the prisoners of technique, and I believe that this was a good thing. You see, it seems that there is a kind of law, to which I have referred more than once during our conversation: in any artistic profession the products are better at the beginning of the history of the art in question.

Let's take the art of tapestry. There is no doubt that the tapestry of Queen Mathilde in Bayeux is better than the tapestry of Beauvais later on under Louis XIV. We can even see, if we follow the history of tapestry, that any improvements worked against the artistic results. For instance, King Henry IV, in the sixteenth century, wanted the art of tapestry to take root in France. So he helped the tapestry-makers to perfect their machines and tools, with the result that tapestry became intricate to such an extent that it became possible to reproduce any shade of color instead of having to show, as in primitive tapestries, a brutal passage from, say, a very intense, bold red to a very intense, bold blue without any nuance in between. Well, with the new tricks of the trade, it was possible to create many nuances and thus to have any shade between a dark red and a light pink—and that was the end of the art of tapestry. It marked the beginning of the imitation of nature, which is sometimes a very dangerous thing to do artistically speaking.

The same is true in the profession of moviemaking, where I am sure that any perfection of technique works in the end against the artistic result. Now, because of this perfection in technique, there is very little that I have to do. I have to be sure that the actors do their acting properly, and to make certain that the color of the furniture or the drapes is not too ugly, and that's all. It's nothing, really—not a big job. And when it's finished, it's finished. Other people take care of the cutting, just as someone else took care of the photography (and very well, too). My job becomes a kind of supervisory one. But to me supervision is not art; art is a matter of doing things with your own hands. And modern art is often inferior because we have first a designer and then someone who carries out the designer's plan. Take this chair. It was made during the sixteenth century and today, if it were to be shown in a museum, the whole world would admire it and many other chairs fashioned during the same period. Why? Because the man who conceived the chair, who designed it, and the man who made it with his own hands and tools, were the same person. That's very important.

All technical refinements, then, discourage me. Perfect cinematography, larger screens, high-fidelity sound, all make it possible for mediocrities slavishly to reproduce nature; and this reproduction bores me. What interests me is the interpretation of life by an artist, and in the process the expression of his personality rather than the copying of nature.

Yet today it is almost impossible in a movie to have the same man doing everything and thereby creating a personal piece of art. I still do it myself, but I may be one of the last ones. And it is a very big job because the technique is at such a level of perfection, an awful lot of time must be invested in any one film project. My last movie took me more than a year, which is ridiculous. In one year I should have the time to tell twenty stories; I had twenty in mind but was able to tell only one. That is why, now, I am no longer such an enemy of other forms of artistic expression as I once was. I'm starting to write novels and stage plays; I love television. Unfortunately, with the improvement in cinematic technique, we have had to give up the old conception of handicraft and become—like so many modern people—specialists.

Now I'm probably more a specialist in storytelling than in anything else. And to tell a story by way of the camera, the typewriter, or the stage, to me is more or less all the same these days. I'm sorry about that because I believe it marks the end of civilization as we once knew it. I may be too pessimistic, but still I love the making of my first pictures when, you know, we had to push a little cart ourselves to create the effect of a traveling shot. I remember a movie I made where I even developed all the film and printed it in my own kitchen! That was a wonderful experience, I must say.

Now about theme. I suggested to you (when we were talking about neo-realism and Hollywood style) that form is not so important, that only what we have to *say* is important. That would mean, then, that theme or content is important, but, actually, I don't believe that, either. What *is* important? I don't know exactly, but in Shakespeare there is one thing I love perhaps the most. It's the fact that each character talks differently and *is* different, according to the people with whom he's confronted. Let's take one of Shakespeare's heroes. If he talks to a servant or a workman in the street, he talks as either of these people would. If the hero talks to theater people, he talks like an actor. And if he talks to a king, he speaks in verse. Terrific!

Today, by contrast, all we hear about is "consistency of character." Contemporary critics think that Shakespeare's plots are naïve or unbelievable, that they are unrealistic and his characters inconsistent. Well, who is consistent in life? I know that I, myself, am not consistent, and I don't think anyone around me is consistent, either. We are shaped by many external factors in our lives; the environment is terribly important in influencing our actions, and that environment changes. Only the man who remains in the same room surrounded always by the same people, the same furniture, the same air temperature, only he is "consistent"; any other man, affected as men are by the outside world, cannot be consistent. He changes as his surroundings do.

Well, now, I said that I don't believe in form and I don't believe in theme, and if I don't believe in theme I don't believe in what people call the "message." So what do I believe in? I believe in something that I find extremely difficult to express. Perhaps I cannot express it. I believe in a kind of aesthetic marriage or melding between the external world, which changes all the time, and our bodies, our selves, our souls—which desire to interpret that world. When this combination or incorporation is something genuine, unexpected, a work of art is the result. If what is created is just the banal repetition of what we already can see anywhere, well, we have nothing and that is the end of that.

BACHMANN: *You say that a work of art is only a work of art when it expresses the constantly changing relationship between people and the world that surrounds them, but what is it that enables such a work to survive without change for generations and generations?*

RENOIR: I think that a work of art is always an individual affair. There are some conditions, however, under which the creation of art is easier for the individual. Let's say that style can give to the artist some tools that are handier than any tools he would have to create for himself each time. This is why artists often adhere to what was done before them, until they get tired of it and want to try something new, with some new tools. Neo-realism is one of those simple new tools.

BACHMANN: *Now about style: when you say that in every picture you make you like to discard what you have previously learned and find a new style, are you always successful in finding that new style before you begin filming? Or do you—as I would presume—develop your new style, and the ideas for how to achieve it, as you go along?*

RENOIR: As I go along, and even after that. Unfortunately for me—or fortunately, I don't know—I am the kind of person who can understand a question only once he is confronted with it. For instance, I understand the meaning of a role when I see the actor play the part—not before. It's only then I understand that, in the dialogue for this particular portion, I wrote only half of what I had to say and have to add things, or I need to be more precise, or some of the material is repetitious and must be cut. The actor thus brings me closer to my own story. This is one of the kinds of marriage or melding, between oneself and the world, that I was talking about. When you arrive at this stage of writing and directing—which to me are really the same thing—you realize that one can't write a great stage play without being at least partially involved in its direction, too, which is to say be "married" to the play's actors and even its designers.

You know Jean Giraudoux in France, right? Well, Giraudoux is supposed to be a great stylist, and everybody believes that he wrote all his dialogue very precisely before giving the script to Louis Jouvet for rehearsals—wrote it, as it were, with a diamond pen on gold sheets of paper. But not at all. Giraudoux used to write very fast and not too precisely, then he got extremely precise after seeing the rehearsals. And during rehearsals all of a sudden the sense of a scene—paradoxically, a scene that he himself invented—became clear to him. He realized that he had written down a scene without knowing exactly what he wanted, and only by watching—I should say spying on—the actors perform the scene could he understand its full meaning.

Probably Molière and Shakespeare did the same thing. They both used to write for their actors. They knew that such-and-such an actor would be wonderful in, say, the part of a king, and, just for the pleasure of seeing this actor play a king, they used to write a play about a king. That's very important: it's the way art should be practiced and theme realized, for it bespeaks a connection with human reality.

BACHMANN: *This is, in a sense, a revolutionary point of view, because I was speaking recently with someone who expressed himself very strongly to the effect that, unless a creative artist has complete control (and foreknowledge) of what he intends to do, he is no longer a creative artist. He is only an experimenter who has created something by accident. And this person completely disclaimed the validity of any creation by accident or empirical method—the very kind of method you seem to espouse.*

RENOIR: I am absolutely convinced that a great artist only two or three times in his life has a clear and complete vision of an artwork in his head beforehand. It's very possible (but not sure) that Molière had it for *The Misanthrope*. But if what I know about many great artists is true, then they were for the most part experimenters. They experimented all the time, testing and trying; they were mainly like a sculptor who molds the clay with his fingers and, after he sees the shape, understands that by pushing the clay a little more to the other side, he can give to this shape more meaning or even a new one—a meaning he didn't have in mind before starting to work.

The same is true of landscape for a painter. A landscape is nothing and doesn't count for anything; yet it counts very much because it is the reason why the painter paints the painting. The landscape is the inspiration, but even inspiration is the wrong word. I should say the landscape is the "reason-for"; it is the "accident." But we need such accidents. The painter in front of his landscape starts with the idea that he is just going to paint it, that's all; but if he is a real artist he discovers so many things in the landscape—and even more in himself through the landscape, unconsciously—that he may just create a great painting.

BACHMANN: *I've never been able to understand why, in sculpture, people always prefer the sculptor who works in stone over the one who works in clay. Yet here are expressed the twin artistic poles we've been discussing. If you work in clay you can always add and subtract as you go along, whereas in marble you must always know in advance what you are going to do—because once you've taken something away, you can't put it back and thus you are bound by the limits you yourself have created. Like Michelangelo.*

RENOIR: This is true, but it is partly due to the fact that we place too much emphasis on theme nowadays. I am absolutely convinced that the best sculpture in the world is probably the sculpture in cathedrals;

the sculpture of the Middle Ages is probably the highest point of our art in the West. And I have the feeling that never once did those artisan-artists care about theme. As a matter of fact, the theme was always the same, as it is in Shakespeare. After all, Shakespeare took his themes in some cases from the cheapest Italian fiction—stories that were quite banal, nothing really. But he made them great because of his own constant communion with the world of which he was a part.

So when some people say that chance or accident must not play a role during the creation of a work of art, I believe they are wrong. It's unfortunate, by the way, that the most important manifestation of the Christian religion is called Communion. The result is that people now believe Communion means only to swallow a piece of bread in church. But that's not true. Communion means to be together—and to take a lot from your fellows at the same time as you give a lot to them. That's the real meaning. And, in this sense, a work of art is a communion. During the making of a work of art you must be in a constant state of communion, you must give and take. And if you don't do that, your creation is purely a creation of the brain, and the brain is only a part of the body—and not necessarily the most important part, I might add.

I want to go back to theme, to its fundamental unimportance. You know, in the Greek tragedies—which many of us consider to be great art—the dramatists used to tell to members of the public a story they already knew. Let's take the Atreides in Thebes. Well, everybody in the theater knew the story of the Atreides. They had heard it a thousand times, and just to make sure the audience wouldn't be caught by vulgar surprise during the performance, the Greek chorus used to tell these spectators the story again, once more, to make certain that they knew it. Today, of course, productions are based on an entirely different conception. Shows are founded on surprise alone—what they call suspense. Well, I'm trying to fight against that as well. I believe that a production should be based on feeling—again, on the idea of communion. I mean a communion among the artist, the actors, the audience, and the wider world. After all, when you listen to great music—let's say a piece by Mozart—it's a direct conversation that you're having with him. Mozart is sitting there in a chair, you're sitting next to him, and you proceed to have a talk—in a musical language that is pleasant and even moving. And I believe that the less Mozart or any artist talks about himself, the more, finally, he gives of himself in communal terms.

The first artist who started talking too much about himself is Beethoven. He was great but he was already a romantic. Now take Mozart: his life was hell. He was unhappy, he suffered from illness, and he was poor—paying rent was a problem for him, as was getting enough to eat. Yet his music is always delightfully gay, always light and easy. I don't quite know how to express myself here, but I feel, nevertheless, that because Mozart didn't make his own suffering the subject of his music, his suffering is even more moving and his music even greater.

BACHMANN: *In experimental cinema we often find the opposite problem in filmmakers who are just starting out. Over here in America we have a large group of young people who feel that they, too, want to rebel against the sugar-coated version of reality that Hollywood has been serving up for so many years. And these individuals have made a number of so-called experimental films—somewhat avant-garde yet slightly different. But the only theme ever touched upon in this work is the theme of the moviemaker himself. These artists talk only about themselves, in your terms, and this is the reason that none of these pictures is truly great. I think there's a connection here with what you said earlier about the Northern nature of man versus his Southern characteristics.*

RENOIR: Yes, the heart must not too often be worn on the sleeve. Better, or more decent, to hide it a little bit. Now, about the people making movies in a club atmosphere in America: I've seen some of these pictures and find them extremely interesting. In any case, they are probably the best hope for the future of world cinema, for such amateurish daring can result in new creativity that can only be good for the medium.

BACHMANN: *Do you think these experimental films that you've seen over here are, on the whole, good pictures? Are they "involved" or engagé?*
RENIOR: I haven't seen enough of them to judge. But let's say that theoretically—in spite of the fact that I don't like theories!—I trust people who are eager to make movies in such an impromptu way.

BACHMANN: *Well, I would tend to agree with you. I was just asking because of what you said a minute ago—that if an artist displays too much of himself in his art, then its relationship to everything else, the quality that really makes it artistic, suffers and the work loses all chance of permanency. Yet, if you look at some of the French avant-garde films of the 1920s, they are as good today as they were.*

RENOIR: Yes, that's true. Let's say that the French during the twenties were very much helped by other artistic movements. The cubist movement in painting, for instance, helped young filmmakers in France a great deal; cubism gave them a desire not to be dry and clean-cut—or is it clear-cut?

BACHMANN: *You mean a desire to be stylized? Stylized in the sense of abstracted or geometrically formed?*

RENOIR: Yes, yes. I think that the influence of painters on the moviemakers of Paris in the 1920s was beneficial.

BACHMANN: *Do you think that the comparable films you've seen here in America, the experimental ones being made today, are of equal quality?*

RENOIR: No, not yet. But we must not forget that the French films we know now, the ones that have survived, are the best of the period. There were also many bad pictures made at that time—works that we no longer remember. And here in America time, or history, has not yet made its selection; we are confronted with a great amorphous mass of movies in which it's difficult to discern ultimate, individual worth. But ten or twenty years from now, only the best out of this lot will be remembered and re-seen. Perhaps then, again, people will talk about a golden age: the Golden Age of the American avant-garde cinema in the 1950s.

BACHMANN: *What film or films would you make if you were free from the extra-artistic limitations of sponsorship, censorship, and the like?*

RENOIR: I am interested in filming a number of subjects, and all these projects take into full account the non-artistic limitations of which you speak. As far as I'm concerned, though, commercial considerations and censorship regulations work in my favor in many ways, because they force me to look at things with a subtler eye. And I am not the only one who has been or is in this situation: the history of the arts is full of aesthetic development in the midst of the worst tyrannies, of a financial as well as a political kind. If I were absolutely free, in other words, I would probably make the same kinds of movies I am making now—but I might make worse ones.

Cinema and Television: Jean Renoir Interviewed

ANDRÉ BAZIN / 1958

Shortly before his death in November 1958, the French critic
André Bazin interviewed Jean Renoir for France Observateur. *This*
movie director has recently been working on projects for French
television, and he is among the first of the leading European
filmmakers to approach the new medium.

RENOIR: I am preparing a version of Stevenson's *Dr. Jekyll and Mr. Hyde* for television. Although I've transferred the story to the present day, and to Paris, my adaptation is still faithful to the original. I'm going to introduce the program with a little talk, as if what the viewers were about to see had to do with something uncanny that really happened a short time ago on a street in Paris.

BAZIN: *When you're making a television film, Mr. Renoir—shooting more or less off the cuff with several cameras—how do you manage to keep a sense of actuality or continuity in the direction itself?*
RENOIR: I would like to make this film—and this is where television imparts something valuable to me—in the spirit of *live* television. I'd like to make the picture as though it were a live broadcast, shooting each scene only once, with the actors imagining that the public is directly receiving their words and gestures. Both the actors and the

technicians should know that there will be no retakes; that, whether they succeed or not, they can't begin again.

In any case, we can shoot only once, since some parts of this movie are being shot out in the streets and we can't afford to let the passers-by realize that we're filming. Therefore the actors and technicians must feel that every movement is final and irrevocable. I'd like to break with conventional cinematic technique, and very patiently build a large wall with little stones.

BAZIN: *Obviously, this kind of film can be made much more quickly than an ordinary motion picture.*
RENOIR: I've just done a shooting script, and the result works out to a little under 400 shots. For some reason, I've discovered through experience that my shots usually average out at about 16 to 20 feet each, though I know it sounds a bit ridiculous to gauge things in this way. Anyhow, I imagine that 400 shots will give me a film of about 6,500 feet—in other words, of average length.

BAZIN: *Are you thinking of showing the picture in the commercial cinema as well as on television?*
RENOIR: I don't know yet. I'll probably try it out eventually with a traditional movie audience. But I think that television now has sufficient importance in the public mind that it can accept films "presented" in a different way. I mean that the effects achieved on live TV are no longer entirely dependent on the will of the director and the cameraman—the camera can produce effects almost by chance, as sometimes happens when you get a wonderful newsreel shot.

BAZIN: *But doesn't television present a classic problem in technique—that of the quality and small size of the image? The Americans seem to lay down certain rules in shooting: the main actors, for example, have to remain inside a sort of square in order to keep the action always in the picture. Do all these restrictions of the medium frighten you in any way?*
RENOIR: No, because the method I'd like to adopt will be something between the American and the French approach. I believe that if one follows the American television technique, one risks making a film that will be difficult for audiences to accept over here. But by adapting these

techniques, one should be able to arrive at a new cinematographic style that could be extremely interesting. I think it all depends on the starting point, the conception.

In the cinema at present the camera has become a sort of god. You have a camera, fixed on its tripod or crane, which is just like a heathen altar; around it are the high priests—the director, cameraman, assistants—who bring victims before the camera, like burnt offerings, then cast them into the flames. And the camera is there, immobile—or almost so—and when it does move, it follows patterns ordained by the high priests, not by the victims.

Now I am trying to extend my old ideas, and to establish that the camera finally has only one right—that of recording what happens. That's all. I don't want the movements of the actors to be determined by the camera, but the movements of the camera to be determined by the actor. This means working rather like a newsreel cameraman. When a newsreel cameraman films a race, for instance, he doesn't ask the runners to start from the exact spot that suits him. He has to manage things so that he can film the race wherever it happens. Or take an accident, a fire. It is the cameraman's duty to make it possible for us to see the spectacle, rather than the duty of the spectacle to take place for the benefit of the camera.

BAZIN: *I think what you have just said brings out the real problem of film versus television. In practice, there are, strictly speaking, hardly any really creative artists in the cinema: there has been a variety of artists who come together, pool their ideas, then translate and record them on film. And the actual filming itself is very often secondary. The real creative artist in the cinema is someone who can get the most out of everything he sees—even if he sometimes does this by accident.*
RENOIR: That's the point. The creator of a film shouldn't at all be an organizer; he shouldn't be like a man who decides, for instance, how a funeral should be conducted. He is rather like the man who finds himself watching a funeral he never expected to see, and sees the corpse, instead of lying in its coffin, getting up to dance—and then notices the corpse's relatives running about all over the place instead of weeping. It is for the director, and his colleagues, to capture this and then, in the cutting room, to make a work of art out of it.

BAZIN: *Not only in the cutting room. Because I don't know whether, today, montage is so essential. I believe we should begin to look at the cinema in a new way, and to start with abandoning all the old myths. The cinema at first was a technical discovery; and everything, even editing, was subordinated to that. Then, in the silent cinema, montage took on a precise meaning, because it represented visual language in the absence of audible speech. And from silent film we have inherited this myth of montage, though it has lost most of its meaning. Consequently, it is in the images themselves that the creative artist should really bring his observation to bear, his own moral view, his particular vision.*

RENOIR: Yes: when I spoke of editing I was using a convenient phrase. I should, instead, have talked of choice—rather like Cartier-Bresson choosing three pictures out of the hundred he's taken of some incident, and those three are the best.

BAZIN: *Television is still rather frowned upon, particularly by intellectuals. How did you come to it?*

RENOIR: Through being immensely bored by a great number of contemporary films, and being less bored by certain television programs. I ought to say that the television shows I've found most exciting have been certain interviews on American TV. I feel that the interview gives the television close-up a meaning that is rarely achieved in the cinema. The close-up in film is essentially a reconstruction, something prefabricated, carefully worked up—and, of course, this has yielded some great moments in the cinema. This said, I believe that in thirty years we have rather used up this type of shot and that we should perhaps move on to something else. In America I've seen some exceptional television shows. Not because the people working there have more talent than in France or anywhere else, but simply because, in a town like Los Angeles, there are ten channels operating constantly. In these circumstances, obviously, one has the chance of finding some remarkable things.

I remember, for instance, certain interviews in connection with some political hearing. Here, suddenly, we had a huge close-up, a picture of a human being in his entirety. One man was afraid, and all his fear showed; another was insolent, insulting the questioner; yet another was ironical; the next one took it all very lightly. In two minutes we could read the faces of these people: we knew who they were. I found this tremendously exciting—and somehow an indecent spectacle to watch. Yet this indecency came closer to a knowledge of humanity than many movies.

You know how many setbacks I have had during my film career. Well, I realized that the pictures that were the most complete failures with the public were precisely those that, in a little projection room before a dozen people, pleased the most. Take the example of my film *The Diary of a Chambermaid*. It was very badly received, mainly because of its title. People expected to laugh their heads off at a movie with Paulette Goddard called *The Diary of a Chambermaid*; they didn't, and they were dissatisfied. In the early days of television, a TV company bought this picture and it is still watched with admiration by enthusiasts. Thanks to television I've made a great deal of money out of it. I thought that I had made a film for the cinema; in fact, without realizing it, I'd made one for television.

BAZIN: *If movie audiences at first looked to motion pictures for something richer than television could give them, perhaps now, accustomed to the limitations of TV, they are ready to accept something simpler from the cinema again. This might mean a reconsideration of the conditions of film production.*
RENOIR: At present, if a film is to be sure of a sale in the French market, it has to be a co-production. To be sold abroad, it has to consider the tastes of different audiences, and one ends up by making movies that lose all their national character. But the curious thing is that national character is what attracts international audiences. So the cinema is in danger of losing both its individuality *and* its market.

BAZIN: *So the answer, as you see it, is that films should be able to recover their costs in the home market, and should in consequence be made more cheaply?*
RENOIR: Exactly. For instance, I hawked the script of *La Grande Illusion* around to all the film companies for three years and no one would touch it. But at that time they did not have the excuse of not wanting to take risks since films were paying their own way. *La Grande Illusion*, for instance, had recovered its costs after its run at the Marivaux Cinema in Paris. Money was easier to come by in those days and one could experiment. The trouble with the present cost of movies is that

you either have a sensational success or you lose a lot of money. As a result producers play it safe, and when one plays it safe art is no longer possible.

Nonetheless, I have a sort of faith in the immense stupidity of the men who run gigantic production enterprises. I believe that they are always naïve children, rushing headlong into what looks as though it ought to bring them money. I think that the word "commercial" haunts them, and provided they bring out a product that is theoretically commercial they are quite happy. The word "commercial," in the cinema, means a film that has no daring, that seems to be made according to certain preconceived ideas. But a commercial picture isn't necessarily one that makes money.

BAZIN: *You once said to me that the commercial label went to any movie whose aesthetic ideal was the one desired by the producer.*
RENOIR: Just that; and I don't think this ideal derives from anything more than the practice of a naïve, incomprehensible religion—and one that even works against producers' own interests. I don't believe that these men are powerful enough, or cunning enough, to be Talleyrands trying to remold the world in their own image.

For instance, for film production to continue as it is at present, it needs a well-organized, stable society. It is in the interest of the producers to maintain a certain standard of morality, since if they don't do this, immoral films won't sell. But at the moment they are more and more producing movies that undermine all the accepted rules for social—or, better, commercial—survival. If you like to see Miss Brigitte Bardot making love simultaneously to her lover and her maid, it's because you think this is prohibited. But too many pictures like this will make people think that such activity is normal. Well, these movie people are going to ruin themselves.

BAZIN: *Yes, the producers have ended up by creating ersatz substitutes for human emotions.*
RENOIR: During the one hundred years of romanticism, it was possible to score a great theatrical success by relying on the fact that the daughter of a workman couldn't marry the son of a duke. And this was because people believed in social differences. Society, by maintaining its

faith in social divisions, also maintained the conditions under which drama of this kind could flourish. To be sure, every work of art contains a little morsel of protest. But if this protest turns into destructiveness, if the system blows up, then the possibility of such drama vanishes at once. That is what is happening now. We have got to the stage of little amorous unions like the one I just mentioned with Bardot. Next, I suppose, a father will be part of the threesome, making love to his daughter. Then it will be her mother, and what comes after that? The moment will arrive when no one knows how to outbid the last player.

I am sure that the great quality of the early American cinema sprang from an American puritanism that put up barriers to American passions. When we saw Lillian Gish, who was about to be assaulted by the villain, we trembled because such a violation meant something. Today, what can you feel about the rape of a girl who has already had sex with the whole town?

Certain restrictions, then, are extremely useful for artistic expression, and though it appears to be a paradox, absolute freedom doesn't permit absolute artistic expression. We can only hope that people will reconstruct the barriers, as they did, for instance, in painting. Cubism, after all, was nothing but a deliberate constraint adopted after the exaggerated and destructive liberties taken by post-impressionism.

BAZIN: *It has been said that modern society and modern art have been destructive of humanity; but television is an aid to humankind's rediscovery or rejuvenation. Television, an art without traditions, dares to go out to look for the new man or the new woman. And you, Mr. Renoir, seem to be looking, in TV, for that* commedia dell'arte *spirit which has always attracted you.*
RENOIR: I think there is another reason for my interest in television. It may be because the importance of technique in the cinema has declined during the past few years. When I began in films, you had to know your trade thoroughly, to have every technical skill at your fingertips. We didn't know, for example, how to create a dissolve in the editing room; so, because you had to do it in the camera, you had to be absolutely clear in advance about when you wanted the scene to end. Nowadays a director would waste time on the set if he concerned himself with such a technical problem. He thus becomes something much closer to a theatrical director than a literary author or cinematic *auteur*.

Let me give an example of what I mean from art history. The Bayeux Tapestry is more beautiful than the modern Gobelins tapestry. Why? Because Queen Mathilda had to say to herself: "I haven't any red, so I'll have to use brown; I haven't any blue, therefore I must use a color like blue." Obliged to make use of crude contrasts, constantly struggling against imperfections, she turned her technical difficulties into an ally in the creation of great art. If the job is technically easy, the spur to genuine creativity doesn't exist; and, at the same time, the artist is too free to apply his invention to different artistic forms. Today, in fact, if I conceive a story for the cinema, that story would do just as well for the stage, for a book, or for television.

All the industrial arts (and, after all, the cinema is fundamentally an industrial art) have been great at the beginning and have become debased as they perfected themselves. The same thing is true, for instance, in pottery. I once did some work in ceramics myself, trying to rediscover the technical simplicity of pottery's early days; and the best I could manage was a false "primitivism," since I deliberately rejected all the developments over time in the potter's technique. So instead I plunged into a genuinely primitive trade by comparison: the cinema.

But the cinema is moving in the same direction. The people who made those fine early American or German or Swedish films weren't all great artists—some were very indifferent ones—but all their pictures were beautiful. Why? Because the technique was difficult to master. In France, after that splendid first period of cinema, after Georges Méliès and Max Linder, movies became worthless. Why? Because we were intellectuals trying to make "art" films, to produce cinematic master-pieces. In fact, the moment one allows oneself to become an intellectual instead of an artisan, one is courting danger. And if I am now turning towards television, it is because television is in a technically primitive state which may restore to artists some of the fighting spirit of early cinema, when everything that was made was good.

Jean Renoir and Television

JEAN-LUC GODARD/1959

At the end of 1958, several of his projects having momentarily fallen through (in particular *Trois Chambres à Manhattan*, starring Leslie Caron and based on the novel by Simenon, as well as *Le Déjeuner sur l'herbe*), Jean Renoir started work on *Le Testament du Docteur Cordelier* with the backing of R.T.F. and Jean-Louis Barrault in the leading role. The film is currently being edited, following the most revolutionary shooting in the whole of French cinema. The techniques of live TV (that is, a dozen cameras recording *en bloc* scenes carefully rehearsed in advance as in the theatre) have enabled the director of *La Règle du Jeu* and *Eléna* to prove that he really is the groundswell behind the New Wave, and that he still leads the world in sincerity and audacity.

JEAN-LUC GODARD: Le Docteur Cordelier *is, I believe, a modern adaptation of Stevenson's celebrated* Dr Jekyll and Mr Hyde?
JEAN RENOIR: Absolutely not. No, not at all. Or at least not as people suppose. I had no intention of doing an adaptation. Let's say, if you will, that it was in a sense memories of reading Stevenson's book that gave Jean Serge and me the idea for *Cordelier*. Actually, the film's proper title is *Le Testament du Docteur Cordelier*. But there was on our part absolutely no attempt at or preconceived idea of transposition, in the real sense of the world. I feel very strongly about this.

GODARD: *In other words, it's the crystallization of a literary reverie?*

RENOIR: Yes, that's *Cordelier*. You know, one is always inspired by something, even in producing the most original thing in the world. Sooner or later one must set off from a point, even if nothing of that point remains in the final result. It's like Racine and antiquity.

GODARD: *Or like* La Règle du Jeu *and* Les Caprices de Marianne?

RENOIR: Exactly. But this time I have improvised even more than usual, although in a rather different way, conditioned by television methods. I have a tendency to be a little too theoretical when I start work. I say what I want to say a little too clearly, as if I were delivering a lecture, and it's very troublesome. But gradually it begins to come right.

GODARD: *And television, with its particular methods of shooting—several cameras, several microphones—has confirmed you in an approach which has been yours for a long time?*

RENOIR: Yes. Television made me discover things which I could not have discovered, or only with a great deal of difficulty, on a film set. What I was saying to you about actors and the reactions they bring to something—which one would be crazy not to take advantage of—well, in a television studio you are forced to let these extend to the entire technical crew. The technicians are obliged to become actors—invisible actors, but with their part to play in the creation of the work.

Of course in a film studio you can sometimes give a certain responsibility to the boom-operator, the focus-puller, or the dolly-man. But in television you are forced to do so. Quite simply because there are nine or ten cameras rolling at once, and each of the nine or ten operators is sole master in charge of his viewfinder. Everything depends on having a good understanding from the start. My job is simply to bring these various forces together, as a watch-maker assembles the various cogs and wheels of his mechanism. Then one starts it off, and each of these cogs adds its own personal note to the final concert.

GODARD: *The opposite, in fact, of the system whereby the director has sole control of his world?*

RENOIR: Let's say rather that here everyone becomes his own master and his own servant too. One very gratifying thing about television is this sort of keenness in the entire crew, because everybody feels that he really is responsible. I was feeling my way tentatively, but I think I learned a great deal. And if only for this reason, *Cordelier* is an interesting experience. I think it enabled me to define certain principles of shooting which, if not entirely new, are at least different from those currently in use in the cinema.

What I like about television is that it obliges me to indulge in collaboration, between theatre and cinema for example. Thanks to the small screen, I have at last found a means of expression which enables me to shoot each scene in dramatic continuity.

Basically, however, there is nothing very new about what I have done. All Charlie Chaplin's films were shot on this principle. They are divided into sequences, each one being a complete story. Once the starting-point of a scene has been established and the mechanism set in motion, then the development depends on the actors. And the important, the essential thing is that the development of a scene must not be artificial. When one is able to follow an actor in continuity, one is leading him, in spite of himself but thanks to him, towards public confession. And this is more or less the subject of my film. Cordelier will, I believe, be a touching character because he is led to make a confession.

GODARD: *What do you think of the fundamental division between television and cinema which exists in France?*
RENOIR: I think it's a pity. My job is to devise and to create entertainments, and I cannot conceive of specialization. I believe that art today is moving more and more in the opposite direction to industry. In the latter, people are constantly specializing. An electrician knows nothing about aeronautics, and conversely. Whereas in the artistic field, the reverse seems to be happening.

Nowadays a man of the theatre can, I believe, bring a lot to the cinema; someone working in television can bring much to the theatre, a film-maker to television, and vice versa. There is not one art which is cinema, another the theatre, a third poetry, and so on. All the media are good because there is only one art of entertainment. At present in France film and television people do not get on very well together. But this is simply because television belongs to the State and the cinema to private concerns, because television people are paid by the month and cinema people by the week.

GODARD: *So the division is purely arbitrary?*

RENOIR: Of course. At all periods people have jumped from one art to another. Take Molière: he wrote ballets or tragedies if he felt like it. And today no one feels obliged to present *Le Bourgeois Gentilhomme* at the Opéra-Comique on the pretext that it is a singing and dancing entertainment. No, it is performed in the same theatre as *Le Misanthrope*. So why should anyone try to force me to shoot *Cordelier* at the Boulogne or Saint-Maurice studios instead of in those of R.T.F.?

I am an author determined to express myself. And I think an author has the right to express himself where he pleases—in the sawdust ring, on the boards of the Opéra, in front of a Cross of Malta camera or an electronic one. What difference does it make? It seems there is a move to prevent my film from being shown in cinemas on the pretext that it will have been shown on television. But they forget that ultimately the only judge is the public.

The Reminiscences of Jean Renoir

JOAN FRANKLIN AND ROBERT FRANKLIN / 1960

QUESTION: *I would say your pictures were much more in a documentary style than what they think of as "commercial."*

JEAN RENOIR: Documentary style is true for certain of my pictures. It's not true for all of my pictures, because it happens that several years ago I discovered something. I discovered that the truth is not outside but inside. I discovered that it was like the commedia dell'arte, which has nothing to do with outside reality; it is acted by people dressed as Columbine, Punchinella, Harlequin. Well, these are not real—and yet it is more real than any picture with actors made up as real coal miners, let's say, or streetcar drivers.

In other words, my last pictures are even an attempt to escape from outside reality. For instance, I started to do it almost completely—almost wildly—in my picture *The Golden Coach*, with Magnani. I don't know if you saw the picture. Well, it is exactly a fantasy, not real at all—but it is about something very real. It is about the theater, about the transposition of real life into artificial life, which is very important to me.

This is why, when you said my pictures were mostly documentary, it was true in the beginning. In the beginning I tried to be helped by the reality of appearances in my pictures. I don't anymore.

Q: *We always think of the French film industry as much more liberal in the subjects and stories they can film, and we think of ourselves as quite benighted and backward. Have you found this true at all?*

RENOIR: No. I don't think it's true. I believe that for instance the pictures by Kazan in this country are as true as any other pictures anywhere in the world. And I believe that if the French pictures are
sometimes a little more serious, may I say, than the American pictures,
it is only because in France the industry is not as strong as in America.
Yes, I mean that a producer in France is not a powerful man. A producer
in the United States is very powerful. In France, a producer is just a man
who is trying to produce a picture, and to produce a picture, of course
he needs money. He also needs actors, and he needs many collaborators,
and to get those collaborators he has to deal with people. That means
that a director in France frequently becomes a producer. French pictures
and Italian pictures seem better because they are more the work of an
author. That's the only reason.

Q: *We have our Motion Picture Producer Code here, which limits subjects
that can be put on the screen.*
RENOIR: Yes, that's true. That's true, but I don't believe that any censor is bad. I even believe that a strong censor can help very much. I
believe that when you are entirely free, you don't know anymore what
to say. I believe, for instance, that the wonderful quality of the early
American pictures was probably due to the fact that the United States is
a puritanical country, that for instance the point of view about sex of
most of the writers writing screenplays was a puritanical point of view.
That is wonderful—something you have to go over. It was very good to
have to fight.

I'd like to give you an example, because I don't believe that I'm very
clear; but may I say, for instance, that in the time of Louis XIV, a man
like Molière was more powerful in his criticism against society, against
nobility, against medicine, against religion—as in *Tartuffe*—than people
were in a time when everything was free—since he had to be very careful and to use symbols and to go around the aim instead of going
directly to the aim; he had to have talent to express himself. And his
criticisms, his satires, are more powerful than the satires in the time
of complete liberty.

What I say is a bit of a paradox. It doesn't mean that I'm in favor of
the censor. I just mean that practically the censor is not so much
against talent as we believe.

Q: *He seems to be against content and story, rather than against talent.*
RENOIR: Yes. You know, to me, the belief in the story is your own
belief; in any storytelling business, the story doesn't count. What
counts is the way you tell the story. And you can be very strong with a
fairy tale by Pierrot, and you can do very well with a very bold story by
Françoise Sagan. That doesn't matter. What counts is the personality of
the artist. And what I have against the film industry, or against the
censor—more against the film industry—it is not that certain stories are
forbidden. That I don't care about. I don't mind at all. It is just that the
film industry is against personal expression. They believe in a formula,
because this formula was already successful. When I say one formula, I
should say a hundred formulas, but formulas. I don't want to follow a
formula. They are afraid of novelty, they are afraid of personal expression, and to me that's the wrong thing. But I'm ready tomorrow to
work in a country with a very strong censor, where I would be allowed
to tell only certain types of stories, only a few stories—even where I
would have to tell the same stories all the time, to repeat them—if I was
free about the way in which I like to tell them.

You know, André Gide said something; he said, "In art, only the form
counts." I believe he was right.

Q: *I'd like to ask about some of your famous pictures.* La Grande
Illusion—*when was that made, and can you tell me the story of it being
made, how it was put together?*
RENOIR: Well, I wanted to shoot this picture for one reason. I knew,
and I still know, and I'm still convinced, that the turning point of history is the war of 1914–1918. The world changed. We can divide the history of the world in very wide periods, and we can say, for instance,
that between the fall of the Roman Empire and the end of the Middle
Ages, we had a kind of period which is about the same. It is a period of
religion, it is a period of work in common, it is a period where the individual had to express himself without any signature—and that was very
important and great.

Well, the Renaissance is the next period, a very important period. It
is the period of the signature, and we can understand the period if we
think that it started with Gutenberg, the printing, and Luther, and that
means the possibility of praying in your own language. That means the

end of "whole" Christianity, the end of one world, the beginning of many little worlds named nations.

But I believe that now we are at the end of that. I believe that the idea of nations, for instance, is absurd. You believe that you are an American, and I could believe that I am a Frenchman. That's not true. We just belong to the Western world. The division of the Middle Ages, between Byzantium and Rome, is here again. The name of Byzantium today is Moscow, and the name of Rome is Washington, but it is exactly the same situation.

Well, to me the war of 1914 is exactly the break—for many reasons, for social reasons. For instance, the women started to work during the war of 1914. Before that war, women didn't work in factories. They wore long skirts and long hair, and they were behaving, thinking, very differently. A woman, a girl, as you are, was unknown before 1914. After 1914, they were exactly as you are today. Why? Because they had to cut the hair, cut the skirts, and work in factories, that's all. Or to work in an office.

You know, they became a new sex, very different from the female sex as we knew it before '14. That's something I wanted to express, and I thought that to express it by telling it very directly was wrong. I thought, Let's tell a war story, and during this war story—I should say, besides this war story—maybe the feeling will be given to the public that this war was the big chance, was the border, the frontier, between the Renaissance and the new Middle Ages in which we are living today. But many people don't know that we're living in a new Middle Ages. They still believe that we are living in a different age.

That's the problem. That's my problem, the film industry—they don't know that we're in a new era. That's the reason for *Grande Illusion*.

Q: *Would you begin by telling me the circumstances under which you went to Hollywood? When did you go?*
RENOIR: I arrived in New York with my wife, who is here, and with Saint-Exupéry, the writer. I arrived the eve of New Year's, the last day of 1940. The next day was the first day of 1941. I can tell you that the contrast between the streets of New York—full of life, and the people blowing on small trumpets and wearing funny hats—and the cities of Europe was something unbelievable.

Well, I went to Hollywood, where I had a contract with 20th Century Fox. The head of the producing department of the company was Darryl Zanuck.

I was very happy with my first picture. Very nicely, Darryl Zanuck suggested I should make an important picture with an important star. I wasn't too much interested in that, and I picked out a story, a script, written by Dudley Nichols, and that's the way I became a very close friend of Dudley Nichols.

The shooting of this picture was something very simple. After all, I suggested to Darryl Zanuck that I should go to Georgia to shoot the picture in Georgia. When I suggested shooting it there because the action took place in Georgia, they were very much surprised, because they were thinking: Why, when we have such beautiful studios and beautiful locations, with all the technical adjuncts, why go to Georgia?

Well, Zanuck was a wonderful man, and he understood what I had in mind. We went to Georgia, where I shot a big part of the picture. Of course, other parts of the picture were shot on the stages in Hollywood. That was my first American picture, *Swamp Water*. I liked it. I liked the story, and I believe I didn't choose too badly the actors, and I believe the company was happy, because we made money with the picture. As a matter of fact, it gave me also the opportunity to do something I always liked very much—to discover young talents. I made the picture with actors who were unknown at the time—what we used to call stub girls or stub boys—and I don't believe that Zanuck even knew their names. The girl was Anne Baxter, and the man was Dana Andrews, and after this picture they became very well known. That's to tell you that my first experience in a Hollywood studio was very pleasant.

But at the end of this experience, I understood that my experience had been pleasant just because it was my first picture, and I had something in my favor, something which helped me very much doing this first picture. It is that I didn't talk English, only just a few words, enough to direct actors, but not enough to discuss with the bosses. During the discussions, when I was feeling that I was going to "lose party," I was switching to French, and as they simply didn't understand French, the discussion was in my favor.

But at the end of the picture, I was starting to talk a little bit of English, and to lose this wonderful weapon, not understanding what people said and not being able to explain yourself. It's why I decided to abandon work in major studios. Very nicely Mr. Zanuck gave me my release. He understood that I wanted to work in a different way. After all, in Europe I was used to working very poorly (financially), not to make any money, or to make very little money when by chance I was making money, but to be absolutely free. I managed to do it very nominally; I had to follow a kind of policy. I know that I'm wrong, but that's the way I am, I'm too independent to exaggerate—that's why I decided to try to work in a different way.

Q: *Are you and Mr. Zanuck friends today?*
RENOIR: Oh yes, very good friends. You know, I left the studio being absolutely happy, even delighted about my relationship with Zanuck. He is not only a very honest man, but I believe he is a great film man. He knows the work, really. He's not only a boss who sits down in an office; he's a man who knows perfectly what's going on in the cutting room and is himself a very good cutter. He's a remarkable man; I admire him, and I believe he likes me, because when we meet each other, we like to be together and to talk, but probably we wouldn't like to work together. That's a different question.

Q: *You never found him difficult?*
RENOIR: Oh, no. Never. But the rules which are necessary in the conduct of a big studio are rules which are not too good for me.
    Now, I don't want to tell you about all my experiences. The only thing I can tell you is that my Hollywood work was very much connected with my friendship for Dudley Nichols. It was after this first picture that we remained very close friends. We attempted several things together, and finally we wrote a story together. I had brought a story from Europe, a story about a teacher who is a coward, who finally becomes a hero, just by chance, during the Occupation. Dudley liked the story, and we wrote it together, wrote the screenplay together, and shot the picture with Charles Laughton as the star of the picture—and the picture was very successful. That was for RKO. That was an independent production, Dudley Nichols and Jean Renoir. And this way of producing pictures pleased me very much. That was *This Land Is Mine.*

Now, my other experiences in Hollywood were also very pleasant. Maybe the best one was *The Southerner*. You know David Loew very well—he produced the picture, in association with me. The picture has no story. We just shot the picture very pleasantly. I must say that it was wonderful to work with David Loew, because David Loew is a very courageous, competent man. I will always remember when the stars of the picture—the man and the woman who were supposed to be the stars of the picture—went through my script, because I wrote the script entirely. When they saw my script, well, they were very disappointed, and they said, "We won't shoot it." And David said, "Well, so you won't shoot it, that's all."

So he took people who were not too well known at the time and who were wonderful actors—Zachary Scott, who used to play very different parts at Warner Bros., and Betty Field—I saw her yesterday, I had the pleasure to have dinner with her, and Betty Field was more a stage actress. She wasn't very well known in the movies. And we shot the picture, and it did very well.

But still, in spite of this happy experience, something was wrong. Something was wrong, and you know, it didn't work so well between me and—I won't say Hollywood, but I would say the industry, the professional Hollywood, the American film industry. I believe the trouble with me is that I consider that a film is just a way of expression. I don't believe that you are born a film man. I believe that you are maybe born a storyteller, and that's what I'm trying to be. I don't say that I've succeeded always, but I tried to tell stories. Now, with those stories it happened that it was easy for me to tell them through the medium of movies. That doesn't mean that movies are the only thing in the world for me. I'm a storyteller before being a movie man. That's the trouble between me and the industry. The industry can never recognize me as one of them. I was always an outsider, and I'm still now an outsider. Though I'm 65, on my last picture in France I had the same difficulties as with my first picture. It is exactly the same thing. I'm terribly happy about that, because it keeps me fighting all the time. It keeps me young and vigorous. That's much better.

Each picture I make—strangely enough—the first reaction of the industry, of the exhibitors or the salesmen, is, "I get some silly business of Renoir's." And it is a silly business, because I've discovered that I'm silly, and I know it, but I like to be silly. I believe that an artist should be also a fool. If the artist is not a fool, he's not an artist. Now, how do you expect to have a fool getting along with an industry where everybody is so serious—where everybody has a good bank account, listens to the radio at the same hour every day, goes to the tracks to gamble with horses, and to the club? You know, after all, they are more serious than bankers! When you see a film actor or a film director and a banker, the banker looks exactly like a silly boy compared to them.

I must tell you something. Very often in France, or anywhere in the world, or even in America, mostly in New York, people tell me, "But, Jean, you know, you didn't get along very well with the people in Hollywood—but that's not surprising, that's Hollywood."

I say, "No, that's not Hollywood. That's the film industry, and the film industry is the same in the whole world."

Practically, it is not the big brass of the film industry who are against me. They are in my favor, all of them. They do what they can to help me. But they are caught in a system. You know, there is a word in the film industry, "commercial"—but commercial doesn't mean to make money. I make pictures which make money, but they are not commercial, because they don't correspond to a certain style—a certain style which is supposed to be the commercial style. Now, it happens that my pictures, even if they make money, are supposed to be noncommercial, just because they are a little surprising, that's all. People up to now didn't accept the idea that an author of film is an author. They believe that an author of film is a kind of contractor who must put together different types of patterns and build a building like the Waldorf-Astoria. They don't understand that you may like to build a small house, but to build the whole thing to design, to plans, and also to put every brick one above the other yourself. That's exactly what I'm trying to do.

Q: *You have worked with some of the finest actors in the film industry, both American and French. Can you select your actors?*
RENOIR: My relationships with actors are good, even excellent, for one reason—I'm a frustrated actor. To me, to be an actor is a wonderful thing, and I love to act, and sometimes in my pictures I act myself, but I act very badly. I'm a bad actor. I'm a ham. The producer asked me,

begged me, not to act. If I could, I would be an actor, but I cannot. That's why I love actors and I get along very well with them.

Now, very often people ask me the difference between American and French actors. I would say that there is no difference, an actor is an actor. You know, to feel that there are differences between Hollywood and Paris, between an American actor and a French actor, would be against my conception of the world, because all my policy, all my behavior is based on what I told you: we are in the beginning of the new Middle Ages, and the division among nations is finished. I mean, within the Western world. To me the world is no more divided vertically with barriers. The world is divided horizontally. You see what I mean? You have the world, or the nation, of the artist, and then you have the nation of the farmers; you have the nation of the businesspeople.

May I tell you something? There is more connection between a businessman from Shanghai and a businessman from New York than between a farmer from Shanghai and a businessman from Shanghai. You understand what I mean about this division of the world? Today, if you talk to a French farmer—well, believe me, the conversation will be very much the same as the conversation with a farmer in Ohio. Very much. But if you talk to an American artist and to an American banker, you will find two citizens of two different nations.

Q: *You worked with M. Louis Jouvet?*
RENOIR: I worked with Louis Jouvet—of course I did. I can say nothing about Louis Jouvet. He was a fantastic actor. As a matter of fact, I never directed the actors. I'm not a director. As I told you, I'm a storyteller. I just manage to convince the actors to play in a certain way. But the physical means, the physical devices—that's up to them.

You know, you have one way of directing which is the normal way. The director says, "Look at me, I will act the scene." If he directs a girl, he will pantomime a love scene with the boy, taking a high voice to imitate the girl. And then he says, "You saw me? Now you do just the same."

That's ridiculous, because the most important thing in the world is respect for human beings. Well, if you respect human beings, try to respect the personality of your actors, and try to help them to find their own personality, and not to force them to adopt your own personality. You understand what I mean?

Q: *This works with a great actor like Louis Jouvet and a young person without much experience?*
RENOIR: It is the same thing. You know, either you are an actor or you are a nonactor. If you have a nonactor who chooses to insist—well, you try to get along with tricks with the nonactor in order to finish your picture and not to have a catastrophe, and not to hurt the feelings of the poor creature who believes he is an actor. But you know, that's a little trick on the side. But let's suppose that you work under ideal conditions—I mean, with actors. In this case, allow them to do the job as actors.

Q: *Mr. Zachary Scott said you were a great pleasure to work with.*
RENOIR: Well, I am happy with that, because it was exactly the same thing on my side. I loved to work with him. As a matter of fact, since *The Southerner* was finished, I tried very often to work again with Zachary, but you know this world is very strange. It seems that you meet each other by chance and you never find again a way to work together. I'm sorry for Zach and for me, and more for me.

Q: *In closing—when an audience comes out of a theater after seeing a picture, what do you suppose they should bring with them?*
RENOIR: Well, I cannot talk about general audiences, because I do not know them, but I can talk a little bit about the audiences of my pictures, because of course their gaze is terrifying for me, as for any author. I try to understand even more. Well, in my case, something happens, very often. It is that, one, I have basically one audience in the world, people under 20, kids. You know, very often I have insisted to my producers to put a sentence on the marquee so the film could be forbidden to people who are more than 20. How you say in English? Adults only? I would say: "Children only."

No, really, my audience is young. Now, there are a few old people who also like my pictures, but when they grow up and are sophisticated and look for reasons, I am not as lucky with them as with the very young ones.

For instance, my last picture in France, before the picture starts in the different movie theaters in big cities, I ask to show the picture to the university pupils, and it was a great success. It was also successful in the theaters, but no comparison.

Now, I have also another opinion about audiences. It is that a picture must not be the work only of an author or of actors or technicians; it must be also the work of the audience. The audience makes the picture, as well as the authors; and it seems to be strange, because you could ask me how the audience can make a picture which is already shot, done, printed.

Well, a picture is different with every type of audience, and if you have a good audience, the picture is better. It is a mystery, but we are surrounded by mysteries.

I must tell you something—I don't believe in science. The only part of science I believe in is the statement of Mr. Einstein that everything is relative. And since I don't believe in science, I believe very much in mysteries—like for instance an audience can help to make a picture which is already finished. I have nothing against that. I believe it.

Q: *I should think if you felt that way that you would have gone into producing plays instead of pictures.*
RENOIR: You are right, and that's what I am starting to do now. I wrote two plays, and I have a third one in preparation, and I wrote an adaptation of a play by my good friend Clifford Odets, *The Big Knife*, that was shown in Paris very successfully. I am an enormous fan. What I like about the stage, it is full of surprise. When my first play was presented in Paris, and Leslie Caron played the lead in the play, it was in a very charming theater, the Renaissance. But you feel that everything is so intimate, compared to the movies, that you feel like taking the box of the man that's selling popcorn during the intermission and selling popcorn yourself to the people, just to help a little bit.

Q: *Have you worked closely with the cameraman? I should think you'd be fascinated by the possibilities of the camera.*
RENOIR: I always worked closely with cameramen, and more now, because now I just invented a new system of shooting pictures. On my last pictures I shot them, one with eight cameras together, and the other one with five cameras. And I must tell you something—when you have five cameras, you cannot hang a viewfinder for each camera, and the cameramen are the bosses. That means they must cooperate with the whole story, with you, be a part of the screenplay and be a part of the picture.

A Rehearsal with Jean Renoir

VIRGINIA MAYNARD / 1960

*Jean Renoir spent the second semester 1959–60 at the University of
California, Berkeley, as Regents' Professor of English and Dramatic
Art. One of his projects there was the production of the world
premiere of his play* Carola *with a student cast.*

One of the first things the visitor to the rehearsal notices is the
pleasant and relaxed atmosphere, the absence of tension or strain. Jean
Renoir, charming and agreeable, sits casually chatting with the students
or with Bob Goldsby of the Department of Dramatic Art, who is assisting
him on the production; laughs appreciatively at the impromptu antics
of the young song-and-dance man who plays the janitor in his production; rises with continental courtliness to greet the feminine members
of the cast as they wander in. "Please sit here, Madame," he says, bow-
ing to the visitor and indicating the Victorian love seat which has been
placed for his use before the rough "stage" of the rehearsal hall. "I'm
sure it will be much more comfortable than those hard chairs, and
there is quite enough room for both of us, you will see."

The student-actors familiarize themselves with the embryo "set"—the
dressing room of a French actress, Carola, and the adjoining hallway,
back-stage of a theater. There is a massive Georgian dressing table for
Carola on stage left, a chaise lounge stage right, a French chair downstage
center; flats to indicate the rear wall, spaces for doorways and windows.

From *Theatre Journal* 13.2 (May 1961), 92–98. © The Johns Hopkins University Press.
Reprinted with permission of The Johns Hopkins University Press.

"This is the first time we have had any props to work with," Renoir says as he sits down. "Not that they are essential at this point, but Larry, our student stage manager, has found them, and they will be convenient perhaps in making a frame for our play. I always like to begin by neglecting entirely the technical problems and concentrating on the expression of character. So far, we have been blocking scenes roughly as we read through the lines, and letting the actors find the meanings of their parts. Up to now, I have been here mostly as author, helping the actors as best I could to understand what I have tried to say in this play. Perhaps tonight I shall be a little more the director."

The twenty-year-old girl who is playing Carola tries out the revolving chair before her stage dressing table, testing it in various positions as she looks into the mirror, then out at the imaginary audience.

"How is it, Deneen?" he calls out. She smiles, and nods excitedly.

"A very talented girl," he says to me, "most sensitive and very capable for one so young. It is a hard part she is playing, an embittered thirty-year-old woman of the world. But good acting is certainly not chiefly a matter of age and experience."

He anticipates my next question. "I must say," he continues, "that I have not found it necessary to change my method at all because the actors are students and amateurs rather than professionals. Of course, I have worked with nonprofessionals many times in my life before, both on the stage and screen. But my thought in this project is to help the students understand the professional approach to directing and acting, and so I continue to work as I always have. My approach, I may say, is perhaps not the usual approach to the direction of acting, but is the result of certain beliefs of my own, in working for a certain style in show business."

Despite his relaxed manner, Renoir is very much aware of the time; and promptly at seven-thirty, when the last actor has made his appearance, he rises and signals for quiet.

"O.K.," he says, "we begin. And now that I know you all a little better, I want to try something new—which is to throw you right into the situation. Tonight we go fishing. [The director of *The River*, who has included rivers in so many of his pictures both for their symbolic and pictoral values, has many such figures of speech.] And I may say, I hope, I think, we catch quite a bit of fish."

The stage manager calls places; the first act begins. The actors of the play-within-a-play enter the stage dressing room. There is Carola, her maid or dresser, a young actress, and an old actor. Renoir watches intently. Suddenly he stands up.

"Excuse me," he says, "I'm very sorry to interrupt you so soon when you are doing so well, but there are some things that perhaps we can do a little bit better. It was very good, but the opening is very important, and to me it's perhaps easier to fix little things from the beginning. All the audience is sitting out here wondering who are those people. I don't think we have told them sufficiently yet."

He turns to the boy who is playing the old actor. "Who are you, sir?"

The boy looks surprised. He holds up a pair of fuzzy slippers, a dilapidated shawl. "Why—I'm Parmentier, the old actor."

"But you cannot tell me that if I am sitting in the audience watching the play. Perhaps you should put down the shawl and slippers until you can tell me who you are without them. Your first line must establish your character. I believe you are right, what you do with it, but I believe we should think about it more. From the very first line people are going to say 'Who is this old man—what is he doing in this play?' The weak voice—the gestures—what you do now is very good, and I believe it will work the way you do it. But perhaps we could do more. This is an old man who is very nasty, very vicious, entirely self-centered. We must try to establish this from the first. I am not going to tell you how. I believe you will find a way. Try in any case."

The boy nods, looks thoughtful, and goes back to the entrance, practicing his part soundlessly. Renoir turns to the very young girl. "And Josette. You have not many lines so we must make each one count. We have a line in our play, 'There are no small parts, only small actors.' Remember that. Your part is as important as any in the show. You have a function in this play. You are a Cassandra-type character, a chorus, the voice of France, angry and hostile at the occupation of the Germans; bitter, hating the Germans. Every part is a synopsis of something, and you are a synopsis of these things. In every line you say. I know you can do it."

He turns to Carola. "You are the queen. The way you walk into the room, the way you sit down, the way you say your lines—everything must mean 'I am the queen and I know it.' I have been asking you to read your lines the way you would in everyday life. Now I want you to add something: a kind of elegance which affects to be cold even when you are emotionally involved. You must guard against too much emotionalism in these scenes and save your emotion for later in the play, when you must show it. Now you are cold in the manner of a lady of English high society, who is afraid to say what she thinks or show a 'vulgar' display of emotion. This will not only add to your character at this point but will make a nice foil for your maid, who is always herself—Mireille goes overboard about everything—while Carola is wearing a mask over her real feelings."

The young actors chatter excitedly about these new concepts of their parts. Someone asks eagerly, "Can we do it again?"

Renoir smiles. "Yes, we will do it again, probably many many times before we have it just as we like it. We will no doubt make many wrong starts and have to begin again. Excuse me if I am so severe now, but the reason that I am so much insisting at this point is that I believe that if you once start *being* the character, you will know what this character would do in specific situations. Now let's go through it again."

They repeat the scene, with such good effect that Renoir does not interrupt them until sometime after the entrance of a new character— the theater manager in the play. This Campan goes through a complicated scene with Carola, at the end of which Renoir calls a halt.

"Excuse me, but I would like to work on this scene for a while. It is very difficult, and I think perhaps we should give it some time. It is not that you are not doing very well—indeed you are, for so soon in rehearsals—but this is a little habit of mine with which you will no doubt become soon familiar. Sometimes I see a little scene like this, sometimes it is only a line, that seems to me to be like a key which could open the understanding of the actor to all the lines of his part. This is such a scene. If we try too much tonight we will be like tourists taking a trip to Europe who see everything, and yet see nothing; it would be better to stay one month in the same place and learn to know it. We must not be like tourists in this play and just look the situation over. Better to stay with this one small scene until we know it thoroughly. So let's go over it again. Sid [to the young man playing the theater manager], perhaps you are trying too hard to get the 'frustrated actor' feeling into your part. Your interpretation is correct—Campan doubtless does have a poetic inspiration at this point—but the way you do it doesn't quite come off. If you begin again in an absolutely casual manner, perhaps we can find where to go."

Sid explains that it was his idea that the "ham" in Campan was beginning to show in this situation.

"Perhaps it is," says Renoir, "but let's do it without the ham. And this time not so fast. It's like swallowing a meal—you have to make it your own. You cannot swallow it whole."

Sid tries the scene again in a more restrained manner. They go through it several times.

"Much better," says Renoir. "Now we have the bread and butter, perhaps we can afford a little ham."

Sid tries again, with, someone suggests, just a trifle too much ham. But Renoir is pleased. "Of course the whole thing is too obvious now, but let the man think. He's diving in. When we decide to dive into cold water we do it with both feet. And we usually come out all right."

They go through the scene again, this time with better results. There is one line Renoir doesn't like. "But I never like to show an actor how to say a line if I can help it," he remarks. "If I must, I wait until I know the actor well enough so that I can imitate him—in other words, say it with his personality applied to my understanding of the character or situation. Even then I would hesitate to indicate the feeling with which it is said. The feeling, I think, is the actor's own private affair. This scene is very difficult," Renoir continues, "but I think when Sid gets to the bottom of the meaning of the words he will have it. To me, good acting is so much a matter of understanding every syllable of the lines, and finding the right mood in which to say them."

He allows the act to go on for some time, then interrupts again. "Excuse me, I hate to interrupt you when you are doing so well. But now that you are getting the feel of the parts, there is a little something else I would like to add. I have the feeling that you are all doing your own parts very well, but that you are not paying enough attention to the other characters on the stage with you. You are acting, but not interacting. And after all it is human contact—the relation of one human being to another—that is the life of the show. Of course, it is very early in the play to start this perhaps—when you are not quite certain of your own roles—but I would like you to try in this little scene we have just finished.

"When Campan asks Carola to have a 'little chat' with General Von Clodius—to keep the theater from closing—Carola reacts to him verbally . . . she knows what this 'little chat' means. But there are two other women in the room who also know what it means, and who sympathize with Carola. They must react silently to this 'little chat.' I would like to feel that all three women stand together against Campan, present a united front against him. That is not so easy to do, Mireille and Josette, as if you had a line—perhaps you will find a look, a gesture, a motion of the body which will convey your feeling. But remember that you are never isolated. People in the play are never alone. Around each character is the life of the play, and it is only when we feel this sense of life, of a group of people acting together, interacting in human contact—it is only then that we have great moments in the theater. I ask you to think about this now, while we have a five minute break to stretch ourselves and perhaps have a drink of water."

Most of the students make a beeline for the drinking fountain or light cigarettes, but several cluster about Renoir. The General and Colonel Kroll of the Gestapo, two characters who have not yet made their appearance in the scenes being rehearsed, have questions about their parts.

The young man playing the role of General Von Clodius says he can't quite believe the General is really in love with Carola.

"He is, believe me," says Renoir. "And if you cannot with reason believe this, I advise you to act the part instinctively as it is written, and you will find your rationalization after. The General looks and speaks coolly, intellectually, but inside he is burning like a twenty-year-old boy. With his aristocratic German education he cannot show this at all times—only in his weaker moments—but the feeling is there, is intended to be there. I believe that in acting, as in any other art, inspiration, or instinct, is more important than reason. The reason is there, but it comes after. The rationalization for making a film, writing a piece of music, comes after the fact, not before. I believe this very strongly. *Act your general,*" Renoir counsels the young man, "as though he is in love with Carola, and you will find your general in love with her. Believe me."

Now "Colonel Kroll" brings up his question: he cannot quite believe in his Gestapo colonel, who, at the end of the play, gives Carola and the General a chance to escape, although Kroll has caught the two aiding in the escape of a French underground agent.

"But believe me," Renoir replies, "this is the character I have created. He is a very complex person, and I think I have made it clear in his

character that he could do this. You are upset because this colonel is
not a stereotype. All my life I have fought against the cliché, the gener-
alization. If it is shocking, if it is unusual—then I am glad. Believe me, if
I had my characters do what they were 'supposed' to do I would be a
very rich man. I would have five Cadillacs in my garage."

Someone else wants to know how Renoir's method differs from that
of Stanislavsky. Renoir considers:

"I believe that I differ from Stanislavsky mainly because I am not a
Russian."

Everyone laughs.

"No," he goes on, "I am quite serious. What I am trying, of course, is
the Stanislavsky method of identification. But I am never able to forget
that there is a world around me—that around this plot, this play, life is
going on. Stanislavsky played in a world limited by the play—by the
story. Outside of this world there was nothing. I believe this is why
Stanislavsky's direction was so magnificent: his actors were entirely
involved in the life of the play, no longer in lives of their own.

"It is a basic difference in a matter of approach, and in a philosophy
of life, in fundamental beliefs. I am perhaps too much of a humanist to
be so specialized. My work is always connected with the outside world.
I cannot forget—now, for instance—that you are a student with exams
to study for, that this boy perhaps has personal problems, that this girl
may not be able to come to all the rehearsals and so become as perfect
in her part as I could wish, and so on. I cannot be ruthless with other
human beings. I cannot ignore their right to be considered by me. It is
perhaps—very roughly—just the belief in democracy rather than
tyranny, the belief in the other fellow's rights, even if they seem to
intrude on my own.

"This play, *Carola*, illustrates what I am trying to say. It is about a girl
who tries to shut out the outside world, to pretend that the German
occupation of France does not concern her, to rid herself of all unpleasant real-life situations by living only for her art. She cannot do it. The
real world intrudes upon her in the person of Henri, the French agent;
in the person of the German general; in the stories about Jews, the
crimes of the Gestapo—until she can no longer ignore it.

"I can no more ignore the outside world," continues Renoir, "than can
Carola in my play; and so of course my approach to directing differs from

Stanislavsky's accordingly. I compromise all the time. But, strangely enough, I believe that it is by compromise that I get good results. That is, good results for me . . . since, to me, the good result is not a perfect achievement, but to get out of a play or a film or an actor a little bit of real humanity rather than a perfect performance. To me, that's sufficient.

"But here are our actors all ready to go again, and we must not keep them waiting. There's just one little part I want to do over again."

He turns to the stage: "O.K., let's start with the scene where Campan is telling Carola he wants her to have a 'little chat' with the general—top of page seventeen; and don't forget your interacting bits, Mireille . . . Josette . . ."

They run through the scene.

"Excellent, excellent," cries Renoir, "I had the feeling that time of a roomful of people really talking to each other, understanding each other, interacting. Now, let's do it again, and, Deneen—when you come to the part where Campan tells you the name of the general you're to see, I want you to act as though you'd just seen a ghost. Turn around in your chair when he says 'General Von Clodius' and look at Campan as though you were in a castle in Scotland and there was a ghost. Then, after a moment, repeat 'General Von Clodius' in a voice that will tell us all you are feeling. Can you do it, Deneen?"

They begin. But when they arrive at the place where Carola is to say "General Von Clodius" the actress is silent. Everything stops.

"Well?" prompts Renoir. " 'General Von Clodius?' "

"I can't," says Carola.

"Oh, come," says Renoir. "You can. Of course you can."

Still she sits silent, a strange look on her face. She shakes her head.

Renoir gets up, crosses to Carola's dressing table and talks to the girl in a low tone. The director sits down in the girl's chair, turns to Campan, who repeats his cue line:

"General Von Clodius, in charge of all the defense installations on the whole Western front."

Renoir turns slowly in the swivel chair, faces Campan, makes his face blank with shock. "General Von Clodius" he says, in a stunned voice.

Campan continues his lines: "What's the matter?"

And Mireille asks, "You know him?"

Now Renoir gets up, and Carola sits down.

"General Von Clodius, in charge of all the defense installations on the whole Western front," says Campan, cuing Carola in once more.

Carola turns, gives Campan a blank look. She opens her mouth, but no words come forth.

"Well?" says Renoir.

Carola bursts into tears.

"I can't—I just can't!"

Renoir pets her. "But of course you can."

"I don't think Carola would say that," sobs the girl. "She would just look at him—and say, 'I can't'—and begin to cry."

Renoir studies her a long moment.

"Well, let's try it that way," he says, and takes his place in the "audience."

They play the scene. It is very effective—highly emotional—the first bit of emotion Carola has shown in the play.

"Well, I must say that is very good," says Renoir. "You've found something there that is better than the way it is written. Well, that's all for tonight, boys and girls. Time to go home."

Carola comes up to Renoir, very upset over her tearful outburst.

"Well, you were right," says Renoir, "and believe me, don't worry about a few tears—without tears I'm afraid we would have no play."

The students gather up their books and begin to wander off.

"Compromises," says Renoir. "You see, there is another case in which a compromise proved itself. For ten seconds tonight we had instead of a very young actress playing a part, the manifestation of a real human being, the real Carola.

"Oh, they don't always work out so well, I'll admit," he muses. "I'm afraid a great many difficulties I've had in my profession have come from my habit of considering the other person, sometimes too much.

"Tell me, why should I, rather than this girl who is playing the part, say how she is to do it? After all, an actor's instinct may be just as good as the director's. At any rate, I have to respect it."

As we go out the door, he shrugs his shoulders. "Even if I were wrong, that's the way I was born, and my father was just exactly like that before me. And I prefer not to change. I'm too old to change, anyway, even if I wanted to."

Conversation with Jean Renoir

LOUIS MARCORELLES / 1962

LOUIS MARCORELLES: *Can I begin by asking a question about your new film,* Caporal Épinglé? *What subject have you chosen for it?*
JEAN RENOIR: I didn't choose it, someone put it up to me. I didn't know the story, but after reading it I thought it was a subject that suited me very well, one I could feel at home with. It's like *La Grande Illusion* in that it's a story of escape, though naturally with all kinds of differences. The fact that it's an escape story interests me in itself, because one enjoys repeating oneself, returning to the same sort of framework and finding the variations in it. Of course this is an entirely different film from *La Grande Illusion*: the action takes place in 1940 and that means it belongs to another world.

LM: *What do you feel the differences really are between the two periods—between 1915 and 1940?*
JR: Well, twenty-five years amounts to a generation. And the great turning point, of course, was not the last war but 1914. The people of the last war come after the turning; the people of 1914 were still riding towards it, quite unaware that any turning point was coming. The characters in *La Grande Illusion*—Boeldieu and Maréchal and Rosenthal—would be amazed if anyone told them, "You know, in a few years these ideas about nations will have disappeared. There will be no more nations." They might understand perhaps that there would be social change, a merging of classes—there's enough talk about that in

Originally published in *Sight and Sound*, 2.31 (Spring 1962). Reprinted by permission.

La Grande Illusion. But it would never have occurred to them that the world could be politically divided in a different way. . . . And money is shared out differently, so that the people in charge are different people, belong to another race. Europe in 1914 was still in the hands of the politicians, even if they were already servants of the great industrial and financial interests. Now politicians have ceased to count for much: we're in the age of the organisation men, the planners. Wasn't the 1939/45 war above everything one of organisation? It was really organisation—in the factories as much as on the battlefield—that defeated Hitler.

LM: *About social themes: in* La Grande Illusion, La Règle du Jeu, La Marseillaise, *and I think also in* Diary of a Chambermaid, *you're showing us a society divided "horizontally." Do you think that the attitude in* La Règle du Jeu, *for instance, is already out of date; that there aren't any longer these rigid class divisions?*
JR: Of course nothing is ever fixed or absolute. And I really feel that the distinctions one establishes in one's own mind are only valuable because they help one to understand what's going on around one. I don't think they represent anything final. . . . I often try to work out why I've adopted certain theories which seem fairly arbitrary, and I usually fall back on the comparison with speed. Drive in a donkey cart down a narrow lane, with the trees practically brushing past you, and you can have the illusion of fantastic speed. Record it on film and it looks wonderful. But if you're sitting in an aeroplane, judging your speed by the time it takes the sun to move behind some object on the ground, you might as well be stationary for all the sense of movement you have. You need standards of comparison to measure speed; and I think it's rather like that with theories.

LM: *Yes, but I believe you've never cared much for general theories. All I meant, simply, was that if you were to return to* La Règle du Jeu *today, you might see it rather differently.*
JR: Well, I don't know about its value as a film, but I do feel that *La Règle du Jeu*, like *La Grande Illusion*, is a sort of reconstructed documentary, a documentary on the condition of society at a given moment. And of course that society is very different now. External reality is often

the expression, the symbol, of an interior truth, and I suppose that even in their clothes people are now all pretty much alike. Certainly it's difficult now to distinguish between a Boeldieu going to the theatre on a Saturday and a Maréchal doing the same thing. There are differences, naturally, but they're much more subtle, more interior, and they're gradually being wiped out. It's possible that between Boeldieu's son and Maréchal's there may be no difference. It's extremely possible.

LM: *National barriers and class barriers may be breaking down, as you say, but we live in a world with two great divisions—East and West. Do you think we can establish real co-existence? Do you see any breaking down of these barriers?*

JR: Yes, up to a point . . . I believe implicitly in the Tower of Babel, and I think all those stories like the one about the Tower of Babel, with which ancient history is dotted, are not meaningless. The stories may be symbolic, things didn't happen just as they've been narrated, but stories like this are all really getting at the same point: the tendency for humanity to come together. Politically, this is the history of the world—the history of the Roman Empire, and of all the later attempts to reconstruct the Roman Empire. At the moment, obviously, the world is split in two; and I suppose that the barriers *are* real ones, though my instinct tells me that they're not. We may be part of an intermediary period, when really big divisions—there are several in the world, after all—are going to replace the old swarm of small nations. But the unifying forces exist too, above all in the way of living and in the coming together of languages. It isn't even always an international thing, after all. It wasn't so long ago, for instance, that when an Italian theatre company from Rome played in Turin the audience couldn't understand the actors. But now, with radio, television, the cinema, they've invented a kind of standard Italian. I must say I regret it. It's just like England, that boring English of their radio and television.

LM: *I think there's a movement now in England, though, to get away from this, for actors to use their local accents. Do you know England well?*

JR: Not at all well, but what I do know is in a family kind of way; through family connections. I adore England and I'd like to live there: people live there very agreeably.

LM: *I've heard some Englishmen say that* The River *is one of the most authentically English films ever made. So you must have a certain fellow-feeling with the English.*

JR: Oh, really it's very simple. My sister-in-law is English, so I do know a bit about English family life.

LM: *What about the English cinema? The English have no equivalent, for instance, to our own New Wave, the break-through of young directors filming independently.*

JR: Yes, but things don't happen simultaneously in all countries. After all, the game was really opened by the neo-realists in Italy, and it wouldn't surprise me a bit if the English were to come in and give us something absolutely unexpected. . . . Look, for instance, at the way English life and habits are changing. I can't stand the kind of literature which likes to over-simplify national differences—you know, the English are so cold, the Italians are warm, the Germans are heavy. But of course there *are* national characteristics: the climate, the way one eats, the way people move about the streets, the fact that traffic goes on the left—all this does add up to something. A few years ago, English manners depended on tremendous restraint; they didn't break the ice themselves, and they respected the ice that formed around other people. Lately, though, in one hot summer I've seen English journalists behaving more like Neapolitans than the Neapolitans themselves. I remember one session at the Savoy Hotel in London, where in five minutes we were all drinking, shouting, bullying each other. It was a lot of fun, and it wasn't at all like the conventional image of England.

LM: *It seems to me a pity that there isn't more of this freedom, this letting rip, in English films. The English cinema is so very respectable.*

JR: It's very, very respectable, but sometimes it's found in that respectability a kind of genius. . . . The terrible thing about the cinema is the way it uses up everything. It exhausts ideas, stories, brands of stories, and suddenly it finds itself faced with a kind of gulf, a ditch across which it must leap to capture some new and absolutely unforeseen territory. We're not talking, obviously, about eternal masterpieces: clearly Shakespeare always had something to say, and he didn't have to jump any ditch. But it's a situation ordinary film production is likely to run

into every five years or so. In France the New Wave has been lucky
enough to jump the ditch. In England the same thing could happen.

LM: *English cinema has always been best known for its documentarists,*
people like Grierson and Flaherty. Do you think a move might come from that
direction?
JR: Oh, it's all a question of people. New movements come into existence through certain people—in France through the *Cahiers* group, the
Cinemathèque. In England the documentary movement was created
by a particular group, around Cavalcanti, wasn't it? Cavalcanti played
a big part in English documentary.

LM: *Well, what do you think about documentary in general, about its*
importance to cinema?
JR: Of course it's important because it's the only school that exists. If
there were any other way for young directors to get a start, well, I don't
know. . . . It isn't that documentary is the only possible school theoretically, but in practice it amounts to the only one, and I don't see how
a young director can begin in any other way. In any case, it's the way
most of our own directors of quality *have* begun. Look at Resnais, for
instance: his documentary studies of painters enabled him to enter into
direct contact with certain problems.

LM: *To get back for a moment to England . . . You probably know about*
the group who've been called the Angry Young Men, and the importance they
attach to the idea of commitment—the feeling that cinema and theatre ought
to reflect and criticise the society around them. Last Sunday, for instance, I
was talking to an English critic who'd just seen Truffaut's Jules et Jim, *and*
who said that he found it quite unimportant because "it's not a committed
film." This seems to me a bit ridiculous, because from Truffaut's point of
view of course the film does have a commitment. I'd like to know what the
word means to you.
JR: Well, of course it has a meaning. But I feel about this word "commitment" or "engagement" as I do about most general ideas: they take
on value only when they move to the particular. You're driving along,
and you see a very poorly dressed man limping down the street: do you
take him into your car or don't you? This is a commitment, isn't it, of a

very precise kind? But as to commitment in a general sense . . . You know I can't believe in the general ideas, really I can't believe in them at all. I try too hard to respect human personality not to feel that, at bottom, there must be a grain of truth in every idea. I can even believe that all the ideas are true in themselves, and that it's the application of them which gives them value or not in particular circumstances. . . . No, I don't believe there are such things as absolute truths; but I do believe in absolute human qualities—generosity, for instance, which is one of the basic ones. Truffaut's film is a good one, in my opinion, because it has this generosity. Of course it has its faults, but these are failings with which I sympathise. I sympathise egotistically, because they are exactly the failings of my own last films, exactly the same . . .

LM: *Have you entirely given up your activity in the theatre, or do you still mean to go back to it from time to time?*
JR: I haven't given up anything. It's just that things turn out in a certain way, and lately I haven't found anything in the theatre that really catches my imagination.

LM: *I seem to remember that about three or four years ago you were quoted as saying "I've said almost everything in the cinema: I find a kind of freedom in the theatre . . ."*
JR: In the theatre there is greater freedom because there is discipline. The awful thing about the cinema is the possibility of moving about exactly as one wants. You say, "Well, I must explain this emotion, and I'll do it by going into flashback and showing you what happened to this man when he was two years old." It's very convenient, of course, but it's also enfeebling. If you have to make the emotion understood simply through his behaviour, then the discipline brings a kind of freedom with it. There's really no freedom without discipline, because without it one falls back on the disciplines one constructs for oneself, and they are really formidable. It's much better if the restraints are imposed from outside.

LM: *Do you feel that the cinema now—that's to say, with its ultra-mobile cameras, portable sound equipment and all the rest of it—gives you almost the same freedom as the theatre?*

JR: For me there's one very interesting demonstration, a kind of open door, and that's François Reichenbach's films. To get the quality of expression, of sound and vision, with the means he employs . . . I think it's tremendously important.

LM: *I believe you've worked with a good deal of freedom on your own new film. Was it shot in a studio or on location?*
JR: Mostly on location. Very little studio.

LM: *Did you work on it alone?*
JR: No, because with this kind of subject . . . Isn't there always this old problem of external reality? Of course I'd like to be someone like Chaplin and get away from it completely, but I'm not strong enough for that. I try, quite often, and the attempts usually go adrift; and I know really that if I have some slight contact with external appearances, this helps me to penetrate more deeply to the interior of the characters. I knew something about the lives of prisoners of war, but not directly, not first-hand. It happens that there's a very talented director, Guy Lefranc, who was a prisoner himself and for whom the subject means something very special—like the Bible for a believer. I asked him to help me, and he's given me this sense of first-hand knowledge.

LM: *I believe you've kept on with the techniques of your recent films,* Dr. Cordelier *and* Le Déjeuner sur l'Herbe. *Does this mean shooting with three or four cameras simultaneously?*
JR: Generally three. And we've mostly recorded direct sound. There's nothing dubbed in the film—oh yes, there is one scene, a short one, where it was raining so hard that you couldn't hear the words.

LM: *When you're using this number of cameras, does it make difficulties in the editing, in matching shots? Are there different light levels, for instance?*
JR: No, we take all that into account. I'm working with Renée Lichtig, the same cutter who helped me on Dr. Cordelier and Le Déjeuner sur l'Herbe, and she's used to this sort of juggling about. In fact, with this method of shooting, the editing becomes essentially a matter of selection and assembly. I'm not faced with a mountain of film which

can be so reconstructed in the cutting that something which started out as a comedy can end up as a tragedy.

LM: *What struck me about* Dr. Cordelier *was the extraordinary freedom your methods seemed to give the actors.*
JR: Here too, I hope, here too. I haven't used the identical technique, because the subject doesn't lend itself in the same way. Not all subjects do . . . I can't see Jean Rouch, for instance, going off to make one of his African films with half a dozen cameras. He obviously needs one camera, and needs it in exactly the right place. But there are no theories, no general rules. All one can say is that with some scenes and subjects it's an unbeatable method. You get this freedom for the actors, and you get a kind of emotional progression.

LM: *But I suppose you have to rehearse very carefully just the same?*
JR: Of course, you always have to rehearse; and you rehearse even more thoroughly when there are several cameras, in order to pin down an emotion and even quite simply to follow through on physical movement. It *is* easy to lose time on this business of matching shots, even when you're just trying to match physical continuity. You take a close-up, and then comes the medium shot which is to follow it in the montage, and which is filmed the next day, and everyone on the set is asking "Was he like this; wasn't his voice sharper; no, not at all, it was less sharp . . . I promise you it was exactly like this . . . I had my elbow bent just this way . . ." And then the cinema finally becomes a job for the continuity girl, and then a job of composition and inspiration. For myself, I'd really rather call a truce to all these problems and shoot the scene in one go.

LM: *In* À Bout de Souffle *Jean-Luc Godard is trying to get away from the standard editing devices, the artificial linking shots and so on, to use a much more fragmentary kind of montage. What do you feel about this?*
JR: Yes, yes, it's excellent . . . But I must tell you that I don't really bother much about linking shots, physical devices to link action. The thing that counts as far as I'm concerned is the emotional link. I feel that the development of thought and feeling in an actor is indispensable—at least to my kind of film. I don't see how I can

expect to establish a relationship with an audience if I don't manage to give it continuity of emotion through a character.

LM: *Throughout your career, I suppose, you've always referred back to realism, however many forms it's taken.*

JR: With constant efforts to escape, since realism annoys me. But it does help me to divine just a little of the interior truth, which is the one vital thing. In effect it has to do with knowing what someone is really like, what stuff he has in him. Then, once one has got at him, one has to make the audience see it too . . . But, you know, everyone really only makes one film in his life, and then he breaks it up into fragments and makes it again, with just a few little variations each time. There's one so-called quality that's more overrated than almost any other: imagination. I've just been writing a book about my father, and I'm delighted to find that he felt this too. He really detested imagination: he thought it was the greatest possible hazard for the artist.

LM: *Because it's too capricious . . .*

JR: No, not that. It's simply that my father was a modest man who didn't believe that his inventions were important enough or varied enough to concern the public. He thought that the artist's proper function was to absorb material, to digest it and to pass it on. The form didn't matter: it could be Picasso's cubist form, or Mondrian's abstracts, or his own figurative technique. But he didn't believe in the idea of man as God, able to create out of nothing. He really subscribed to that text by Lavoisier which you must know: "In nature nothing is created, nothing is lost, everything is transformed . . ." Well, there you are.

LM: *A few years ago, I believe you were quoted as saying that directors ought to be able to make films for art-house distribution, that there should be more of these cinemas throughout the world and that production could be financed through this kind of distribution. Do you still feel like that?*

JR: Yes, but it's still an ideal, an intention, rather than a fact. I think something like this will happen, and I'm encouraged by the increasing number of different types of cinema. Cinerama, for instance, clearly doesn't attract the same audience as the one which goes to the Publicis Cinema to see Truffaut's new film. These are two entirely different kinds of enterprise. . . . When I say different audiences, though, I ought to stress that I don't necessarily mean different people: of course every human being is potentially a member of all sorts of audiences, depending on whether he's feeling in the mood for Wagner or for a music-hall.

LM: *I was talking recently to Truffaut on this subject, and he said that he didn't want to make films just for specialised audiences, that he wanted his films to reach everyone. I think he's a little ahead of his time, because I can't see* Jules et Jim *doing the same kind of business as* The Guns of Navarone. *But I'd like to ask you about this question of contact with the public.*

JR: I can only give you my own opinion, and I rather think I agree with Truffaut. You must make films to reach everyone. If you don't, you split up into your little private groups, you become pretentious, and in my view you lose the sense of what the cinema is really about. It is, essentially, a mass art; and we must accept that, we must take it for what it is. I don't believe that in our age the differences between the various forms of expression are so great that we need to try to bend one form to ends which aren't proper to it. You know, the cinema becomes a mass art simply because of the distribution system: there is a negative, or maybe several negatives, and you take whatever number of prints you want, and there you are. We wouldn't have to talk about a mass art if there were only one copy of each film. Anyhow, if you want to practise something that *isn't* a mass art, heaven knows there are plenty of other ways of expressing yourself!

LM: *All the same, as you've said, different films do appeal to different audiences. Do you think this is something for the business men to sort out— to fit the film to the market—or does it mean that directors should consciously make films with certain audiences in mind?*

JR: Naturally, it's firstly a matter for the business men. But there's another reason why the situation is quite different from what happens in the theatre. A playwright can write for a certain actor—Giraudoux for Jouvet, say—in the assurance that his work will reach the public. But there's no reason for a film director—for tomorrow's Truffaut— knowing that the Publicis audience has taken kindly to his film, to say to himself, "Well, I'll make another film which will come out at the

Publicis. . . ." But why not? It would give the artist a wonderful feeling of security. In fact the only harmful thing about our job is this fact that it's commercial. We are obliged to please too many people, because it's the condition of the job. If you start out with the idea of pleasing every-one, however, of course you end up satisfying no one. One has to start with the idea of achieving a certain objective, uncovering a certain truth, and if the mass public accepts it, so much the better. One makes films for them.

LM: *I suppose there are likely to be more and more different kinds of films, and perhaps a more widespread diffusion of films. Do you think there is also going to be more room for individualism?*
JR: There will be more specialisation, I suppose. There's no reason why entertainment shouldn't move in the same direction as the rest of life. When I was at college, for instance, one either read science or the humanities; one did Latin or one didn't! The division stopped there. Now there's a frantic kind of forced specialisation, and the subjects which students have to absorb are so complex that they are forced to select, to limit themselves. It will be the same in entertainment, the same in everything.

LM: *Do you think that the cinema has absorbed part of the theatre public?*
JR: No, I really feel rather the opposite. . . . I see our age as one of great specialisation, as I've just said, particularly in the professions, but in some ways we're moving away from specialisation, for instance in the field of technique. If I have worked in the theatre, it is only because technical development is such that at the moment a director is not exclusively a film director. . . . When I started out in films, you know, the director had to do almost everything himself. He practically devel-oped the film himself; and of course it was tremendously exciting. Then all these technical preoccupations shut us up in our own little world, just as the old-time craftsmen were enclosed in the world of their par-ticular craft. A man who made barrels, for instance, would never have thought of making tables: he had too much to learn about his own craft. Now you make a barrel with a machine, all in a few minutes, and since you can make a table just as easily, why not have a table as well?

The New Wave directors know their craft; but there are a tremendous number of directors around who know absolutely nothing about the technical problems of their job. They really haven't the first idea about photography, or about what happens when you develop a film, or about sound recording. The director simply comes along and says "I want such and such a scene," and the technicians do it for him. So people now have their general ideas, their artistic ideas, and the artisan has given way to the artist. And this is something to regret, because great art is made by artisans and not by artists.

LM: *Then you can't be very enthusiastic about the Hollywood tendency towards super-spectacles, bigger and bigger films?*
JR: I enjoy watching some of them. But I get far too much pleasure out of doing the odd jobs on a film to want to get tied up in an undertaking where one becomes a kind of general, with a whole staff at one's disposal. The general doesn't have any fun; the really entertaining thing is to be a corporal giving riding lessons to half a dozen men, teaching them how to hang on to a horse. That's where the fun is.

LM: *You worked in Hollywood for some time, and might go back there. Were you as free and happy as in France?*
JR: But of course!

LM: *You obviously like America a lot. What is it that you get from it particularly?*
JR: Oh, many things . . . Americans may be less subtle in their attitudes than Europeans, but they're also less bitter. In America you can still sit in a shop and have a chat with the grocer's boy about the development of the local bus service or about pre-Columbian art, or whatever it may be. It isn't so easy in Paris. Try to interrupt your butcher by chatting to him while he's chopping up the cutlets . . .

LM: *Are you irritated at all by the American emphasis on technical perfection?*
JR: Certainly not, because I have a great regard for good technique. I've spent my time in France bullying the laboratories to get better results, I've always tried for perfect camera movement. . . . The danger

for America, as I've said, is that everything becomes so perfect the director doesn't have to know anything about technique at all. But I despise technique—despise it while I'm working, I mean—because I really do know it. And if you don't know it all, I don't see how you can expect to make first-class films.

LM: *Quite a long time ago, in some interview or other, I believe you mentioned a director called George B. Seitz who had worked with M-G-M on the Andy Hardy pictures. I think you quoted him as a case of an artisan who really knew his job.*

JR: Yes, perhaps. I'll try to tell you what I had in mind. I believe that the dangerous thing in a director's career is to make films which earn a lot of money. After a really big box-office success, people turn their backs on you, they don't want to suggest films to you, you're out. But have a good flop which has cost millions, and people love you, they fall over themselves to get you to work for them. . . . It really isn't a paradox: it's true all over the world. Now, I gave as an instance the case of this gentleman who directed the Mickey Rooney pictures, and who kept Metro rich for years. I wanted to know the name of this director, and no one could even tell me who he was. Well, here is this fantastic thing: here is this man who earned more money for the cinema than almost anyone you can think of, and no one even knew his name. Isn't that proof, if you want it, that money doesn't count in the cinema?

LM: *I know you've always had a great sympathy for the American cinema. Was Stroheim someone you admired particularly?*
JR: Yes, yes. A great character.

LM: *You cast him in* La Grande Illusion, *and when you were making* Nana *I believe that you were . . .*
JR: Naturally I thought of him. He was a great influence.

LM: *And do you feel about Stroheim that he was someone who helped to bring together European and American trends?*
JR: Oh, he was like all the Americans: there are very few Americans who are really American and nothing else. Take someone like

John Ford, with all his Irish sentimentality. Or take Chaplin, who's an American artist whatever he likes to say, but whose films would have been quite different if he hadn't been born in England. My feeling is that America hasn't yet achieved a complete fusion, that the melting-pot hasn't worked completely. America is still a club for discontented Europeans.

LM: *I believe you're now an American citizen.*

JR: I'm both French and American. And of course I have an American family: my mother's father was American—at least he emigrated to America—and I have all sorts of American relations.

LM: *I'd like to ask you about one last subject: about critics. It seems to me that in a sense criticism is an impossible job.*

JR: It's a very difficult one. I try to put myself in the place of the critic.

LM: *And being a critic makes you want to make films yourself, because the more you put the questions, the less clearly you see the answers. You want to take a hand in the thing yourself.*

JR: That was my father's idea. Given that painting isn't, as Truffaut says of the cinema, a mass art, my father insisted that finally one was painting for other painters.

LM: *But what do you expect yourself from a critic? Is there anything he can give you?*

JR: That depends on the critic. A man like Bazin, for instance, gave a lot, but probably this was not only through his criticism but through what emerged from his writing as a whole. He had a kind of vision of the world shaped by the cinema, and what he wrote went beyond criticism. In fact the criticism was secondary, and I think this is true of most really good critics. When a critic simply writes that a film is good or bad . . . well, anyone can make mistakes.

LM: *Do you think criticism can play a really constructive part? Do you feel, for instance, that the influence of* Cahiers du Cinéma *has been a constructive one?*

JR: I believe that modern critics have helped towards the formation of certain trends, certain groups in the cinema. The cinema today isn't the creation of *Cahiers,* but obviously *Cahiers* has done quite a bit towards it. And that's all to the good.

LM: *Today we're experiencing a certain reaction after the first enthusiastic response to the new cinema. What do you think about that—is it an unfair reaction?*
JR: It's all extremely unimportant. The New Wave came, and after it there was bound to be a counter-reaction. It was inevitable. But it's absurd to suggest the New Wave doesn't represent the cinema of our time: of course it does. One can say that very good films are being made outside the New Wave, but these good films don't give cinematic expression to this world of 1962. In a few years there will be another movement, with another name, or no name, bringing something else with it: so much the better.

LM: *I read recently something you were reported as saying . . . I can't quote it exactly, but it seemed to me marvellous. You said something like this: "I'm not ashamed of changing my mind, at least I'm not afraid of setting out, looking for something, without knowing where I'm going . . ."*
JR: Well, what matters is the action, not the target. Of course one needs general ideas, but they must be so deep-rooted, so profound, that one hardly knows one has them. You have to start out in a certain direction, and keep to it, but in the way that migratory birds follow a line instinctively, without knowledge. I believe the artist ought to be like that. And then the conscious part of his mind goes into the detail, into action, into doing. An eighteenth- or nineteenth-century idea which has caused immense trouble is this one of targets. "Do this and you will be rewarded"; "work well and you will have money for your old age." It ought to be done for the pleasure of the moment, the pleasure of working well.

LM: *Finally, I'd like to ask whether you believe that there's a return at the moment towards individualism.*
JR: Towards individualism? Alas, yes, because we've had quite enough of individualism. The myth of the mass, the myth of the

individual . . . I don't believe in them anymore. People want to react against the crowd, and so they get the idea that when a young woman writes a book explaining how she makes love, the things that please her, this is exciting. Well, it doesn't excite me. I'm sure she's right to make love, but that's her affair, not mine. . . . I believe in the individual, as I said at the beginning of this conversation, when he reflects the world and tries to explain it. I believe in the individual if he knows how to absorb. It's imagination that we ought to be afraid of.

Jean Renoir on Love, Hollywood, Authors, and Critics

JAMES R. SILKE/1964

There is a certain ego which permits one to question men of the caliber of Hitchcock, Hawks and in this case Jean Renoir. There is also a fear which admits to the falseness of that ego. Filled with both, I drove to Jean Renoir's home in Beverly Hills one evening about seven. I was totally absorbed with his films and my mind was sorting out questions about his various creations. Upon arrival, I was greeted by Mr. Renoir himself, complete with a pair of comfortable slippers and an even more comfortable smile. We entered his home and went into the living room. Immediately I realized that I had forgotten something of great importance about the man I was to interview. Completely consumed with Renoir the film maker, I had forgotten Renoir the painter, his father. The room was a living museum of Renoir paintings with a few by his friends Matisse and Gauguin. I quickly explained my confusion and with a gentle gesture of his hand he said, "Make this your home," and left me to be with his father for ten or fifteen minutes. Upon his return, I found that the beginning of the evening was an apt prelude to what was to come, for upon meeting Jean Renoir, ego and fear are banished by his presence.

I: *Critics in the United States have written the opinion that you and your films have grown old and become sentimental, no longer have the bite of the early films, are exploring the same things over again. What is your response to this? How do you feel about it?*

From *Cinema* (LA), 2.1 (February 1964, pp. 12–14, 36). Reprinted by permission of James R. Silke.

R: I have no response. People are perfectly free to think what they want. Myself, I love to make pictures but I love to make pictures the way I feel. I make pictures when I have the occasion to make pictures. Now, about the critics, well, to be even very frank, I don't . . . I don't read them.

I: *I see. You don't read critics at all?*
R: Oh, well, I do. I must say, I love good reviews and I hate bad reviews, of course. I'm extremely sensitive to reviews. But I believe that everybody is free and if people believe that I lost a little bit of my fighting spirit, well, they are free to believe it. And may I say they are probably right. They are probably right because I don't believe that to fight is so important now.

I: *That's what I hoped you might talk about now. I felt that some of the brash youth, the bite, the attack, that I saw in the recent showing of* Rules of the Game *was not nearly as beautiful as the things I saw in* The Elusive Corporal. *Now is this wrong? Are you yourself conscious of a mellowing?*
R: I don't know if you are wrong or right. I did it without any purpose, in any case. I love *The Elusive Corporal*. I love the subject, I love the theme, because it is a way to show how vain and useless is a war. In *Grand Illusion*, for instance, I'm perhaps a little more aggressive against war. Now I don't believe that we even have to be aggressive. It's too late.

I: *Too late to be that aggressive again?*
R: Yes, because the values which we thought were eternal when I wrote *Grand Illusion*, well, I found out that they are not eternal at all. They are just very promisory. And, practically, what remains is just the value of the human being, that's all. The rest is pure propaganda. Or perhaps it's pure imagination.

I: *Can you specify some of these less transitory values?*
R: Well, I could specify one. And one is human solidarity, is human friendship. I believe that the human contacts are more important today than they were before. For one reason: the general contacts are disappearing. The nation is not as important as the nation was when I was ten years old. When I was ten years old, you know, I was a Frenchman,

and to me there was only one thing existing in the world and that was France. And all my little friends were exactly like me. Slowly, with travels, with the airplanes, with films, movies, TV we learn that after all there are other peoples who exist all over the world. And perhaps they also have their points of view. And so I do believe in aggressive pictures, in fighting pictures, in violent pictures, but I believe that the violent is justified only if it is about a personal point of view. Not about general ideas. The general ideas have become too weak.

I: *In other words, the one concern you have now is the individual.*
R: The individual, the human beings and their souls. To me the salvation of the world is the human being. And what is wrong often in art, it is that art is trying to find out, to realize anything *but*—without being interested in the knowledge of the human being. For instance . . . you know there is a desperate search for the human being today. For instance, in painting. The proof of this search for the human being is abstract art. What is abstract art if not the desire by the artist to reach the public directly, without having to go through the subject. Without having to go through a trade, through a model, through a house, through a landscape, you want to give yourself to the public directly without any intermediary. And it's why I believe we arrive at the time of the author. Today the author is very important. The author is important because the author may in several fields reach the public directly.

I: *Do you think that you could make an abstract film in that sense?*
R: Excuse me, I didn't say that at all.

I: *No, I'm just inquiring . . .*
R: No, no, no, excuse me. I believe that abstract films are maybe possible only with cartoons. If you show human beings on the screen, you cannot be abstract, it's impossible, unless you hide them with a certain makeup. But it's just a makeup. You see through the makeup very quickly. But I believe that abstraction on the screen is absolutely possible, and I saw beautiful abstractions on the screen, but through the means of cartoons. If you have actors, those actors still have a spirit, they have a head, hands, legs, and you have to deal with their reactions, which are flesh reactions.

I: *Then has your relationship with the human being in the film, with Jean-Pierre Cassel, for example, become more important now, this human relationship, than it used to be?*

R: Oh, yes. I don't know if in my next film I will do it, but now my wish is to be closer to the individual problem, to the human being, and to forget more and more about certain old beliefs like the plot, like, may I say, the background, photographic perfection. I don't believe that photographic perfection is important in a picture. You know I believe that Hollywood will take its place in the history of the movies as the first and foremost one with the silent pictures, as the first and most important one with the beginning of the talkies. But the Hollywood of today won't count at all. It will be entirely forgotten. And I give you the reason. They are honest, and they believe in perfection. That's very dangerous. You have not to be honest in picture making. You have to be in love with human beings. And that's all. Now about perfection. Perfection is a deadly weapon. You know people, very honest producers, you know, they are very honest, they believe in what they do. And you know they gather on the set: "Let's make a good picture!" I believe that to make a good picture has no importance. I believe that to make a good picture is perfectly useless. What is important is to make a picture in which perhaps for one second the public will reach a human being. And that's all.

I: *Is this new to you, is this a concept you've recently arrived at?*

R: No, it's not new to me, it's not new to me, but it is more clear. I always believed it, but I believed it without realizing that it was so important. Now I know it is important!

I: *Don't you feel, too, that Hollywood as a collective place is becoming less important because the individual movie maker is now becoming so important?*

R: Well, perhaps there will be a rebirth of Hollywood and I wish it. It would be wonderful!

I: *If not of Hollywood, perhaps of the individual movie maker. You, for example, are still in Hollywood . . .*

R: No, I am not in Hollywood, I am not in Hollywood. I am in a place on a little hill where I have a nice garden and where I'm very close to my family, my son is living in California, my grandchildren are living in California, but I have nothing to do with Hollywood. I don't know them. I am a complete outsider in Hollywood. I make my pictures in Paris for only one reason: number one, I can write my own screenplays in French. In English, I don't feel so safe. My English is a little rusty. And I like better to write my screenplays in French. Number two, and that's the most important reason, in Hollywood they don't ask me to make pictures. In Paris, they do ask me! That's a reason, don't you think so!

I: *That's a very unfortunate reason, but a cogent one. Have you seen any of the New Wave films? Truffaut? Resnais?*
R: Oh, yes. And to me, I admire them, I like them. I believe they were perfectly useful, they arrive at the right moment, and may I say that they are playing a big part in the history of the picture business because they are representing what I said, the importance of the author. You know the picture by the New Wave may be bad or may be good, that's not so important. To make a bad picture is not important. I repeat, I insist, the idea that the aim of the picture business is to make good pictures is perfectly stupid. Ridiculous. Excuse me, do you believe that the comedies by Shakespeare are perfect? No! But they are great!

I: *They are great.*
R: Okay. You know, in other words, we have not to be perfect, we have to be great. And we have to admit it and to be ambitious and to believe in them. We have to believe not in perfection but in greatness. Now, the importance of the New Wave is that they brought—well, I did it before them and some other people did it before them, but they did it more obviously, they did it with more gusto. They brought the idea of the author, they brought the idea that the picture is the work of a certain man, of a certain author, just as a novel is the work of a Mr. Victor Hugo. And that's good.

I: *Do you believe any Hollywood directors have this authorship?*
R: No, not even the ones who are the masters who can do anything they want. No. You have wonderful directors in Hollywood, and you have some geniuses who are certainly making wonderful pictures, and they make those wonderful pictures the way they want. But they are not *trying* to express themselves. You know they ask ten good authors to

write a wonderful screenplay, and the screenplay is perfect but this screenplay is not at all the expression of the great director.

I: *You then differ from the position of the New Wave critics when they name Hitchcock and Hawks as the two leading directors in the world today?*
R: Well, you know, Hitchcock is very different. Hitchcock manages to influence his screenplays and to bring to the screen a certain style which is a Hitchcock style.

I: *It's always Hitchcock.*
R: It's always Hitchcock, and to me that's good. That's good.

I: *There's an authorship . . .*
R: There is authorship with Hitchcock.

I: *Are you familiar with Howard Hawks?*
R: Yes, yes, yes. I'm familiar with his work, but you know, there is a . . . you know, who is the Hollywood director I admire the most? I admire Leo McCarey. And I believe that this man about 15 years ago brought to the screen a certain kind of light comedies, if you remember the comedies of Leo McCarey with Katharine Hepburn and Cary Grant. You remember? They were good! To me that was a great personal style, and a style which can be expressed only in Hollywood. To me that was a very good moment of the movies. There is another thing. You know, I'm talking about the author, because I'm an author and you always fight for your own sake. But don't believe that I don't admire some expressions, some artistic expressions, which are the expression, may I say, of a general belief. Of a crowd. For instance, to me, the greatest expression of Hollywood is probably the western. I don't think that the western could have been done anywhere else. And the westerns to me are as good as *la commedia dell'arte* in Italy. It is very much the same thing. You know stock characters, you know instead of having a doctor, we have the sheriff, we have the hero, the villain. Well, believe me the westerns are great, they are still great on TV.

I: *How do you regard John Ford?*
R: John Ford is a great man, no doubt. John Ford is the man who gave a certain nobility to the westerns. But the western could exist

without John Ford. The westerns are something very strong and John Ford is just, may I say, the best one among the western makers. But he is a man who is the head, who is the top of the group. You know, with the New Wave, the New Wave is very different. Each one of the New Wave is just himself without any connections with anything else.

I: *You believe their authorship is more personal, more individual.*
R: Much more. Much more. Now don't forget that the New Wave perhaps will be another failure. That doesn't matter. They will have brought to the movies the idea—well, they didn't *bring* it—they *added* to the idea of authorship. And that's very important.

I: *And they are more important as individuals than as a collection of individuals?*
R: Much more. Much more. What happens is that they were all friends and they all started together. But you know, there is no connection, there is no similarity between the work of Resnais and the work of Truffaut. They are two opposite poles. But it happens that they work together at the same time and people put them under the label of New Wave, that's all.

I: *The critic's affliction! Do you feel this human idea has invaded all the arts, this human idea you mentioned earlier?*
R: Well, yes, with art, it is just a reaction against the fact that our civilization is the civilization of the crowd. Now when you belong to the civilization of the crowd you have only one idea. It is to find the individual. This reaction is very normal.

I: *For creative people.*
R: No! Also for the public, for anybody!

I: *They start to seek themselves?*
R: Take the books which are successful today. They are books which are really the expression of the author, books in which you can read the author through the writing.

I: *Will you name a couple so this idea becomes clearer to me?*

R: I will name what I have in mind, a book which is not new, it's already ten years old. But, for instance, it is the first book of Mlle. Sagan, Françoise Sagan. This book was a very good book. But much more important, it was the direct expression of Miss Sagan. People who were reading this book were not only reading a book, they were having a meeting with Miss Sagan. That's very important. Take the book by Nabokov, *Lolita*. You know, it is a confession by Nabokov. Nabokov is sitting down here, and the reader is here, and Nabokov says, my dear friends, don't you think that young girls are more attractive than middle-aged girls? Well, I think that they are better! You know, and I'm in trouble! Or someone else may say, and what do you think about sodomy? I like sodomy, you don't like it, well, that's too bad, I think I like it. Well, it's a confession, it's a private conversation.

I: *Do you think this can be maintained through, say, thirty or forty novels, this . . . ?*

R: Ahhhhhhh! That's a very different question. And this is, perhaps, a very sound question. And perhaps you are putting the finger on one fact, which is the fact that so many authors are the author of one book.

I: *And film makers?*

R: And film makers are the author of one film. Very often. You know, everything they have in themselves, they tell it. When it's told, it's told. That is the only way to do what we call today a work of art. That's the only thing which is interesting. Perhaps we are like the monsters of Greek mythology. The monsters Hercules was fighting against. Perhaps we are to devour the people who are giving us pleasure. And the author who gives us all his soul, all his spirit, well, we're to kill him, perhaps. It's possible.

I: *Do you think there's a lack in an author who is not able to continue to grow, to go on writing new things, maybe he's not big enough inside?*

R: Long ago, a friend of mine who is a great author, that's Marcel Pagnol—you know he wrote *Marius*, *Fanny*, *Cesar*—well, Marcel Pagnol is a good friend and a great man. And he told me, Jean, you know an author is like a battery. You accumulate electricity during a part of your life, then you give. And when you are empty, you are empty. Well, I said "Ohhh, how wonderful is your statement." But I didn't believe it. I don't believe it. I believe that the real author is a man who can reload the battery constantly by contacts with the world. Yes. I believe that the constant contact with human beings reloads the battery. And if the man is a real author, if he's talented, he will give again, again, and again, like a good peach tree. After all a peach tree gives peaches during his whole life and he stops to give peaches only when he dies. If we take the real, great authors in the history of literature . . . for instance, let's take an author of novels, the medium of novels being very close to the medium of film. Let's take the greatest French novel writer, Stendhal. Stendhal was not a professional author, he was not a professional writer, he was an amateur. And he was working with different jobs, he was a consul somewhere, he was working for a business company, and about every three, four, five, ten years he used to write a great novel, a novel which is now considered as a masterpiece and as a model for all the novels in the world. That's the way he wrote *Le Rouge et le Noir, The Red and the Black*, he wrote *La Chartreuse de Parme*, he wrote, you know, but so many! And he wrote them very quickly. He wrote the *The Red and the Black* in 40 days. Yes! Well, I believe this man is a good example of the real genius who can reload, reload his batteries.

I: *Dumas, Père.*

R: Dumas, Dumas did novels. Dumas is a phenomenon. Balzac is a phenomenon. Balzac until the end of his life wrote, wrote and wrote. No, I was taking the example of Stendhal because Stendhal probably in the history of French literature will remain as the top. Probably.

I: *And a love in his work for the human being.*

R: Oh, yes. Oh, yes.

I: *This is a criticism I have had of movie makers, that they have fallen out of love with the human being, with life.*

R: Most of them don't like human beings. They love tricks, camera movements, lightings, you know, and effects. They are purely technical.

I: *And even from the standpoint of life, I think they are looking for the "effects" of life, the sordid, the ugly, the stark, the new, the horrible. And it's decadence that has set in.*

R: Yes, yes. Well, you know, it's a very normal phenomenon. When Rome arrived at a period of decadence, the Roman public loved to go to the circus and to see Christians devoured by lions or burned to death in flames. You know, they loved it. And it is the same thing now. It is the same thing now with our public. They love violence. It is just a proof that we are at the end of a civilization. Don't you think so? You know, when you need to witness violence to have a kick, to be happy, I don't believe it's so healthy.

I: *Do you feel then that there is a responsibility upon the author to show a different direction?*

R: I don't believe that responsibility in an author ever worked. I don't believe that any author ever did any good because he was feeling a responsibility. I believe some authors instinctively feel a certain love for the human being, and they will do a lot of good, I hope. And some of the ones don't, and that's all. But I don't believe that is on purpose. As a matter of fact, I don't believe that in life *anything* is on purpose. Let's take a very small and very vulgar example. You know, you have people, and I myself was one, who want to do a picture because it would be a message. And you lose money! I myself did it several times in my life and I made bad pictures that way. On the other hand, you make a picture just because you feel like it, you feel that making the picture you would be happy, and perhaps you *help* a little bit in this picture. In other words, may I say that I know that I'm old-fashioned today. But I say, it may seem ridiculous, but I believe in instinct more than in intelligence. I'm even a little suspicious of intelligent people, of too intelligent people. I believe that intelligence without instinct doesn't give any results.

I: *I don't feel you're old-fashioned! I feel what has happened is that we've developed a new establishment, and what you're saying is, in fact, very unorthodox for our time.*

R: Very often I give an example about our own world, about very trivial things. Very often, just for fun, I ask friends what's the color of the flag. And they say it is blue, white and red. It is the French flag or the American flag, they are blue, white and red. And I take some samples of blue and you know the flag is no more blue, it's pure imagination. The brains are gaining upon our senses, we have no eyes, we don't see that the flag is not blue. Now the blue of the flag is a kind of dark purple, very close to the black, very close to the violet, it's not a blue anymore. But people say blue, white, red! You know, take a bottle of wine—and I did it also—you take a bottle with the label of a very good Bordeaux wine and you put a California wine in the bottle. People are delighted. Yes! You know, believe me! Believe me, the brains work more than the senses today. And to me, the only way to do good art is to have the senses working more than the brains.

I: *In what directors do you feel this policy is working best today?*
R: My favorite director today is Truffaut. I love Truffaut. I believe this boy, you know, he senses here, at the tip of the fingers.

I: *Who of the Italians would you name?*
R: Well, I'm still . . . I like Fellini. And there is a man—I don't like him too much as an actor, but I like him as a director—I like De Sica. As a director. To me *Shoeshine* will remain a great picture. And *Miracle in Milano*, did you see it? It's a great picture. And I like Rossellini. Very much.

I: *Have you seen the new Antonioni?*
R: No. Not yet. I like Antonioni, very much. The Italians are gifted for picture making. They are gifted. The only thing is that they may easily ruin a great thing. You know they may easily ruin all the Italian film making and nobody knows why. You know, they may all of a sudden . . . you know, we need a certain discipline in life, and the Italians may grow out of the discipline very easily. For instance, take Rossellini. He's an enormous man. He's a fantastic man. But all of a sudden Rossellini could believe that he has to make a picture, absolutely ridiculous, and he would make it. He would make it, believing that it's good. You know, the Italians are perhaps more—perhaps—more gifted than the French, perhaps. But the French have a certain discipline of thinking which helps them not to go overboard. But I like Antonioni. *La Notte* is a wonderful film.

I: *What about Sweden? Ingmar Bergman?*

R: Oh, Ingmar Bergman is a wonderful case because he's the only good businessman in the movie business. Yes. You know this man, number one, is a state employee. And he is paid by the month. And he knows that the next month he will have money to buy bread, which is very important, number one. Number two, he's got a kind of troop, a kind of stock company, and they are acting on the stage and acting in the movies. That means the costs can be shared between the stage and the movies, and that's very smart. Finally, Bergman manages to make good pictures for little money. He knows very well that with the little money he spends for a picture, with the art theaters all over the world which would in any case take his pictures, he will pay the cost of the picture. Well, I don't believe that 20th Century-Fox can say that. No, he is the only good businessman in our business.

I: *That's quite a pertinent comment.*

R: May I add that he has got plenty of talent, and he is an author because you can look at a film by Bergman just one minute, and you know it's Bergman. You know each frame is Bergman.

I: *Who of the American directors do you feel stand up as authors? You named Leo McCarey, and we talked about Hitchcock.*

R: Of course, you can recognize Wyler in his work. I must confess I didn't see any pictures by Wyler since about ten years ago. I didn't see *Ben Hur*, I didn't see the last pictures. I believe Billy Wilder is very personal. What he does is wonderful, it's fascinating, it is very personal, it has a personal touch, no doubt.

I: *Have you seen the Robert Aldrich films?*

R: I saw some of them. I think he is very good. I believe that another good director could do the same films. I do not get the feeling that it is absolutely personal with Aldrich, but it is very good, it is perfect.

I: *A type of authorship comes through in his style, don't you think?*

R: There is a type of authorship, but to me not sufficient. The authorship should be more than that. But I believe that if Aldrich was working in a kind of industry where authorship was possible, he would be a great author. I just believe that he is too shy.

I: *He is very bold in what he does, but even here that's not enough, perhaps?*
R: Excuse me, to be bold about stories, about statements, you know, is nothing. You must be bold in the making of pictures, that's very different.

I: *One of your pictures that I enjoyed most was the* French Can-Can.
R: Oh, yes.

I: *Which I thought marvelous. It bubbled with excitement.*
R: You saw it?

I: *Yes. It was a wonderful film and it didn't get widely shown here.*
R: No! None of my French pictures were ever shown properly in America but *Grand Illusion. Grand Illusion* was shown properly.

I: *Why is that?*
R: Because the French producers are badly represented in America. For instance, my last pictures, I made them for the oldest corporation in the world. That's Pathé. Pathé is an old lady and she is represented in America by a very nice friend, a friend of mine in New York, he is a wonderful man. But Pathé cannot give him the means to, you know, to reach the different exhibitors.

I: *I see. Pathé doesn't give him financial means for promotion, advertising, publicity?*
R: Yes. You see they consider that when a picture comes here, the picture is paid by the French market. And every American penny is a benefit. Then why to worry about the American market?

I: *That's unfortunate for those of us here who love good films. How did* The Elusive Corporal *do locally at the Beverly Canon?*
R: Ohhhhh, I don't know. I didn't go. I went the first day but, after all, it lasted two or three weeks, I don't know, not too much. I don't believe it did very well, I don't think so. I don't know, but I don't believe it.

I: Picnic on the Grass *played a lot here. . . .*

R: *Picnic on the Grass* was very successful, I think. And I'm very happy because I have some interest in the picture!

I: *In* Corporal, *Jean-Pierre Cassel I thought particularly fine casting for a Renoir film.*

R: Ohhh, he is a magical man! Well, you know, this man, number one, is very French, and I believe that the Corporal had to be typically French. And Cassel is typically French. In life he is not typically French, in real life he—you know, many of the Frenchmen are Catholic, and he is a Protestant. He is a Protestant, yes, he is a Protestant. He comes from a village near Nimes where the Catholic and the Protestant don't talk to each other! Yes! You know, he is one of the heirs of the people who revolted against Louis XIV. He is a good man. A very good man.

I: *Did you select him because of any particular performance?*

R: I selected him because of a performance in . . . I don't remember the name of the picture. . . .

I: The Love Game*?*

R: Yes. *The Love Game.* I liked the picture, and I was anxious to have Cassel to play in my picture because I thought this man could have a certain lightness, and a certain sense of humor. I didn't want *The Corporal* to be heavy.

I: *No, it had a lightness. There was some talk here, you know, of a lack of hatred of the Nazi in the film.*

R: This is true. During the picture I edited very much because I thought I would make a picture where you don't show some of the horrors which were committed by the Nazis. Perhaps it's not fair. On the other hand, you cannot treat a big question like the Nazi question in only one picture. My picture was about French military prisoners, and those military prisoners ignored entirely what was going on with the Nazis. The Nazis were just the enemies, that's all. And, you know, I talked with almost fifty different prisoners of war who had been in Germany during the war, and many of them tried to escape, and I believe that the way I showed in the picture is the real spirit, that's the way they were thinking. And I was interested in the picture because of *that*, because I believe this can't last—this importance given to details, this unimportance given to the big questions. I believe that was the characteristic of the last war. You know, the other war, when I wrote *Grand Illusion*, well, I was in this first World War. We were all of us then believing in the importance of this war. We were absolutely sure that we were rescuing humanity, that we were bringing democracy to the world. We were absolutely sincere and dedicated. During this second war, not at all. During the second war, the prisoners knew very well that they were victims of a fantastic misunderstanding. For instance, one thing about the Americans. In the beginning of the war, the American newspapers were extremely patriotic—let's go, let's beat the German! And the French took it for granted. They thought with such articles in the American newspapers, they are going to be here! Tomorrow! Well, the Americans didn't come. They came much later. And that gave to the French a certain skepticism, they didn't believe in anything but in what we said, human friendship. Human beings. They abandoned any great ideas, and that's why I love the Corporal. *The Corporal* is the expression of what people think today. Today, you know, we are finished with great ideas. But, perhaps, we are more deep in our personal friendship, perhaps a friend can sacrifice himself for his friend more than before. But he won't sacrifice himself for general ideas. To me what is good in our days is the spiritual going back to the basic beliefs, the belief in friendship, the belief in love, the belief in your children, the belief in the woman you love. To me that's very important.

I: *The film maker in America seems even more possessed with big ideas and tries to make films about these great messages.*
R: That doesn't mean anything today. Even the post powerful incentive in the world today, which is perhaps the communist idea, which pushes people in the Congo, and causes revolts in South America. In Europe they don't believe in it. Not a bit. But they don't believe in the opposite either. But they do believe in the love of a girl, or they do believe in the friendship with a man, and to me that's good. You know, when you think too big, it's purely intellectual, it's purely with the brains, it's not with the sense. Real love is made of contacts, touching, seeing, the sound of a voice, that's more important. Don't publish my

interview because I would be in trouble! Cut everything which is
unorthodox!

I: *Well, I think it's unorthodox but essential, what you say.*

R: As a matter of fact, the greatness of this country comes from the
fact that the growth of the country, the way the country grew, was individual. Not so long ago, America was made of farmers who had almost
no connections with the next farmer. There was the family, the friends,
that formed a little country inside a country. And there is still a little bit
of this spirit in America, and I believe that is the greatness of America.
Europe was submerged with general idea, too many. Now they know it's
wrong, they are trying to go back to the basic truths, the basic feelings.

I: *To sum up, then, would you say that this philosophy, this love that
you've expressed for the human being, takes a consciously directed form in
your films?*

R: I don't know. I don't know. No, I'm not trying to do it. I am not
trying to enlarge my feelings. I'm just trying when I make a film to be
absolutely sincere and not to write one word which is not the expression of my feelings. And that is all.

Jean Renoir: Interview

JAMES D. PASTERNAK / 1964

PASTERNAK: *Tell me about your last silent film.*
RENOIR: My last silent film was a light comedy—a military comedy—named *Tire-au-Flanc*. It is an old French play which is terribly funny—I don't say my picture, but I say the play. It is typically a commercial live comedy for the big public. And it was a very successful film, in spite of the fact that sound was coming.

P: *Did you find the transition from silent to sound difficult for you?*
R: No, not at all. As a matter of fact, the sound helped me.

P: *In what way?*
R: I found a certain pleasure in using the sounds. I started to be interested, not so much in words, but in sounds. In the expression of the human being helped by the emission of sounds. The sounds may be a cry, a whisper, perhaps not a word, perhaps not a sentence. To explain myself, I must quote a conversation I had often with the wonderful fellow who played the part of the actor in my picture *The Lower Depths*. His name was Le Vigan. We used to say we should make sound films, but not talking films. We should invent an international language which would be no language at all. The actors would never explain things, but would emit sounds. You know, like a bird has sounds, or a dog: quee-euee, qua-qua, pa-pa, kee-kee, woo-woo, wee-wee. That would be the dialogue. But not at all logically built

From *The Image Maker*, ed. Ron Henderson, Richmond, Va.: John Knox Press, 1971, pp. 33–39. Reprinted by permission of James D. Pasternak.

words and sentences. Of course, that cannot be done. But that was a way to express what we were feeling about sound.

P: *Do you think that the sound films today are meeting their fullest potential? We seem to have just these strict, very realistic dialogue films.*

R: It's because people are constantly confusing. People are paying too much attention to the plot, to logic, to the logical approach to the making of the film. It is the eternal fight between the intellect and feeling. Probably we need both if we want to do something of certain value, but we must not neglect feeling. The intelligence is taking over all the time. But there is also another thing: the separation between the creation and the execution, which is very wrong. If you want the execution to follow the creation, the creation must be very clear. The creation must be logical. It's why you need a definite language of definite words.

P: *The younger French directors today seem to be preoccupied with ego, with projecting their own personalities in a manner of speaking.*

R: Yes. That's a very normal reaction against the fact that the author for years was absolutely neglected in the motion picture business. Even in many pictures now, you have no author. You have people working on a certain task. They work together, but you don't feel that it's the work of an author. You replace the actor and nobody will notice it. You replace anybody in the production and nobody will see it, even the writers. The writers write in a certain standard style and it's very difficult, you know, outside of the very good ones, of course. Also the music is standard.

If we follow the history of art since the beginning, great art was always born by a complete mixing between the conception and the creation. By conception, I do not mean the story. The story belongs to everyone. If we take any great art, the art of the theater, for example, the stories are about the same all the time. The stories were repeated at other times by different authors, and finally the one who had genius did well, and that is all. But when we see *Romeo and Juliet* we don't think of the eternal author who came before Shakespeare. We think of Shakespeare.

P: *Hunting for a motif, then, is not so important?*

R: It is important because, strangely enough, if your motif is not good you are lost. But the *creation* of the motif is not important. What is important is to *choose* the motif.

P: *To bring yourself to the motif you take?*

R: Yes. What is the motif? The motif is exactly what the landscape is for the painter. It's not the landscape which makes the painting, it's the painter. But you need the landscape. Even if you are an abstractionist, and even if you don't copy the landscape, you need it.

P: *In the New American Cinema, perhaps the preoccupation is totally with landscape—with the abstractions.*

R: Yes, very much.

P: *Have you seen many of the underground films in this country?*

R: I saw a few of them, but not many. I saw, for example, this excellent film about Negro kids in Harlem. The director is a woman. . . .

P: *Shirley Clarke? The Cool World?*

R: Yes. It was very good. I believe such a picture is useful for the American movie industry.

P: *What do you mean?*

R: It's very useful because what is missing in America is a sense of reality. And when you are Charlie Chaplin you don't need reality to be real. But when you are not Chaplin, reality may help you, and it may help the American director more than any other director in the world. There is in America a certain tradition of hiding reality—of making up reality. For years and years, reality was much too beautiful in American pictures. It had nothing to do with reality. This reality was the reality which was existing in the spirit of the American public. And the film-makers were giving to the public the reality they wanted. And now, even if you have art pictures and war pictures with people dying— blood, etc.—well, it's another make up–adding reality. Reality has to be recreated, of course, by the author—the world as it is. Photography— pure photography doesn't exist. That's out of the question. Everything must be recreated by an author. But if the author has certain values he gets a certain feeling of reality. After all, what's the main thing great men can do for us? It is to remove what is hiding reality. And we need them because we are too weak to do it ourselves.

P: *It's a funny word, "reality."*
R: Yes, it is confusing. Perhaps we should say "truth." But reality does exist and doesn't exist. It does exist only if it is recreated by somebody, by an author, by an author who can be named an author. Many people believe that they are authors, but are not authors.

P: *Are there authors in Hollywood today?*
R: I think so. I believe, for instance, that in the pictures of Mr. Billy Wilder, you feel they are *by* Wilder. There's a certain "Wilder touch" which is obvious.

P: *Is this because he writes the film as well as directs it?*
R: Probably. But even if he did not write it, his influence would be big enough to give a certain shape, a certain style to his productions.

P: *Because he has that much control over the film?*
R: Yes, but also because he's got a certain conception about what precisely a film should be, and his conception is strong enough to influence everybody—cameraman, actors, etc.

P: *Do you believe that those of your films which were most personal were the result of your collaborating on the script? I know that you preferred writing the script when you could.*
R: Well, I couldn't *not* collaborate on a script. And I couldn't for one big reason. I change everything when I'm shooting. I have to improvise. That's my nature. I have to improvise because I probably don't have a big imagination, and when I'm working on a script, or when I'm working on a script with a collaborator, I don't see all sides of the question. Sometimes I realize what the meaning, the deep meaning, of the scene is only when I shoot it. All of a sudden I say, "but this scene seems to be brilliant, seems to be well-written, but doesn't mean

anything." I missed the point up to now, and the point is that I see it only because I saw the actors rehearse, and something was sounding forth and you hear it, you know, like a bell with a little crack. Well, you need a bell without a crack. So, you have to relight the scene, or change something, or push the actors in such a manner that the words acted in a certain way mean something else.

P: *That calls for an almost supernatural producer, someone who will give you total freedom.*
R: Doesn't exist!

P: *Doesn't exist?*
R: No! He doesn't exist. Now I have a proposition for something very interesting, but you know I cannot work within the frame of a well organized industry.

P: *And Hollywood is still too well organized?*
R: Perhaps. That's possible. But in Hollywood today you can do very much. Don't forget this: most of the producers are free producers now. They don't work for the studios anymore. The studios just give them money and release the films, and that's all. Hollywood today is probably the best place in the world to make pictures. I would like to make films in Hollywood. I would love to. It is still a wonderful tool, perhaps the best tool in the world, for the making of pictures. The only thing which stops me in Hollywood is the problem of language. You know, in English I have no ability. What I write is not subtle. And it tires me to present a project in English. It's not my language, and to work in a foreign language is not easy.

P: *You say that Hollywood is the best tool. But often Hollywood's films are just that—tooled. They're just crafted out.*
R: That's true, but sometimes you have a genius. After all, if I'm making pictures now, it's because of the Hollywood pictures. When I was a young man, I used to go to movies very often. And my favorites were the American pictures. I didn't consider the other ones at all. Chaplin, Stroheim, Griffith, they were my masters.

P: *And the actor in film?*

R: The actor in film? Well, our master—the greatest of us—Mr. Chaplin, is an actor. Stroheim is an actor. *Was,* poor Stroheim!

P: *Poor Stroheim?*

R: He's dead, and that's too bad.

P: *I thought for a second you were referring to his experience in Hollywood.*

R: Yes, but after all, no. The possibility for production of Stroheim was finished with the big organization of the industry. You know, it was either Stroheim or Thalberg, two equally talented men. But Stroheim represented the director as I conceive it—exactly. As a matter of fact, when you say that Truffaut, for instance, is free to make a picture the way he wants, that's how Stroheim used to work. The industry has to go through a certain period of organization. And they did, and brilliantly! They gave beautiful products. The comedies by people like Lubitsch, for instance, were magnificent, were brilliant. I believe that today, fortunately, we are back to the time of the author. I don't know if I can still enjoy that, but I'm happy to see that it's coming, even if it's for the young ones.

P: *Would you say, then, that Thalberg was an Erich Pommer?*

R: Yes. And he was also a genius. He had the feeling of what the movies should be in a certain period, in his time.

P: *But didn't this hurt some of the directors who might have disagreed with him?*

R: I know, but this period was not a period for directors. That was a period for stars and producers. Life is changing, and an art or an industry goes through different phases, and we must accept those phases as they are.

P: *What phase are we in now?*

R: It is very difficult to forecast the future, but I believe we are coming back to the time of the author, because of the normal reaction against the spirit of the crowd. The crowd was the master for years. The crowd is still the master in politics. But I believe that we have arrived at a certain period where the individual is very important, perhaps too important. As a matter of fact, in certain manifestations the individual is so important that the individual stinks, to my own taste. Sometimes I feel like yelling, "enough with the individual!" Sometimes I feel that I would like to see, but it's impossible because everything comes when it has to come—the question of periods is important in art—but I just wanted to say that sometimes I feel an immense, a fantastic love, a fantastic interest for early ritual art. For African art, which is purely religious, or for the very primitive days of Greek art.

P: *Do we need religion in our films today?*
R: That I don't know. The period, the very religious period of the Russian Revolution—when I say religious period I mean the period when the revolution was so young that people living in Russia and the world, since they're communists, were devoted to their creed as much as the early Christians were to their creed—got beautiful pictures. A picture like *Potemkin* is certainly very close to a religious picture. I mean that behind such a picture, you feel an absolutely sincere faith. But, should we say belief instead of faith, perhaps?

I wrote something for a religious review not long ago. Just one page. There is now within the frame of the Church, mostly the Roman Catholic Church, a great interest in modern art. The new buildings, the new churches, are extremely modern, designed by very audacious architects. It represents a complete revolution in the idea of the building of churches, statues and symbols. If there is a new religious art, if there must be a new religious art, it has to be connected with the rest of life. And this religious art can exist only after a certain religious revolution is accomplished in the minds of the people. I talked very briefly in this article about what religion was during the Middle Ages, which was a great religious period. Religion then, and even before Christ, was a part of life. Religion was the very thing. Religion was the theatre, music, any form of art. A meal was a religious function; to make a child with your wife was a religious function; to die was a religious function; to be born was a religious function. Religion was the organization of the whole life. Not only the organization, but the feeling, the conception, the understanding, and art. You didn't need the individual; you didn't need the author. You didn't need the author because the conception was so strong. And I believe that this organization gave us, is the reason for, the masterpieces we find when we dig the soil in Greece or in Asia, or anywhere. But today everything is separated.

We live in a time of specialists. Everything is specialization. A man works as a lawyer. When he is in his office, he is a lawyer, and a very good lawyer, and he doesn't think of anything else. He is trying to help his clients; he is trying to be a good lawyer. Then he breaks for lunch with friends and they're interested in a certain sport. He becomes a sportsman. He is exclusively a sportsman during the lunch. In the evening he will be the good father and the good husband. The little wife will come: a little kiss, a drink, you know, the children: how is the school? the children were good in school, yes—the father. In religion, every Sunday (or every Saturday if he's Jewish), he's a religious man. All of a sudden he turns a page, he forgets exactly all the rest, and he becomes religious—and deeply religious! During half an hour, one hour, he's a religious man. In the early days of any religion, that was absolutely different. Life was a whole: including religion, including lovemaking, including the meals, including making a living. Everything was together, and that's very different. It's why we cannot hope to remake the masterpieces of the Middle Ages because they belong to a period when the organization of life was different.

P: *Is that to say that our masterpieces won't be as good as the masterpieces of the Middle Ages?*
R: No! It's why the individual, the author, slowly replaces the general conception due to religion. And I believe that now our only hope is man, is the author.

P: *And the author is really, so to speak, a man of God.*
R: He is a man of God. No doubt. But, you know, the author has a terrible responsibility today. Terrible! The responsibility of somebody making a statue during the Middle Ages was very little. The statue was a part of his life. The making of a religious gesture for the sculptor was the same as preparing the bread for the wife. But today the author

is a specialist, and to me what is difficult is to see how many functions
a specialist should take. And I believe that the only way to give the
specialist a certain importance is to give him many functions. By many
functions I mean, for instance, in the movies to make him the producer, the writer, the author, and frequently the actor.

P: *You've seen many of Bergman's films, I'm sure. Here is religiousness in
the most literal sense of the word.*
R: Yes, exactly. But a very special religion. It is puritanism, but a puritanism that is very interesting. We must not discard puritanism from
the reasons for the quality of the early American pictures. The early
American pictures were perfectly puritanical, and they were great.

P: *How do you mean puritanical?*
R: I'll give you an example. The way love, physical or spiritual, was
treated in American pictures. I mean the love of a young man for a
young girl, or of a young girl for a young man—the way it was treated.
You had the feeling that before the young girl could join the young
boy, all the obstacles in a puritanical society were working against this
love. They had to fight, and it was very difficult. You know what it
was like in a small city: the gossips, the fear of religion, etc. The love
affairs in the early American pictures were treated in a very puritanical
way, and they were good. They were very good. That helped. That
helped Mr. Griffith, for all the love affairs of Mr. Griffith are puritanical,
and they are great. They are magnificent.

P: *There was this tension. You knew the audience was with them.*
R: A tension and a difficulty. The things were not easy. Let's tell the
story of a young man and a young girl, and they would like to sleep
together. Well, it happens that the young man is a knight in the time
of King Arthur. And to conquer the young girl he has to climb a
ladder to reach her at the top of a feudal tower. That, to me, is very
interesting, because the ladder is very dangerous and there are archers
with arrows ready to kill him. Here, you have a story to tell. Now
today, where everything is free, you tell the same story—the young
man whistles and the young girl is in his bed right away. Well, there is
no story.

P: *What about the increasing nationalism of films today? Films seem less universal than they were.*

R: To become universal is very good; but one must dig the little hole on a certain spot. I know very well that each time (and it happened to me very often) I was confronted with producers who were planning an international picture—a picture which will please in America as well as in Italy—it will always flop. Now when somebody like De Sica makes *The Bicycle Thief*, which is very Italian, purely Italian, it becomes universal.

P: *Are we making American films which are really American?*

R: The only way for the American film to reconquer the world market would be to make American films—great American films. That doesn't mean that those films shouldn't be done by foreigners. After all, in the history of the American picture, some foreigners like Mr. Chaplin made good American films.

You have to study American society to understand it, and to do what an author should do—to absorb facts, to digest them, and to give them back with a certain order, with a certain style, a mature style. What is art? It is the marriage of the personality of the author and of the stuff he observed. The only way to make great American films is to make films expressing in a genuine way what American life is, what the American preoccupations are. It is possible that the questions are too complex now. There is one thing which makes the making of American films very difficult. It is the fact that a big part of the country is prosperous, and it is very difficult to tell stories about prosperous people. They have no apparent problems. It's why the best American films we see are about the poor parts of America. The poor American should be the hero of the future American film.

P: *Why?*

R: Because the problems of the poor man are more complex, more intense, more difficult to solve than the problems of a prosperous man.

P: *And being a prosperous man, then, is like being bored?*

R: Yes. A satirist could make beautiful pictures about bored and rich Americans. That's a kind of satirical possibility. It would be fantastic.

My picture, *The Rules of the Game*, could be shot in America today, very well.

P: *But would Americans be able to laugh at themselves?*
R: That's a different question. I'm not thinking of the success, I'm thinking of the quality of the product.

P: *Can the two be separated?*
R: Well, of course, if you are not successful, you stop making pictures. That's also something very dangerous in picture-making—the fact that you must be successful right away. If not, you don't find any money to make other films. And that's bad because in any other art you have the benefit of time. Van Gogh didn't sell one canvas during his life, but today we know that Van Gogh was a great artist.

P: *In your early films, your early silent films, some of them weren't successful. Yet you were quite capable of pursuing your artistic goals and creating masterpieces.*
R: Well, you know, patience—patience, losing money, luck, all of a sudden somebody coming: "Would you like to make a picture?" You don't know why. I was lucky during my life, very lucky. And always from people who wanted to work with me. I was also helped very often by the actors.

P: *You mean important actors?*
R: Yes, for instance, with *Grand Illusion*. Much of the opportunity to make *Grand Illusion* I owe to Jean Gabin. Jean Gabin was already a big star and he helped me. We peddled *Grand Illusion* in every office of Paris—American companies, French companies, Italian companies—and nobody wanted it. It lasted two years, and Jean Gabin was with me. "I want to play the part." And they said well, a picture with Gabin is very good, but we don't want this story. Finally, I found a man who was not in the movies. He was a gambler and he had won a big amount of money at the stock exchange. And he said, "Well, I don't know what to do with this money. You want to make a picture. Here is the money."

P: *What was the first film that you produced as well as directed?*
R: *Water Girl.*

P: *And that was a successful film?*
R: No, I lost money. I lost my own money with it. It was after *Nana* that I started to make a few successful films.

P: The Little Matchseller *was a successful film, wasn't it?*
R: No, it wasn't a successful film, but, you know, I did it with such a little money that it had to find the money back.

P: *And your first sound film?*
R: *On Purge Bébé.* You know I had very few big productions like *Le Bled,* like *Le Tournoi,* and the producer was afraid I would be too expensive with sound, that I would take too much time. I had to prove that I could make a talking picture without too many expenses, and I picked up a comedy by Feydeau, a wonderful French author and comedian. I took a short play. I took a few young unknown actors, like Fernandel and Michel Simon, and I shot the picture. I wrote the script in six days; I shot the picture in six days; I cut the picture in six days; and after one month the picture was shown at the Gaumont Palace in Paris. It happened that they had a hole; they needed a picture. My picture was ready. They took it, and in one week the cost of the picture was paid.

P: *Your father died in 1919, I believe—is that correct? . . .*
R: Yes.

P: *You were 25 at the time, and I believe you mentioned you were in the trenches when a friend of yours mentioned a Chaplin film you should see. Is this perhaps the point at which you became very interested in films?*
R: Oh, yes. That was the beginning. I didn't decide to make pictures right away, but that was the seed.

P: *The Chaplin films?*
R: Oh yes! I discovered the movies. A wonderful discovery.

P: *How did you come to do your first film?*

R: I was mixed up with a certain group of people making films, but in those days my real profession was to be a ceramist. That was my first trial after the army. And I did like it very much. But I didn't like the fact that I had to have a certain artistic pretense, if I wanted to sell my products. I hated the word artistic. And I still hate it. I accept it because it's so important. Nowadays everything is artistic. But, in the bottom of my heart, I don't like it. You know, you make things, that's all. And they are good or bad. Or they're an expression of yourself or not, and that's all.

The Ruler of the Game: A Conversation with Jean Renoir

PENELOPE GILLIATT/1968

"Look at this," said Jean Renoir in his Paris apartment, bending over an art book. "It is the Annunciation to the Virgin Mary, and the angel is just shaking hands. It is an interesting way to tell someone she is pregnant." He had been speaking French, but now he switched to English and repeated the last sentence, with characteristic absorption, substituting for "interesting" the word "funny," which he pronounces "fonny." The ideas of what is comic and what is interesting truly overlap for him. He looked out of the window and said that the roofs of Paris houses go at angles that always remind him of theater wings. A child was playing somewhere below in this offstage life, and a wife was shouting while her husband strolled away from her, pulling on his cap at a nonlistening slant and then putting his hands in his pockets. "The first films I made were very rotten," Renoir said. "Then I started to make a sort of study of French gesture, and maybe they improved, with the help of my accomplices." The sight of his own gestures as he was talking made me remember one of those fugitive shots which can break through his films so piercingly—a shot in his 1939 picture *La Règle du Jeu* of the plump character played by Renoir himself, the fortunate, poignant stooge, who has just idly let loose the fact that he would have loved to be a conductor. In a shot late at night, on the terrace steps of a grand country house, he can be seen for a second from the back in an image of the clown sobered, conducting the invisible house party inside to the beat of some imagined musical triumph.

From *Jean Renoir: Essays, Conversations, Reviews*, McGraw–Hill, 1975, pp. 13–37.

His big shoulders droop like the withers of a black pig rooting in the dark. Recently, after I had spent some time with Renoir, it struck me that the character perhaps embodies a little of the way he thinks of himself, and that this great, great master of the cinema, who has an amplitude of spirit beyond our thanks, actually sees himself as a buffoon.

Renoir walks with a limp bequeathed by a wound from the First World War. He has a blanched, large face, very attentive, which turns pink as if he were inhaling air when he is interested or having a good time. At the beginning of the 1914 war, he was twenty. Nothing in our benighted century seems to have undercut his sense that life is sweet. He makes films full of feeling for picnics, cafés, rivers, barges, friends, tramps, daily noises from the other side of a courtyard. It is singular and moving that a man whose talent imparts such idyllic congeniality should also have such a tart and sophisticated understanding of caste. In his 1935 film *Le Crime de Monsieur Lange*, for instance, the hero's world of the badly off and hungrily gregarious is pitted against a boss class of steely, swindling fops. The heroic Lange, who murders with our sympathy, is a young man who writes thrillers in the time left over from a dull job in a printing plant. Renoir's murderers are always strange to crime: an unhappy clerk, a down-at-heel, derided lover, a game-keeper—people near the bottom of the heap who take desperate action because they have been driven beyond their limits. The limits usually have to do with what a man will take in punishment to his dignity and his seriousness about how to live, and his gestures state everything. There is the essence of ache and hesitancy in Dalio's double turn, near the end of *La Grande Illusion*, at the door of a woman who has sheltered him while he was on the run from a prisoner-of-war camp and whom he cannot quite declare his feelings for. Renoir's own way of standing reminded me sometimes of a shot of Michel Simon in *La Chienne*, his big head bent in watch over a murdered woman. The tonic passion and lightness of the dissolving shot would be recognizable as Renoir's in a thousand miles of film. So would a special kind of cheerful misrule that sometimes runs amok in a scene, like the time his tramp Boudu, in *Boudu Sauvé des Eaux*, lustily wrecks a room in the process of merely cleaning his boots, carousing around the world with an abstracted serenity in the midst of riot.

When Renoir is in France—he spends a lot of time in America, at a house he and his wife, Dido, have in Beverly Hills—he lives in an apartment close to the Place Pigalle, in a *rue privée* with a black iron gate that is guarded, not very vigilantly, by a caretaker. The little curved street inside is lined with plane trees, and moss grows through cracks in the pavement. There are elegant iron lampstands, and gray shutters on the beautiful, run-down old houses. His apartment is on the second floor of a house with ivy spilling over the front door. The stairwell is painted in a peeling burnt sienna with a turquoise design. It is all very dilapidated and very nice. "I think it's better when things aren't brand-new," Renoir said. "It's less tiring for the eyes." He sometimes speaks of the apartment as if it were an obstreperous old friend with long-familiar attributes, many of them a bit grating but all indispensable. "I like the proportions," he said one day, looking around at the place. "It's not entirely convenient. When it rains, it rains in here." He showed me drip trails at various points, accusingly. "But I like the proportions. If you want to make me happy, you should feel absolutely at home."

In the drawing room, where he works, there is an old-fashioned telephone, paintings by child relatives, comfortable armchairs with springs gone haywire, ancient white-and-gray plasterwork on the walls, records of Mozart and Vivaldi and Offenbach. During the days we spent together talking, Renoir usually wore a tweed jacket and old leather moccasins—with a tweed cap when we went out—and he always had a pen clipped in his jacket pocket. We seemed to spend a lot of time in the kitchen. It has two tall windows, and between them a splendid freehand drawing in brown paint of a window with curtains looped back and a bowl on the sill. He did it himself. He said, "A mirror fell down and broke, and it left a patch, so I put up that piece of paper." I said that it wasn't a piece of paper: that it was a drawing, and looked rather like a Matisse. This so embarrassed him that I had to say quickly, "Matisse on an off day, with a headache." The drawing made a third window to look through, so to speak, when we were having lunch opposite it every day at his scrubbed kitchen table. Renoir's doctor recently gave him a choice of whiskey or wine, and he chose wine. We drank rather a lot of it, and cooked gigot. I mentioned Céline at one point, and he lowered his head and looked pleased. "Greater than Camus," he said. "He was entirely hidden for twenty years. He was not the fashion." Renoir was genuinely unable to think it right that I should have come all the way from New York to see him, and in the end I had to put it as if I were using him as a way station on a journey to my house in England. "I rather hate airplanes," he said. "We should be able to part the Atlantic like the Red Sea and drive across it in a bus. I'm fond of buses." We swapped bus stories.

We caught ourselves in a mirror one day as we were coming into the apartment, talking mostly about actors, whom he distinguishes from stars as though a star were to be removed from the matter with a long-handled pair of tongs. He made a face at our reflections and said, "To be a star and play yourself all the time—a beautiful doll imitating yourself . . ." Ingratiation is one of the few flaws that really seem to scrape on his nerves. He picks up any hint of it fast. He once remarked to a filmmaker whom we both know that there is something that bothers him in Chaplin's films, which in general he admires. He called it "an anxiety to displease nobody." Though Renoir's own films seem expansively charitable, they are altogether uncompromising. "I believe in the Tower of Babel, I suppose," said Renoir. "Not in the story, exactly, but in the meaning. The tendency of human beings to come together. My first attempts at film-making probably didn't find this point. But one gets into practice. When things go badly on a film, I think I will go and raise dogs, and then the crisis blows over. At one moment I feel that a story is terrible and at the next that it's wonderful, and in rare flashes of lucidity I feel that it's neither good nor bad. And so, indeed, quite like everything else. I am very much in favor of intelligence, but when you are at work on a film or a story or a painting I think you have to go on instinct. In *La Règle du Jeu*, for instance, I knew only very roughly where I was going. I knew mostly the ailment of the time we were living in. That isn't to say that I had any notion of how to show evil in the film. But perhaps the pure terror of the danger around us gave me a compass. The compass of disquiet. You know, there is a sense in which artists have to be sorcerers twenty years ahead of their period. I don't mean that they are wiser than anyone else—only that they have more time. And, well, though it is much harder for an artist to do this in the cinema, because the cinema insists on being an industry twenty years behind the public, it can sometimes be done."

He turned out to be thinking now of many young film-makers whom he admires, and to have left altogether the topics of his own pictures and of his own shocking and lifelong difficulties in raising money. At this moment, in 1968, he has virtually had to give up the prospect of making a movie from a very funny script, written by him, which Jeanne Moreau wants to play in. No financing can be found for it. The situation seems commercially unintelligent. It is also an offense, as if Mozart were to be deprived of music paper. A short while ago, another script—a comedy about revolt, which Simone Signoret wanted to do— similarly fell through. In the meantime, Renoir remains not at all bilious and works on other things. He is writing his second novel—his first was called *Les Cahiers du Capitaine Georges*, and was published in 1966— and directing a series of sketches, also by him, for French and Italian television. He always declines to fuss. I had the impression that he doesn't like weightiness of any sort. In 1938, when he was abused by some people for making a film of *La Bête Humaine* that wasn't slavishly true to Zola, he stoutly said that he hadn't particularly wanted to serve Zola, he'd wanted to play trains. "You have to remain an amateur," he said to me one day about directing. "The big problem is not to stop at being a voyeur. Not to look on at people's predicaments as if you were a tourist on a balcony. You have to take part. With any luck, this saves you from being a professional. You know, there are a thousand ways of being a creator. One can grow apples or discover a planet. What makes it easier is that one isn't alone. One doesn't change or evolve alone. However great the distance between them, civilizations move a little toward one another. And the worlds we know, the directions to which interest bends us in our knowledge or our affection, incline to be one in the same way."

A French television unit came one day to direct Renoir in part of the shooting for a long program about him and his father, the painter Auguste Renoir. He needed a companion for a walking scene in Montmartre, and I was the obvious person, although I told him that the only acting I had ever done had been on account of having red hair.

"Lady Macbeth," he said.

"Yes," I said.

He told me what it had been like at school for him because he had had red hair, as his father painted him in the famous childhood portrait. "And who else did they make of you?" he asked, stroking his head unconsciously. "The Pre-Raphaelites?"

"Agave in *The Bacchae*," I said. "For the same reason."

The French sound man said politely, after a long time, that he was getting only a moan from me on his earphones, and could I talk more loudly.

"Her diction in English is excellent," said Renoir.

"Now a new setup," the TV director said, after another long time.

"Which side do you prefer?" Renoir asked me.

I said that the next part might go better from the other side, because of my nose. Renoir took me by the shoulders and had a look at me.

"A girl ran into me in a corridor at school and bent it," I said.

"It's true," he said, nicely, and put me on his other side, and we moved around a lamppost. He held my wrist, perhaps to help himself travel a slope, and then slipped his hand up to my elbow to support me through the prospect of having a seven-word line to say, while he improvized a monologue of incomparable invention and warmth.

Some time later, I asked him about an actor I liked very much in *Monsieur Lange*. Renoir beamed, and said something incidental about his own way of working. "I'm pleased you pick him out. He was excellent, exciting, subdued. However—not that it mattered—it happened that he couldn't remember his lines easily. So the thing was to give him a situation where he had to say what he had to say. Where he couldn't say anything else."

And the same day—"He is the most French director," said the actress Sylvia Bataille, who worked with him on the 1936 film *Une Partie de Campagne* and on *Monsieur Lange*. "The most cultured. He has a sense of history like no one else's. He was the precursor of everything in French cinema now. You know, when he is directing you, he has a trick. Well, not a trick, because that sounds like something deliberate. A way of doing it—a habit, the result of his nature. He will say, 'That's very good, but don't you think it's perhaps a bit boring to do the next take exactly the same way?' He will never say that the next take is to be totally different because in the first one you were terrible. I think the reason he is a great director is that he knows all there is to know of the resolves that people keep to themselves. He knows the human reaction to anything. I'm not very good, but he made me magnificent."

There exists an affectionate French documentary of Renoir directing some actors. He listens to them as if through a stethoscope. Then he may talk of other times, the times of "Monsieur" Shakespeare, "Monsieur" Molière—speaking without sarcasm. Again and again he says, *"Trop d'expression."* He tries to get a highly charged actress to speak "like a telephone operator." There is a big moment, and he tells her not to be sweet. *"Soyons pas mignons."* It is always "us." *"Soyons secs."*

"If actors look for feeling at the beginning of a reading, the chances are it will be a cliché," he said to me. "When they learn the lines alone or when we learn them together—the second being the better—in either case I beg them to read as if they were reading the telephone directory. What we do is to read a few lines that can help the actors to find the part. Pick a few lines that are symptomatic. Now, what happens then is that, in spite of himself, the actor begins to find a little sparkle, provided he forbids it. Whereas if you begin to play with feeling, it will always be a generality. For instance, suppose an actress playing a mother has to speak of 'my son' when he is dead. For most actresses, it is the devil's job for this not to be a cliché if they begin with the sadness of it. And if you start with an idea of how to say it, then it is very difficult to remove it. You should start with the lines quite bare. You see, even in our day everyone is different from her neighbor, or his. We must help an actress to find a 'my son' that will be hers and only hers."

This strong feeling that people are different is obviously part of Renoir's great gift for friendship. I said something about disbelieving and fearing the cool comfort that everyone is replaceable and no one indispensable. He said securely, *"Everyone* is indispensable." We talked about Brecht, whom he was very fond of. They had fun together, loping along the streets by the Seine with some friends, in a gang. "He was a very modest man, you know," Renoir said. "Well, perhaps he was, like many modest men, proud inside. He was a child. It's not so easy to remain a child. And he was also sarcastic, which people never understand. He was romantic but also sharp, and sharp people are not well understood. We had many adventures. We wanted to make films. I remember once we went for money to Berlin, to the king of German cinema. We suggested a subject. He said no. He said, 'You don't belong to the movies.' You see, he was right. On the way home, Brecht said, 'Look, Jean, don't let's make movies. We should call what we want to do something else. Let's call it *Pilm.'* "

When we were back in Renoir's living room after the television shooting, he said to me, "In directing, I don't follow a script very closely. And I think it works best to choose a camera angle only after the actors have rehearsed. I suppose that between my way of working and the one of following a script closely there is possibly the same difference as between Indian music and Western music since the tempered scale. In Indian music, there is a general melody, and this general melody is ancient and must be held to, and then there is also a general note played on a particular instrument, and this note is repeated all the time and keeps the other instruments up to pitch. And so there is a melody and a pitch, and the musicians are free to move around these fixed points. I think it is a magnificent method, and I try to imitate it with actors and filmmaking, up to a point."

We drifted into talking about Stanislavsky. Renoir said that he had learned endlessly from Stanislavsky but that Stanislavsky had "a big problem." He explained, "Often the Moscow Arts Theatre had to speak in front of an audience that didn't know Russian at all—or, if so, not good Russian. It forced the company to make too many clear signals. To shout inner things, so to speak."

We sat in the drawing room on another day. "Excuse me," said Renoir. "My maid is here today and I want to know how she feels. She has a bad eye." He went out and stood talking with her, his head hanging down as he listened, like a fisherman's watching a river. She was insisting that she was all right and could work, making gestures with a dustpan: a short, alert woman, one eye covered with a patch of bright-pink sticking plaster. They stood there for a time, visible through two doorways and faintly audible, like people photographed in the unemphatic style of his films.

"She won't go home," said Renoir, coming back into the room. "She's very strong. She doesn't look it. She's built like a French soldier. Frederick the Great was amazed by how small we were. Just before a battle, he said, 'How can they fight?' " Renoir limped around and got some wine and said, "We lost, I believe." And then he sat down again and went on watching the woman for a while through the doorways. I looked at a photograph pinned up over his desk. It showed a cluster of men in cloth caps sitting on the ground and laughing. The scene looked rather like a factory picnic, but not quite. Renoir said that the picture was by his friend Henri Cartier-Bresson and that the men were convicts. "When their sentences were over, they didn't want to leave the labor camp, so they just stayed. They had their friends, et cetera, et cetera. And also, you see"—he spoke seriously—"I think they'd come to like the work."

We talked about a London prison where I had once lectured and shown *La Règle du Jeu*. He asked a lot of questions, often using the words "interesting" and "interested," which sprinkle his talk, like "et cetera." "I quite enjoy lecturing when I'm doing it," he said. "Not so much when it's over. Doing it is generally the only thing, isn't it? One sees that even with banking, which God knows is a stupid occupation. But when a banker is actually making the money he thinks he needs to retire with, then he is happy, and with luck the retirement never arrives. I suppose I really believe work and life are one, as the Hindus do. When I'm making a film, for instance, I don't know where the divisions are in the job. When I'm writing, I'm cutting the film in my head. And when I'm cutting I'm doing more of the screenplay. You understand, this isn't to say that there aren't terrible days before we start, when nothing is possible." He paused, then went on, "But Hollywood, because it has this genius for departments, has found the perfect way to make pictures that have no sense. A producer has a wonderful screenplay, by wonderful authors—plural—and he puts wonderful actors in it, and then he hires a wonderful director, who says 'That's a little slow,' or 'Please be more warm.' And so—well, it is most efficient, and what it reminds me of is a perfect express train racing along perfect steel tracks without having any idea that one of its compartments contains a beautiful girl leaning against beautiful red plush with a most interesting story to tell. A lot of people who are quite sincerely critical of Hollywood say that the trouble is that the people there worship money, but I believe them to be worshipping something much worse, and that is the ideal of physical perfection. They double-check the sound, so that you get perfect sound, which is good. Then they double-check the lighting, so that you get perfect lighting, which is also fairly good. But they also double-check the director's idea, which is not so good. It brings us straight to another god—or perhaps I should say devil—that is very dangerous in the movies, and that is the fear that the public won't understand. This fear of 'I don't understand' is terrible. I don't see how you can ever understand something you love. You would not say that you understood a woman you love. You feel her and like her. It has to do with contact. Something many people ignore is that there is no such thing as interesting work without the contact of the public—the collaboration, perhaps. When you are listening to great music, what you are really doing is enjoying a good conversation with a great man, and this is bound to be fascinating. We watch a film to know the filmmaker. It's his company we're after, not his skill. And in the case of the physically perfect—the perfectly intelligible—the public has nothing to add and there is no collaboration. Now I am going to be very trite and say that it is easier to make a silent film than a talkie, because there is something missing. In the talkies, therefore, we have to reproduce this missing something in another way. We have to ask the actors not to be like an open book. To keep some inner feeling, some secret."

Renoir's feeling for ambiguity is powerful. He clings to doubt as if it were a raft. I told him about a playwright friend of mine called N. F. Simpson, the author of *One-Way Pendulum* and *A Resounding Tinkle*: wonderfully funny plays that some humorless drama expert in London once lammed into for having no form, though this is a great part of their funniness. After a particularly fierce battery, I remember Simpson—a schoolmaster, to boot, who could have run rings of logic around the drama expert if he had been moved to—sitting on the floor with his back against my hi-fi and saying, his long face no more melancholy than usual, that the man was perfectly right, that the plays had no shape at all. "It struck me at the time that I could have given them a shape," he said. "But it seemed like breaking faith with chaos."

"This question of perfection," said Renoir. "Bogus symmetry. It is one of the reasons modern objects are so ugly. Plates, dresses, colors. If you take the blue of faïence, the blue of delft, it is never absolutely pure, you see. There is nothing quite pure in nature. In the Army, with the cavalry, I learned that there are no white horses and no black horses. They always have a number of hairs that are another color. If the horses were plastic, that would be an unforgivable fault. My father used to talk about this idea. Not about plastic, of course. . . . He had, for example, a small piece of advice for young architects. He said to them that they might think of destroying their perfect tools and replacing the symmetry produced by their instruments with the symmetry produced by their own eye. When he was asked about a school for artists, he said he would like to see inns—inns with the temperament of English pubs—where people would be fed and where they would live and where nobody would teach them a single thing. He said that he didn't want the spirits of young artists to be tidied up. His talk was terribly interesting. Toward the end of his life he would think deeply, perhaps because he couldn't walk. I believe sitting in a wheelchair helped him to think as he did. Often I would suppose he was working, and then just find him sitting, and we would have a conversation much like the one I am having with you. A certain spectrum of life would interest him."

Renoir's cast of mind often seems very like his father's. "As the years went by, I found he was becoming rather a marble bust instead of a man," Renoir recalled. "I wanted to stop that. It was why I wrote a book about him, I think." He spoke about Auguste Renoir's attitude toward prowess, and it defined his own. He said that his father "didn't care for *tours de force*"—that "to his way of thinking, the beauty of, say, a weightlifter was at its greatest when the young man was lifting only something very light." The filmmaker son does that. The world he created in *La Règle du Jeu* spins on his forefinger. We talked about the biography. It is called *Renoir, My Father*, and he published it in 1958. I had the impression that he misses his father daily. We also talked about his books. "I like writing," he said. "Because it doesn't matter."

Another day, we went to see a film. The screenplay of the film—Truffaut's *Stolen Kisses*—he found "very interesting." He said, "It has no suspense. I hate the sanctity of suspense. It's left over from nineteenth-century romanticism. The film is to the point and comic. It is a sort of synopsis of the times, this humor. It is not so much something to laugh at as an attitude toward life that you can share. At least, in *this* film you are permitted to share it. So the film must be good, I think. I like it very much."

We walked out into the cool sun. Renoir inspected the streets and said, "It seems to me that the people of Paris are gayer than usual. Perhaps it's the weather? ["*Il a une telle correspondance avec la nature,*" Sylvia Bataille had said a few days before.] Or perhaps it's still the effect of the events of May in 1968." He looked closely at everything, as if he were going to draw it from memory later.

The taxi we took had a postcard of a Picasso stuck in the dashboard: inevitably, in Renoir's company, it seemed. He instantly leaned forward and started to talk about it. The driver, who chatted with hair-raising responsiveness in the Paris traffic, turned out to be a spare-time painter. "Only to amuse myself, you understand," he said.

"Why not?" said Renoir. "Everything interesting is only to amuse yourself."

The driver, making the taxi lurch horribly, produced a magazine called *Science & Art.* We nearly hit something because he was finding a page to show Renoir and then stabbing a forefinger at the place, leaning over to the back seat with his eyes on the magazine. "Paintings by madmen," the driver explained during a feat with the clutch and the accelerator.

Renoir looked at the page and exclaimed. It showed a schizophrenic's painting, a gilded dream of a Madonna and Child that also had some-thing carnal and pagan about it, like a Bonnard, and something quite free, as things tend to be in Renoir's presence.

The two men talk with passionate absorption about, in turn, mad-men, the Madonna, and paintbrushes. As we get out, the driver gives Renoir the magazine, shakes his hand, and offers his name.

"Renoir," responds Renoir, and he thanks the driver for the present as he climbs out, his bad leg slowing him a little.

"You are of the family Renoir?" says the driver, amazed, moved, something dawning on him, looking at Renoir's face.

"Yes."

"Of the painter Renoir?"

"Yes. He was my father."

The driver goes on looking. "You are yourself, then . . . There was a famous man of the theater and the cinema . . ."

"That's my nephew Claude. A cameraman. Or my brother Pierre, per-haps. The actor."

"No, someone some time ago, a most famous man of the theater and the cinema, I believe."

"Yes, I think you are right, I believe there was once another Renoir who worked in the theater. Not related."

When we were pottering about the kitchen one day at lunchtime, Renoir said severely, "We will not have much. You don't eat, and now I don't eat, either. You must have been easy to ration," and he started talking about the Second World War. He was very kind to the English, even to the food. "Without the English, we should now all be under the jackboot. Yorkshire pudding, Lancashire hot pot. Exactly how is shepherd's pie made?" Just before the fall of Paris, Renoir and Dido joined the flight to the Midi. He took with him some of the most treasured paintings in the world. His own car was in the country, far away. "I didn't know what to do," he said. "At last, it occurred to me: perhaps one can still hire a car. Perhaps the Peugeot people are still working. So we went to the Peugeot factory, and there is every clerk at work as usual, still filling out forms, with the Germans ten miles away. I have to fill out all these forms, and then we have a car, and we drive to the Midi, very slowly, with the canvases of Monsieur Cézanne, et cetera, in the back. A big trek to the south. Everyone who could find a cart or a wheelbarrow. It was a very bad sight."

Renoir has his father's strong respect for touch, and for a kind of conviviality that is unmistakable and moving when he creates it in any of his films. He is a fine friend to spend time with. "One of the things I like about Shakespeare, very much, is that the characters have a great variety of intimacy," he said to me. "They are different according to whom they are speaking to. Of course, Shakespeare had a great advantage over cinema directors. It is one that interests me a lot. He shares it with, you could say, Simenon. You could call it the advantage of a harness. Elizabethan plays and also thrillers are constricted, and that is very liberating. In the cinema, you can do all too much. For example, when the hero of a modern film has a phobia, you are obliged to explain it by flashbacks: I mean, to go back to the time when he was beaten by his father, or whatever thing is supposed to have had such a result. This freedom can be quite enfeebling. It makes one very literal, very anxious to make everything clear, get everything taped. You know, I believe one has to have only a rough idea when one is making a film or writing a story, or whatever. A rough scheme, like a salmon going upstream. No more than that. It's no true help—is it?—to know already where one is going to arrive. In fact, I think targets have done a great deal of harm. This nineteenth-century idea in Europe, and now in America—this idea of targets—has caused terrible damage. Rewards in the future, and so on. Those never come. Pensions. I thought about this a good deal in India when I was making *The River*, in 1949 and 1950. India was a revelation. I suppose I'd been looking for such a place and thinking it was all past, and there it was. Suppose you are interested in Aristophanes, and suppose you go down the street and suddenly see people who are exactly his contemporaries, who know the same things, have the same view. That's what India was like for me. I had been starting to fall off to sleep. In India, you could make a full-length picture just by following someone through the day. A grandmother, say, getting up in the morning, cooking, washing clothes. Everything noble. Among poor people in India, you're surrounded by an aristocracy and a nobility. The trouble now is that the advanced countries are trying desperately to grow better by the mistake of removing the ordinary. We're trying to reach greatness by reading classics in houses that have no cold in the winter and no heat in the summer, and where everything can be done without the natural waste of time. One of the things I liked about India is that the people have the secret of loitering." This brought up Los Angeles, the city famous for picking up as a vagrant anyone who is merely strolling along a street. Renoir was very firm. "All great civilizations have been based on loitering," he said.

Much later, coming back to this point after a loop of talk about food and operetta, Renoir said, "Think of the Greeks, for instance. One of the most interesting adventures in our history. What were the Greeks doing in the agora? Loitering. Not getting agoraphobia. The result is Plato. My film *Boudu* is the story of a man who is just loitering."

Renoir spoke of Satyajit Ray, his helper on *The River*, whose Indian films are much like the ones that Renoir had just envisioned for me, and who feels Renoir and *The River* to be vital inspirations of his own work. "He is quite alone, of course. Most other Indian films are—well, I suppose they would be called uninteresting, though I have to say that they often interest me very much. There is sometimes a wonderful mixture of fairy tales and daily life and the religious, and no one thinks of it as at all comic, because no one is conscious of incongruity. I saw this in an Italian theater once. A little theater, not much bigger than this room. At the front of the stage, a man threatening to kill his mother. In the back, by some trick, a locomotive rushing. It was very fine. Hamlet and railway stations. Genuinely popular. You know what I mean. Every now and then, one gets this in Indian films. In the middle of a story

about Siva and a film star and dancing and so on, there will suddenly
be a god with a mustache who looks like a cop. It is practically the only
question of the age, this question of primitivism and how it can be sustained in the face of sophistication. It is the question of Vietnam."

This question is much on his mind, and he came back to it another
day by another route. "You know, I have a theory about the decay of art
in advanced civilizations," he said. "Perhaps it's a joke, but I believe it
may be serious. It is that people *want* to make ugly things, but at the
beginning their tools don't allow them to. When you find figures or
vases in Mycenae or Guatemala or Peru, every one is a masterpiece. But
when the perfection of technique allows men to do what they want, it
is bad. Perfection of technique—sophistication—has nearly destroyed
the movies. In the beginning, every movie was good. When we see the
old silents at the Cinémathèque, they are all good. This isn't nostalgia.
They are. And, believe me, I know some of the directors who made
them and they aren't geniuses. It also has something to do with puritanism. I'm in favor of puritanism, I think. Not for me. But for a nation
it can be very good, and for art. Those early movies in Hollywood
reflected the decorum of the people, a kind of thinking that I could
not abide for myself. We would demonstrate against it now, I daresay,
including me. You know what I think about all this? I believe that
Creation has a considerable sense of humor. Of farce. The closer we are
to perfection, the farther away from it we are. This makes me think
about Hollywood, of course. The interesting thing about Hollywood,
Beverly Hills, Los Angeles is that it isn't really materialist at all—not in
the true sense, because it obviously doesn't care for the material in the
slightest. In fact, that's the big advantage of Hollywood: the fact that
the buildings don't count. It is therefore a place in the abstract. You are
there—no, I should say that *one* is there, and I suppose I must mean
myself—only for one's friends. When Clifford Odets died, I thought I
wanted to leave Hollywood. He was a prince. Every gesture, every way
of thinking was noble. Although I love Hollywood, I have to say that it
is without nobility. But I stayed, of course. You know what I like about
America? Among other things, the obvious. The generosity. There is a
great desire to share. To share feelings, to share friends. Of course, this
can be a travesty and ridiculous. It can be reduced to "togetherness"
and the vocabulary that could find such a word for such a thing. But it

also has to be said that there exists in America a stout attempt to do in language exactly the opposite, to make things noble. For instance, calling tea a beverage, calling a barber a hairdresser. It doesn't work, but the attempt, in the face of the obstacles—well, it's interesting and nice, isn't it? It is very much harder to live nobly in America than in India. One of the things that are helpful to Indians is the concept of privacy. It is so strong there that to have spiritual privacy they do not even need physical privacy. In America, this concept is not so easy to have, partly because of the ethic of sharing, perhaps, and partly because of the ethic of proselytizing and persuading other people, which Hinduism is entirely free of, and which has arrived so dreadully at Vietnam for America. The problem of caste—of Western caste, of paternalism, et cetera—has led us into this proselytizing. I suppose caste is what all my films are about. Still, any big society is a melting pot, as they say. Take Rome. And the banal melting pot of America that is so much in question at the moment really works pretty well except at one point. The point of the Negro. One forgets that the slaves weren't originally brought by the Americans. They were brought by the French, the Spanish, the Portuguese. The really difficult thing to explain is that the slave owners pretended to be Christians. All men are brothers, and in the meantime the brothers on your estate are slaves. I suppose it has to be recognized that much of the truth about Christianity is about money, and most of the truth about subjection and propaganda is about money. Outside Paris now, there are Arabs living in shacks built out of gasoline cans who make a great deal of money for Paris businessmen. Americans make money out of Negroes, and Frenchmen make money out of Arabs. Every country has a worm in the apple, and the worm in the apple of America is a very tough one."

We went out into the Place Pigalle. "Much changed since the days of my father and Monsieur Cézanne," Renoir said, perfectly cheerfully. There was a night club on the corner which had the present special tattiness of the recently new. "Sensass!" a placard said of a stripper. The whole place was plastered with the words of some arid new Esperanto. "Chinese," Renoir said firmly. "A Chinese dialect that is understood only on this side of the square."

He talked about his new novel. It is about a murder, and based on a real crime that he heard of as a small child from Gabrielle, his father's famous model. It happened in a village between Burgundy and Champagne. "Two murderers," he said. "One with a big nose, the leader, and the other the weak one. At the time of the murder, which was very terrible, the villagers heard the sound of the ax blows on the earth to bury the corpse. The earth was very cold. The sounds seemed to them to be coming from under the earth. That was the way Gabrielle remembered them. They came from the private cemetery. Somebody seemed to be trying to escape from the ground, everyone thought. The cemetery had been made for a man in the French Revolution who didn't want to be buried in a religious place." A while later, considering what the story might be like as a film, he said, "Too violent. I'm an admirer of violent films, but I can't make them. Also, I am scared of them." He was about to spend five days or a week in the country where the murder happened. The name of the village—very near his own family region—is Gloire-Dieu. Someone had sent him a browned clipping of a local song about the crime, which he said had deeply wounded the villagers' sense of blessedness in their name:

COMPLAINTE SUR LE CRIME DE LA GLOIRE-DIEU
Écoutez la triste histoire
Désolant notre pays.
En faisant le récit,
Vraiment on ne peut y croire,
Car le pays bourguignon
N'a pas un mauvais roman . . .

Renoir talked about a lot of other plans. Some that had been scotched seemed no particular cue for regret. The ideas continued to interest him, and it was sometimes quite hard to be sure whether he was describing a plan of his own or the plot of some favorite already achieved: the "Satyricon" of Petronius, for one. He recited the stories of classics in the present tense, and they acquired his own tang. "There is this matron who lost her husband, and she is so much in love she can't bear the thought of being alone," he said, limping along the cobbles and helping me. "She stays in the cemetery near the corpse of her husband. There is a soldier nearby who is watching thieves. The crucified bodies of thieves. The authorities have to have a soldier there, because one thief's family wants to steal the body. The soldier says to the woman, "Don't cry so cloud," and he comforts her so well that after two or three days he makes love, and the family can steal the corpse, and so everyone is happier, except that the soldier has failed in his official task and what on earth can he do?"

Without changing his tone, Renoir went on from Petronius to describe his unmade film about revolt. He had written it in two parts. At no time did he speak of it in the past. "One is a revolt against an electric waxing machine. The other is about war. Two corporals from two armies hide between enemy lines beneath the roof of a kind of cellar. We start with a very polite fight about who will be the prisoner of the other one. In the end, they decide there is only one decent position in the modern world and that is to be a prisoner. But each doesn't like the enemy food. Oh, and now I have suddenly found the ending, in talking to you. I think this is the ending. They change uniforms, and then each can be the prisoner of the other and have the food he likes."

The television show he is doing is "like a revue." He continues, "Some of the sketches are very short—no more than a sentence. There is one sketch of the Armistice, and a burglar breaks a vein in his neck and wakes a sleepwalker and they are the first victims of the peace. Before this, there is a soldier who is told by a sergeant that if he dies before the Armistice he will be right and if he dies after the Armistice he will be wrong. You know what has happened? Patriotism is really quite a new idea to the ordinary citizen. It happens to be useful in politics to pretend that it is a powerful emotion, but it isn't. Not widely. Most people have never thought first of their country; they've thought first of their family. You know, I adore England. I have English relatives. I'd like to live there. People live there very agreeably." (Though I should think he could live anywhere, given friends, just as he can make enjoyable work for himself in strange countries or in atrocious circumstances.)

"The trouble is that techniques change and the actors' style of playing changes," he said. "Just as fashions vanish, so our films go into oblivion to join others that once moved us."

The greatest of Renoir's will never do this, but he doesn't seem to know it. It makes you pause to see a man with such a powerful sense of the continuity of the general life engaged with the form that most deals in quick deaths. He eludes that blow by understanding filmmaking another way, as play. He will sometimes describe a director as *"le meneur de jeu,"* and he calls his friends and collaborators his accomplices. "The cinema uses things up very fast. That's the point," he says. "It uses up ideas and people and kinds of stories, and all the time it thinks it wants to be new. It has no idea that film people themselves change and are new all the time. Producers want me to make the pictures I made twenty years ago. Now I am someone else. I have gone away from where they think I am."

Interview with Jean Renoir

RUI NOGUEIRA AND FRANÇOIS TRUCHAUD / 1968

Last autumn, Jean Renoir was back in France. He had come to prepare a new film: meanwhile, *La Marseillaise* (1937) was reissued in its
integral version, and the Cinémathèque mounted a *hommage* to his
work. He talked to us in his Paris flat on the Avenue Frochot, just
around the corner from the Place Pigalle and the 'Moulin de la Galette'
immortalised by his father, Auguste Renoir.

SS: *A year ago, you came to Paris with your project for* C'est la
Revolution, *which was turned down by the Centre National du Cinéma.
Was it to have been an episode film?*
JR: Yes. I had originally written seven sketches. Then I reduced the
number to five, and even three, because they grew as I worked on them.
I haven't abandoned the project, I've simply put it aside. Maybe one
day I shall try to do something with it, I don't know. In the course of
my life I've worked on a lot of projects that have never come to anything. I imagine it's the same with most people.

SS: *Then you went back to America. What have you been doing since?*
JR: I've had a lot of ideas for new films, and finally concentrated my
energies on the one I'm working on now—a film about a *clocharde*, with
Jeanne Moreau. It's still all a bit vague, and there isn't a final script yet.
I've written one version, but I'm not satisfied with it and won't use it.

Originally published in *Sight and Sound*, 37.2 (Spring 1968), pp. 57–62. Reprinted
by permission.

I'm working on another at the moment. You know, I'm convinced that you only discover the real meaning of a film as you work on it. I don't believe in blueprints. But since the sets have to be built in advance, one has to have a plan, and that's why I'm making one for my story; but I will only discover what the story's about as I work on it, or more probably as I shoot it. One thing I am sure of, it's a good subject. Jeanne Moreau as a *clocharde* is all I need for a starting point, but I don't know exactly what I'm going to do with her. It won't be a series of episodes, but a story with a beginning and an end and it will last about one-and-a-half to two hours, that much I do know.

SS: *Will the film be set in Paris?*
JR: If not actually in Paris, then at least in the North of France. Not in the South, but somewhere where it rains.

SS: *Will this film take up the idea of liberty from* Boudu Sauvé Des Eaux? *The character of the tramp—who also appeared at the end of* La Chienne—*seems to be a recurring one in your work.*
JR: I'm not alone in suggesting this kind of solution. A large number of people today, or at least a large number of young people, are trying to reject the conventions of society and discover a way of life that is less comfortable but more free.

SS: *Are you referring to the hipster movement in the United States?*
JR: Not specially. I think this is something that had to happen. As inevitable as rain after sunshine. Something natural and normal.

SS: *When you were shooting* The River *in India, didn't you also think of making a film about the pariahs?*
JR: Yes. But the main reason one can't make a film about the pariahs, or about any other minority for that matter, is language. I don't think a film about the pariahs made in English or French would be any good. One would follow the life of a pariah family on a boat going down the Ganges, follow all the little things that happen to them, but if they're not speaking their own language, they're not expressing themselves properly. If you use famous actors, French or American stars, the film will be completely false. It isn't possible. The only way to make this

kind of film would be to have a great deal of money put up by people who realised they'd never see it again. Because either the film would be uncommercial, being in a language the general public couldn't understand, or, if it was in a commercially exploitable language, it would be false and I wouldn't want to make it.

SS: *Had you envisaged it as a documentary?*
JR: No, I'd envisaged . . . well, yes, if you like. It depends what you mean by documentary.

SS: *Would you have used amateur actors?*
JR: Yes, or else Indian actors sufficiently familiar with the pariah life and language to give the characters some semblance of authenticity.

SS: *As Rossellini did in* India 58?
JR: Yes, but it would probably have been more of a dramatic film than *India*, which is closer to pure documentary.

SS: *Would you say that* The River *is a fulfilment?*
JR: Oh! I think it's more of a beginning than an end. Shooting that kind of story makes you think about many things, you re-examine your values, and you modify them.

SS: *But* The River *does mark the close of one period of your work, which then opens in a new direction . . .*
JR: Let's put it more simply and say that *The River* brought me into contact with new things, taught me something about things I didn't know, and that this had a great influence on me.

SS: *On a point of detail:* La Tosca, *the film which you prepared and Carl Koch finally directed, bears a strong resemblance to your own work.*
JR: Well, you know, Koch had worked a great deal with me. I've never seen *La Tosca*, but everyone tells me what you have just said. It's because we worked together like brothers: inevitably I had a lot of his ideas and he had a lot of mine. He was a marvellous collaborator—on *La Grande Illusion* and on *La Règle du Jeu*.

SS: *Like Jacques Becker . . .*

JR: Yes, certainly. Becker and Koch were my friends, my colleagues in film-making. For *La Tosca* I shot only the first sequence, and it has apparently been used in Koch's film. And of course we had written a script which for once was fairly precise: since it was adapted from a story that already existed, we couldn't wander away from it, we had to follow the story. Koch, who is dead now, was a really remarkable man, and it's a great pity he made so few films. He could have done some wonderful things. His knowledge of life was very profound, and he also had a sense of the absurdity of the human condition . . . that's very rare nowadays, people seem to take everything seriously. One has to take things seriously, of course—everything *is* serious, but still it has its amusing side even in its seriousness.

SS: *There have been a number of remakes of your films: Fritz Lang* (Scarlet Street, Human Desire), *Luis Buñuel* (Journal d'une Femme de Chambre) *and now Jean-Pierre Melville* (La Chienne). *How do you feel about remakes?*

JR: I think that if the story is good, remakes are perfectly justified. The good stories in history have been used ten or even twenty times over by different authors. Shakespeare never wrote an original plot, but borrowed his stories from the Italian chronicles, from ancient history or from existing plays. And he's the world's greatest dramatist, so if he could do it, so can we. An erroneous belief has taken hold since the Romantic period that the originality of a literary or dramatic work depends on the originality of its plot. In my opinion this is absolutely untrue. The plot is necessary and you need a good one, but you can borrow it from anywhere you like. I even think that to encourage good stories and good films, there ought to be medals, prizes of some kind, for people who plagiarise. We want to encourage plagiarism.

SS: *Of the kind Godard practises in his films?*

JR: Yes, of course, and he's perfectly aware of what he's doing. It's the same with all the classics. Let's take a great classical dramatist like Corneille, who borrowed *Le Cid* from De Castro—all the great classical dramas are derived from an existing source. It's not a question of copying but simply of using the same springboard.

SS: La Marseillaise *has just been reissued in its original, integral form. Was it hard to reconstruct?*
JR: Not so difficult as *La Règle du Jeu*. We had more help. The Cinémathèque was very cooperative, and we were able to use the soundtrack of a Russian print. It took a lot of work, but it always looked feasible.

SS: *Twenty years before Rossellini's* La Prise de Pouvoir par Louis XIV, La Marseillaise *uses the same technique of mingling the general and the particular, historical fact and personal anecdote.*
JR: I still haven't seen Rossellini's film, though I'm hoping to. For me Rossellini is one of the great directors, all his films are important. He's a man who has the cinema at his fingertips; he breathes cinema and thinks cinema, so everything he does is interesting. Rossellini is one of those people who express themselves directly through what they create. His films are self-portraits.

SS: *You once said that* La Marseillaise *was one of your favourite films.*
JR: I don't think I can have said that because I have no favourite film. Of course some of them may have certain sentimental associations . . . but you know, the real source of happiness, not just in the cinema but in any kind of human endeavour, is the fact of creating. Once a thing is done, well, it's done. Of course it's very nice to be applauded by audiences and very unpleasant to be booed: I'll admit that's important, but not *that* important. The real thing, the real intoxication if I may call it that, is in the act of creation: that's what matters, whether one is creating an apple pie, a film, a child or a painting.

SS: *What are your most pleasant memories?*
JR: There have been good moments on all my films, but my most treasured memories have to do with actors. I love working with actors.

SS: *In America, you and Robert Ryan became friends while shooting* Woman on the Beach. *You even wrote the preface to the book by his wife, Peggy Ryan.*
JR: Bob Ryan is a marvellous person. Professionally he's absolutely honest in everything he does. But he was unlucky in happening on a

period in which the American cinema was in full cry after war epics—
all of them highly successful. I can understand people making them,
given that a business has to make money or grind to a halt. If the cinema didn't make money, tomorrow there would be no cinema, so one
mustn't blame the people who make commercial films. But commercial
films consume a lot of talent. People can lose a lot of their feathers in
them. But they also produce people like Leo McCarey, who has never
pushed himself forward and who is often forgotten. He made the
admirable *Ruggles of Red Gap* in 1935, with Charles Laughton, and the
ease and elegance of his work is really remarkable. He is very ill—he was
in hospital when I left America a fortnight ago.

SS: *You have talked on several occasions about the hipster movement.*
What do you see in it?
JR: I believe it's an international movement. It's simply a turning of the
wheel, a querying of the values of the society these boys and girls grew up
in. I think that suddenly they're questioning the motive force behind
most people who work or do not work in contemporary society—namely,
success. Suddenly they're wondering whether success really means as
much as people have supposed. Success, and therefore money. In other
words it's a reaction against a purely commercial society, and I think that,
with only slight differences, the feeling is the same everywhere. I think the
movement of the Red Guards in China is a little the same, maybe . . .

SS: *What do you think of Jean Renoir the writer?*
JR: I don't, since that is me and one doesn't judge oneself. I wrote *Les*
Cahiers du Capitaine Georges because I didn't think it was possible to make
a film out of it, even though I had been asked to. It's a confession, the
confession of a man who lived a great love through a period of history;
but above all it's the confession of a man explaining his reactions in the
face of a period of considerable change, for the world before 1914 and the
world after are entirely different worlds. So it's a witness to this transition
talking about himself. It's so personal, so intimate that I find it very difficult to imagine it translated into images. These are thoughts, not pictures.

SS: *What do you think of the influences or affinities that exist between*
directors? For example, The Southerner *conjures up the King Vidor*

of Hallelujah *and* Our Daily Bread, *the John Ford of* Tobacco Road *and* The Grapes of Wrath.

JR: That's very possible, and I'm glad, because one ought to be open to influences. I'm not at all in favour of isolation. Quite the contrary. I'm in favour of contact with the world; and if you have contact then you can't but be influenced. And besides, they're both directors whom I admire as men. King Vidor is a wonderful person. In the whole of human history there have never been sincere artists who weren't influenced. So of course total isolation is a fight against outside influences, it's like saying "I personally am so interesting, I have such a beautiful soul that I want to serve it up to you on a plate." I prefer the idea of digesting the world, observing it and trying to transform one's observation into something personal, but with observation as a starting point. And under observation I'd include reading books, seeing films or plays, listening to music; these are some of the elements that influence you. Or just contact with the man in the street. I've never tried to influence anyone at all. In effect, when I make a film I'm asking other people to influence me.

SS: *As a director you have made remarkable use of colour. Yet you have used it in only five films.*

JR: I have not made more films in colour because it hasn't seemed appropriate. I think that some subjects demand black and white, others need colour. In point of fact, as we progress further, so more and more subjects benefit from being treated in colour, for the simple reason that the public has grown used to colour, even expects it. Nowadays the black and white film is almost an exception. But in my opinion the danger of colour is realism. I think that in every art one has to retain the possibility of a transposition. One mustn't just copy, one mustn't imitate nature—luckily, colour processes aren't perfect and this copy of nature remains rather remote, so that in practice colour offers other means than black and white of effecting this transposition. I believe the ideal of people working on colour—laboratory workers, chemists and technicians—to succeed completely in copying nature is manifestly false. The day they can reproduce nature exactly, there will be no more cinema. What's interesting is the transposition by a cameraman, by a director or an actor . . . the concentration, the translation.

SS: *Why is it that in the cinema older directors can make stronger, more mature works (Ford, Hawks, Walsh, Lang, etc.)?*
JR: It's the same in all the arts, in any craft. If a writer tends to repeat himself in his later works, it's because he is not a very good writer. But think of Stendhal, for instance. One of his last works was *Lamiel*, a quite extraordinary book, absolutely different from anything he'd done before. Now there are people who are famous for a single novel, a single film, a single picture . . . no, not a picture, painting won't allow that, painting forces the artist into a constant progression because it's a craft in which the technical—or more correctly the material—element plays an enormous part. The danger with the cinema, now that it has become so technically perfect, is that you can detach yourself, forget the problems of translating something through an image or a sound. It's all too easy. The modern director is surrounded by splendid technicians, men of skill and taste who do everything for him. The result is that the director is a bit like the station-master who makes the train run on time but hasn't actually anything to do with the train. This is dangerous and one must guard against it. But this doesn't mean that the director should create the film on his own, not at all; everyone brings his own little bit, and one of the director's most interesting tasks is to coax everyone into expressing himself more fully.

SS: *So the cinema is a constant process of self-examination?*
JR: Yes, of course. With writers it may be more erratic, but it seems to me that with the greatest writers there is a kind of constant progression till the day they die. With painters it shows more clearly. It's obvious that Picasso today is stronger and more profound than he was at the age of twenty; it's obvious that Titian as an old man achieved an indisputable mastery. It's true that Velásquez and Goya . . .

SS: *Would you agree that areas of your work still remain to be explored?*
JR: It sometimes seems to me that people go round the edges of my films. When the Cinémathèque invited me to come along and present one of my films, I chose *Le Caporal Épinglé*. Not that I consider it a great masterpiece, far from it. It's a workmanlike film that I made as best I could; but through it I tried to express certain things which obviously . . . well, which people just haven't grasped.

SS: *Could you have done anything more on* Partie de Campagne?
JR: Absolutely nothing. That's the conclusion I came to. When the film was finished, Braunberger, my friend and producer, said to me: "It has the makings of a feature film. Do you want to try to turn it into a feature?" I said that I didn't think so but I was willing to try. So I tried to write something to stretch it out, but it wouldn't come. Then I said, "If you don't mind, I'll ask Jacques Prévert to help me out." So Jacques and I thought about it and tried to work out something by adding a long prologue and an epilogue to the story. But nothing we tried hung together, it didn't work at all. The whole idea of making it longer was a commercial one; for myself, I had conceived it as a short film, the way it is.

SS: *Do you think television is really an art form?*
JR: Why not? Take the commercials on American TV, for example, they're really extraordinary. The advertisements for General Electric, Ford or Coca-Cola—like some of the French commercials—contain images of astonishing beauty and boldness. It seems to me that these commercials are undeniably an art form, and I love them.

SS: *Do you think you might work again for television?*
JR: If the opportunity arises, yes, especially if I have a really original idea. If I haven't, there would be no point in doing what my colleagues do so well and so much better than I should. But if I get an idea that seems to me a little out of the ordinary, then I should like to . . .

SS: *Do you find there's a real affinity between your own films and those of the younger French directors today?*
JR: I must admit that I feel very close to much of what the younger generation is doing. Their way of thinking is probably very close to mine, and I can understand the sort of affinity that exists between the New Wave directors and myself. Things have to be kept moving. I did certain things, they've done others, and new people will come along to do something else again. The world, life, can never stand still, because immobility means death . . . but of course even death is alive because there is decomposition, which is a very interesting thing. Movement and metamorphosis are essential to our world. The leaves on this tree are starting to turn yellow, then they will fall, and turn into a nice little

pile of compost so that tiny blades of new grass will come up again next spring.

SS: *That's the whole philosophy of* The River, *and one aspect of the theme of liberty which runs through all your films.*

JR: Yes, liberty. And in this context one situation that preoccupies me a great deal is the question of adaptation, the way in which an individual or group of individuals may be accepted by a different environment. *La Règle du Jeu,* for instance, is about the introduction of an aviator—who doesn't belong at all—into a social group which functions very well without him. So long as he's not there, everything works fine. He arrives, and despite his purity, his honesty and his goodness, he destroys everything and is himself destroyed. Films that take place in a prison are very convenient because the characters are automatically cut off, which is a great help in telling a story. With *La Grande Illusion,* for instance, the fact that it's all enclosed within four walls is marvellous: it's a foolproof situation. But it can also be a good thing to get a little lost, because that's often when you produce your best work. For I'm convinced that whatever you do that's good—or bad, for that matter— you do in spite of yourself . . . you don't know in advance that it's going to be good.

SS: *This chance element in creation seems to tie in with the idea of freedom, which you approach in a variety of ways in the sketches that were to make* up C'est la Revolution.

JR: Yes, I had written those sketches very carefully. It wasn't a film about revolution. I had some comic situations which I shall certainly use somewhere else. For instance, one about a husband whose wife is unfaithful. Everyone in the village is trying to put a stop to what they regard as an unhappy situation, but the husband is furious because he wants his wife to deceive him. She brings home a charming young man who shows him every possible consideration, gives him little presents, looks after him, pulls up a chair for him when he wants to sit down— and people want to deprive him of all this! I had also written another sketch about two corporals from opposing armies who are trapped in a completely devastated region. They don't like being there at all because they're in a farm which has become a kind of symbol for the two armies, who keep firing shells at it. So there they are, they want to get out, but if they try to leave their hole they'll be killed. And they come to the conclusion that in time of war being a prisoner is best. It's a nice, healthy life, but the one snag is that you're a prisoner in enemy territory. You're far from home, fed a kind of food you don't like, surrounded by people who speak a foreign language—in other words, you're a foreigner. And of course they don't like the idea. So they decide to change uniforms and get taken prisoner by their own armies. Not a bad idea, is it?

Meanwhile, in London for the opening of *La Marseillaise,* Renoir demonstrated the gentle art of winning friends and influencing people by his patient, courteous and apparently inexhaustible interest in everybody and everything. Even the talk he delivered in his own inimitable way one Sunday morning at the Academy Cinema became "not so much of a lecture as a conversation"—and the audience purred. Some of his themes and anecdotes—for instance, the story of how he and his associates did everything on *La Petite Marchande d'Allumettes* from generating the electricity to developing the negative—are familiar from earlier interviews or articles; others, included in the following extracts, may be less familiar, or are at any rate so irresistibly phrased that they demand perpetuation.

JR: When I started to make films my ambition was just to be successful, I was attracted by the glamour of the profession. Slowly, I discovered that to make films was something much more important, and perhaps a way to discover reality.

It was during the 1914 war: I was a pilot in a squadron, and a good friend of mine was the son of Professor Richer. Professor Richer had discovered something very precise about the inner reactions of the body to certain gases and liquids, and was also working on artificial nourishment; he was a very important man, and I admired him very much for one reason—I didn't understand what he was looking for! One day my friend Richer came back off leave from Paris and told me "My father took me to a movie." Well, you know, I was an officer in the cavalry, now in the air force, and I despised movies; to me movies were characters jerking on a piece of white canvas and shown mostly in carnivals, not even in a real theatre. But Richer said, "My father, who is a great man, told me that there is an actor who may convince you that movie-making is something very important." During my next leave I went to see this actor, who was called Charlie Chaplin; and back at the squadron I told Richer, "I believe your father is right when he says that we are confronted with a kind of revolution: this way of projecting life on a white screen is probably the new artistic expression of our century, the *real* artistic expression of our century."

Then I was shot in the leg by a Bavarian infantryman, and while I was convalescing on crutches, there was nothing else to do and I started looking at movies. In the beginning, I must confess, I didn't like them at all, but I became more and more convinced. I was so much impressed that I even took a projector to my father's house—by then he was paralysed in the legs—and showed him a Chaplin film. He was delighted. Slowly the idea grew in me that I had to be part of this revolution. I had the idea that I was going to be a leader, that I was going to be important. I lost these childish ideas only when I was confronted with the difficulty of the profession, only when I understood that you may have a great idea, but you still have to deal with the industry, with money; and you have to deal with the public. The public likes what already exists, but I dreamed of showing things which didn't exist before me. I was absolutely convinced that if I showed something a little different the public would love me. Which was not true. They just hated me.

To make films may be one good way to discover bits of reality. I believe that one of the most important functions of the film-maker is the destruction of cliché. We are surrounded by cliché. We believe that life is what we are told. Not at all. Life is something very different. Life is a combination of what does exist and what you have in mind: this combination may bring a work of art, may bring one second of happiness, one thing being as important as the other.

When I started to make films we really had to know what a camera is, we had constantly to think of what was going on. The technical dangers are bigger today because technique is perfect, and perfection is terribly dangerous in this world. I even believe that if a woman were absolutely perfect, her nose that of the best Greek statue, the proportions of her body divine, and her character delightful, then this woman would never find real love in her life. To find real love you must be *un*perfect. We hate perfection. We believe that we like it but we don't. We love life, that's more important than perfection. And the terrible thing about film-making is that the people who are important, the masters of the profession, the producers and even the big stars, believe in perfection. Very often people say, "What's wrong with Hollywood is that they think only of money." Money is not so dangerous, not nearly so dangerous as the cult of perfection. Anyway, it's wrong to believe that Hollywood loves money: they love to *spend* money . . .

But with the perfection of technique today, all the solutions are brought to you, anything you want. You want the brightest colours?— the best cameraman will bring you the brightest colours. You don't have to worry about anything. And since the pictures are expensive, you have to use very well-known actors. And the very well-known actors arrive with their solutions all ready—they will deliver the goods as well as they did in their last picture. This means that you are going to see exactly the same actor for the rest of your life. He won't change. Why should he? Not to change brings him a million dollars every year.

The danger is that of finding yourself confronted with answers which are not your own, answers you didn't have to work to find. In the early days, directors had to make their imagination work in order to balance what they were missing with inferior technique. Now that technique is perfect, you must become a great technician and then forget about technique. But first you must be a great technician.

I regret the magnificent innocence of the first films. If I could go back to the time of Hoot Gibson, Mary Pickford, directors like Fred Niblo and Tourneur, I would be delighted. But we can't. We must accept time as it comes.

One day I was talking to one of the most experienced entertainers of our time—Maurice Chevalier, who really knows what success is. I asked him how he chose the songs for his shows at the Casino de Paris, when he appeared alone on stage for an hour and sang perhaps ten or twelve different songs. "It's very simple," he said, "if I sing something new, something they've never heard before, they never like it. Never." So he used to start with songs from last year or perhaps two years before; and those songs, which had been unsuccessful then, were now successful because the public knew them. In other words, if you want to persuade the public to accept a new point of view, to share in a discovery, you

have to play the part of a prostitute, to put on a bit of make-up in order
to attract . . . she may be wonderful inside, but if she doesn't put on a
bit of make-up no one will follow her . . . You have to be a little bit dis-
honest, you have to give something the public can follow, and the easi-
est thing is the action. You must take a popular plot. For instance, I am
sure that initially *La Grande Illusion* was so successful because it was an
escape story. The escape story has nothing to do with my film. But it's a
mask, a disguise, and this disguise made *Grande Illusion* a big money-
maker.

Of course the purpose of any real art is, among other things, to reveal
the artist, to make the artist alive, and to give the public—something
more important than anything else in life—the possibility of a contact,
a conversation. I don't believe you admire a Cézanne painting of apples
because it is a good imitation of apples: you like it because you have a
conversation with Cézanne . . . Forgive me for a personal recollection.
Gabrielle, who was my father's model for part of his life, was with me
in Hollywood and one day she said, "Jean, it's too bad that you don't
own a portrait of your father by himself . . . But after all, it's not important, because you have a little painting of roses and that's exactly his
portrait." You see what she wanted to mean?—that through the roses
and without showing himself, Renoir was showing himself *more* than
through a self-portrait.

La Règle du Jeu was the result of a dream, of something I had inside
myself, deep down. I believe that many authors, and certainly myself,
tell one story all our lives, the same one, with different characters, different surroundings. My preoccupation is with the meeting: how to
belong, how to meet. In *La Règle du Jeu* this preoccupation is quite obvious, not only because someone of different character is introduced into
a certain milieu, but because this character (the flier, played by Roland
Toutain) is pure, whereas the group is impure. The others were good
people, I loved them. People thought that in writing *La Règle du Jeu*
I was criticising society, but not at all. I wish I could live in such a
society—that would be wonderful. But in any case this society was
not pure and the flier was pure. That was the problem I had inside
myself, without realising it at the time.

What pushed me to make *La Règle du Jeu* was an ambition to treat
a subject which would allow me to use the exterior forms of a French

comedy of the eighteenth century. I was also a little bit influenced by Musset, but my ambition was to find again a certain elegance, a certain grace, a certain rhythm which is typical of the eighteenth century, French or English. And that's the way I made the picture. During it, as always, I discovered that my problem was my old problem: what would happen to the stranger who wants to belong to a milieu which is not his. And of course the problem of how the poacher is going to be admitted to the servant milieu. I discovered this only afterwards, but I thought that's not bad, the picture will certainly please. I was sure the public would like it—it was a light picture, parties are not big problems, and the big problems were so well hidden that the audience wouldn't be hurt in their feelings. Well, I was very wrong. Starting with the first show it was a kind of riot in the theatre. I even saw one gentleman who was trying to light a newspaper to set fire to the theatre and prevent them from showing such a piece of trash. And I came to the conclusion that the film was at least a very controversial one. That hurt me very deeply—I was so surprised. I didn't shoot La Règle du Jeu with the idea of being a revolutionary. It was a big surprise and a bad one.

The picture is shown now in its complete version. There is only one scene missing, in which I (as Octave) am walking with Toutain during the hunting party. I'm trying to make him forget about his unhappy love, and I explain that the only women who should interest a man like him, a gentleman, are servants. Choose your mistresses among servants, I say.

One day in Hollywood I read a review of a book by Rumer Godden which ran something like this: "This is one of the best written English books of the last fifty years: it probably won't earn one penny." I thought well, that's a wonderful review, I must read it. I bought the book, I read it, and I understood right away that it had great possibilities for a film. I got in touch with Rumer Godden and asked her publisher to give me an option. Meanwhile, a man I didn't then know was trying to make pictures in India because he had money there. One day this man was travelling in an aeroplane, sitting next to a very charming Indian lady who asked him what he was doing in India. When he told her he was going to make Indian films, she said, "You won't. You may get a picture on a piece of celluloid, but you have to know India to talk about India." This statement was so logical that he was impressed, and asked what he ought to do. She suggested that he should tell an Indian story seen through the eyes of Westerners, so that you would approach India through an intermediary, and mentioned Rumer Godden's *The River*. He'd never heard of the book; he'd never heard of Rumer Godden; but he was impressed by the lady and asked her who she was. She was Nehru's sister. He went to the publisher to try to get the rights to the book, and was told that an option had been sold to a certain Jean Renoir. "Who is Jean Renoir?" he asked. Eventually he asked me if he could buy the option. I told him I wanted to make the film, and he said, "Well, if you're so stubborn, let's shoot it together." So we started. I must add that before meeting him I had visited every studio in Hollywood, even in Paris, trying to find a producer, and everyone answered very wisely: "A picture in India without Bengal Lancers, elephants or a tiger will never make one penny." I tried very hard to see if I could have tigers . . . but it didn't work. Finally I found this man who produced the picture, United Artists took it, and it was very successful.

Quite late I discovered a marvellous method which I owe to Louis Jouvet and Michel Simon, who used to apply it on the stage. It was well known up to the romantic period, and it's called the Italian method—*à l'italienne*. You sit down around a table with the actors, and you read the dialogue exactly as though you were reading the telephone directory: no expression, absolutely blank. You forbid them to give any expression, and you must be very severe, because any actor instinctively wants to give an expression before knowing what it's all about. You read a scene about a mother witnessing the death of her child, for instance. The first reaction of the actress playing the mother would probably be tears. We're surrounded by clichés, and for many actors it's as though they had a little chest-of-drawers, with an answer to a question in each drawer. Drawer number three—"Mother witnessing death of child": and you apply the answer. But if you read the lines without any expression, this forces the actor to absorb them; and all of a sudden—you see them spark. One of the actors has a kind of feeling which is going to lead him towards an interpretation of the part which is not a cliché. It will be his own interpretation, having nothing to do with what was done before.

For instance, with Michel Simon this is the way we discovered Boudu: by reading, reading, reading. One day, without realising it, almost in spite of himself, Michel started reading with the voice of Boudu. I told him, "Here we are, we've got the part." And out in the courtyard, he was walking like Boudu. A Boudu I didn't expect. I didn't know this Boudu five minutes before. This Boudu was new, a creation by Michel Simon, and perhaps a little bit by myself, not the Boudu which had been done a hundred times on the stage.

I hate dubbing. I even believe that in a period of high civilisation, like the twelfth century, if people had done dubbing in films they would have been burned in the public square for pretending that man may have one body and two souls.

Renoir at Home: Interview

LEO BRAUDY/1970

In September of 1970, after I had finished a first draft of *Jean Renoir: The World of His Films* and felt completely steeped in his work, I went to Beverly Hills to interview the man himself. Beyond the pleasure of meeting him after having spent so much time with his films, I wanted to track down some of the more elusive facts about his life and career, and try to get his own sense of the continuity of his films and preoccupations. He and his wife Dido lived near the top of one of those twisty roads that snake up the hills behind Beverly Hills and Bel Air, no names on the mailboxes. Whatever question I might have had about the great French director living in Los Angeles vanished when I saw the house.

There was a beautiful view from the back terrace, even a laurel tree, and the whole atmosphere was like a California version of the Provence around Les Collettes, the farmhouse where, along with Paris, he had grown up. Basically bare wood floors with Oriental rugs on them. White painted brick walls. Even the modern comfortable furniture seemed to fit in with the portrait of the young Jean in hunting outfit painted by his father, the large bust of his mother, and some of his ceramics from his pre-film years. The interview lasted a few hours and ranged widely over whatever subject took our fancy. I did manage to collect some new facts, as well as a few pithy aphorisms to quote in the book. But the interview itself has never been printed. I've put together some intriguing chunks of it here both as an homage to Renoir in the

Reprinted from *Film Quarterly*, 50.1 (Fall 1996), pp. 2–8, by permission. Copyright © 1966 by The Regents of the University of California.

102nd anniversary of his birth and as a testament to the continuing vitality of his work.

Renoir is wearing green khaki pants, the crotch very low, a long beige cloth coat slung around him, a whitish shirt buttoned at the neck, powder-blue socks, and yellowish-brown moccasins. Dido seems perhaps in her early fifties, lithe and active, brown complexion, wearing beige ski pants and a white sheer cotton blouse. She is very solicitous about him, and gently satiric as well. When he is about to autograph my copy of *Renoir mon père*, for which he puts on dark-rimmed glasses, she jokes, "Now, Jean, where is your pen? Do you remember how to spell Mr. Braudy's name?"

Renoir still seems very vital and quick, although he does forget things, or so it seems. It's a strange feeling, to meet someone in whose work you've been immersed and that you know so well. When his memory slips, it's as if he's forgotten his lines. But why should he remember details, all equally immediate to me, many distant to him?

In terms of ideas and wit, he is fine. A lot of his pauses seem due to his imperfect English, a search for the appropriate word. He looks somewhat shrunken from the bear-like presence of his prime (when Jean Gabin called him "Le Gros"), as if he now has a wooden hanger inside his coat. His nose is veined, and dark on one side, perhaps from a recently broken blood vessel. One of his eyes is more closed than the other—the result of a minor stroke? He doesn't talk especially slowly, except in pausing to formulate ideas he wants to get across. I can see how in more robust days his pauses would have been taken as a kind of solidity, not the vagueness one might now—because of his age—assume they were.

He says he is sorry he had asked me ahead of time not to use the tape recorder, but whenever he heard himself speaking English, he blushed. He is very solicitous to make sure he isn't talking too fast, looking down at my pen to see if I have come to a stop. He always has something more to say, and I often find myself asking another question that turns out to be an interruption, because he is about to elaborate on his previous response. And he doesn't really repeat himself very much, unlike Hitchcock, for instance, whose interviews always feature the same handful of anecdotes and formulations.

Despite some apparent disability from his WWI leg wound and his present age, he shuffles and shambles around the house with a jaunty air, not seeming to take much deliberate control over his movements. When he wants to stand up just before I leave, he asks me to hold the small pewter cup that contains his sherry, because he can't get out of the chair while holding it.

As we're talking, he points to where I have rested my drink on a magazine and asks me if I'm married. "It's the act of a married man, whenever he has a drink in his hand, to worry if there are any coasters around." The kind of detail he's so good at. He asks me what I am going to do afterward, and I say I'm going to San Francisco to see my sister and her new baby. And he visibly brightens up, gives a big smile, almost a Renoir cliché. Later Dido asks the same thing, and I mention visiting my sister and my aunts. She says, "So this is a family trip and to your family you've added Jean Renoir." Not to be outdone in compliments, I say, "No, I have Jean Renoir and to him I've added my family." They both smile, although I'm not sure of the difference in meaning and perhaps it just appeals to their sense of humane symmetry.

When I leave, he shakes hands many times, says to send along any questions I've missed and also to tell him next time that it would take so long, that it was such an important interview. He keeps saying I have a whole book there.

LEO BRAUDY: *Did you use the canvasses left to you by your father as a cushion against financial problems, so that you could be more free in your film-making?*

JEAN RENOIR: When I did use them, I used them unwillingly. When I made movies, my only idea was to be successful, to deliver the goods. In spite of myself I was attracted to certain subjects and ways of treating them. I was never entirely successful with business. Since I had the paintings, practically I was more free than the actors, who had no money at all. But I didn't think of it.

LB: *When you sit here among the paintings by your father that you still keep, do you ever think of the contrast between your young painted self in the blue hunter's suit and your older self sitting in front of the painting?*

JR: I don't like to mix emotions with plastic arts. I'm trying to enjoy them without any sentimental feeling.

LB: *One touch that I like very much in* La Chienne *is the Renoir that the two* clochards *are admiring in the gallery window toward the end of the film.*
JR: It happened that it was there and I used it. . . . You know, I must not exaggerate commercial problems. Outside of the fight over *La Chienne* and some trouble with my early talking pictures, I always managed to shoot what I wanted.

LB: *Your own work begins with a more epic canvas and then later in your career you become more interested in pastoral. It's the reverse of what the Renaissance thought was the normal progression for artists: from pastoral beginnings to epic maturity.*
JR: If I didn't try to produce epic films after a certain period, it's mainly because I wasn't confronted with subjects of an epic value. In a way, both of my war films, *La grande illusion* in 1937 and *Le Caporal épinglé* in 1962, are about war prisoners. I started telling the story the same way. Then in the process of making the film not only the subject changed but my mind changed as well.

The 1939 war was not an epic war. It was a war of jails, a war of pro-paganda, a war of cruelty. It was a war for people who weren't the size of the people in the First World War. The people in that war were like knights during a crusade of the 12th century or characters from an episode in Virgil. The 1939 period gives us characters who are more petit-bourgeois. They have greatness of their own, of course, but a dif-ferent style of greatness. The war of 1939 was not a war of epic person-ages. I tried to convey its special quality by a scene in *Le Caporal épinglé* in which the character Ballochet, played by Claude Rich, sits on a toilet and, while fulfilling his natural processes, tells the corporal, Jean-Pierre Cassel, of his dreams to be a hero, and how they have failed.

LB: *You wrote in* Renoir My Father *that your father would have been horri-fied if any of his sons grew up to be a hero.*
JR: He would have believed he was horrified. My father believed firmly that you never act as you plan. Without being an existentialist, he believed, and I believe—perhaps by imitation—that action always

precedes the plan. People are always heroes by accident. There is an unconscious force that makes a certain individual born a hero. In our blueprint civilization, essence is always supposed to precede existence. But I think it was a very intelligent move of Sartre's to insist on the opposite, that existence precedes essence.

LB: *Do we need these accidental heroes today?*

JR: Today it would be a good thing to have more heroes. We need them. And they would probably be very ordinary people. I knew a few people close to being heroes in the First World War, when I was in the Air Force. Guynemer [the French flying ace of World War I], he was one. He was possessed by a kind of strength he didn't really understand. He went off shooting down innumerable planes in a kind of frenzy, perhaps forgetting that there were human beings inside the planes. There's always a kind of inhumanity about heroism. The Garden of Eden had a population of non-heroes.

LB: *What about those people who assume the exterior of heroes, but don't have the insides, who use the panoply of heroism just to impose on others?*

JR: Most real heroes don't look like heroes. The heroic look is a cliché. Gabin [in *La grande illusion*] does not have the appearance of a hero. He's just a man who does his job, without following any theory. Heroes act in a certain way because it's their function, it's their job, to act that way.

The real reason for any picture is to explain a character who is following out his destiny. Boeldieu, the character played by Pierre Fresnay in *La grande illusion*, isn't a hero in that sense. He is a man who thinks in terms of his caste, his cavalry upbringing. When he puts on white gloves before he is to distract Stroheim so that Gabin and Dalio can escape, Gabin doesn't understand. Why the ceremony?, he wonders. My father would have been with Gabin.

LB: *So Boeldieu needs the proper gloves in order to feel he's doing something heroic?*

JR: Yes, and clothing is an important proposition to remember in writing for the screen. We have a saying in French, *l'habit fait le moine*—"the garment makes the man." It's a true saying, but only in a superficial way. If a man becomes a hero wearing the outfit of a hero, it proves that he had something inside he didn't guess was there. His action and the surrounding circumstances make it authentic.

In pictures and real life I hate what we call psychology. I believe so much that we are influenced by our surroundings. The study of the soul of someone living on such and such a street means nothing to me. Every bit in a human being is produced by heredity and surroundings.

The best director in our days—someone who amazed me with his feeling for picturesque locations and strange characters—that's Orson Welles. He's a great creator. The idea of a tycoon is not the same, can't be the same, after *Citizen Kane*. *Citizen Kane* is not what we read before about such people. It is a work that is really due to the observation of the real world and on the other hand it is the complete creation of Orson Welles.

LB: *But with all his troubles, Welles has not managed to make as many films as you.*

JR: But he keeps up the fight against the cliché. That's why he has so much financial trouble. Chaplin has the same ability, only in a different style. The fact that Orson Welles and Chaplin didn't work in Hollywood for a long time was very bad for Hollywood. It was a terrible mistake. Orson Welles represents a case of pure Americanism, but influenced by some Europeans. He brought to Hollywood the idea of a particular world.

LB: *I have always especially liked the way in your films when you're in danger of becoming too solemn, you do something funny or ironic, and when you're in danger of becoming too comic and frivolous, you interject something serious.*

JR: I try to be clever about that. In each film, you discover it slowly: the proper balance. Usually I start on my pictures with the possibility of contrast or of telling a story that is absolutely real but unbelievable in some aspect. I'm terribly attracted by what seems unusual but difficult to understand, not difficult because of the plot but because of the complexity of characters. I try to work close to nature—but nature is millions of things and there are millions of ways of understanding its propositions.

Perhaps one of the things that pushed me to make a film like *La Marseillaise* was to destroy the cliché that people who are possessed by a great idea are necessarily very serious people who speak with a certain dignity and present a certain figure to their followers. Instead I tried to be a witness of the daily life of the participants of a great tragedy. It's hard for an English-speaking audience to get, but I purposely made all the characters speak in very common language. For instance, at the end of the career and almost the life of Louis XVI, he discovers that tomatoes are a very nice vegetable, and he's sorry he hasn't known them before.

What is interesting about the cliché is that you can use it willingly as a frame. Inside, the characters don't follow the cliché. Outside, then, it doesn't matter. But it sets them up.

LB: *That remark reminds me of the way* La Chienne, Le Carrosse d'or, *and* Le petit théâtre de Jean Renoir *all begin with the frame of a proscenium arch or theatre curtains.*

JR: The first episode in *Le petit théâtre* is deliberately a cliché. I was very careful to have a set that looked like a set. It was necessary to have a lot of cardboard and makeup in this story of a beggar and his dreams.

LB: *So the frame is like the clothes on a hero, the habit on a monk?*

JR: Let me give you an example. Suppose a director or producer is casting the part of a sailor. A normal bad actor would work hard in order to have the real costume, the real walk, the real language of a sailor. Perhaps he will even take a trip on a boat to be burned by the real wind of the sea. Perhaps he will buy a real sailor coat from a real sailor. As a result, he will look like a real ham. Let's now try Chaplin as a sailor. He will arrive with derby, little cane, big shoes. But inside he'll be so much a real sailor that he'll be convincing despite the fact that his costume isn't right.

LB: *Doesn't this qualify your long admiration for Stroheim? He was so crazy about clothing detail that he spent enormous amounts to get his actors the right period underwear.*

JR: Even Stroheim's mistakes are interesting. The big problem for a film-maker is the part you must give to the outside truth and the part to the inside truth. The inside should be the only important one.

LB: *What then do you think of General Rolland, the character played by Jean Marais in* Eléna et les hommes?

JR: He's a very weak man. He is the selfish, rich man who likes any kind of adventure under one condition: that it can't harm him. He's too careful to get into anything serious. The real hero of *Eléna* is Elena herself. The kind of hero I admire, who is basically good, is La Chesnaye in *Rules of the Game*. And that whole movie is a result of my belief that we are living in a century of compromises.

LB: *Norman Mailer once described the film director as a kind of general deploying his forces. . . .*

JR: Too many directors think of themselves that way. They are generals who tell the trees to go over there, the people over there, the sets over there. But a director must absorb things, not keep them at a distance.

LB: *In* Le Caporal épinglé, *what does* épinglé *signify?*

JR: It's "pinned"—an allusion to butterflies pinned through the stomach onto a board.

LB: *That's what I thought. But that seems the opposite of the English title.*

JR: It is unfortunately opposite. We couldn't get a good translation for "the pinned-up corporal." "The pin-up corporal" didn't work. So *The Elusive Corporal* was the only one anyone came up with.

LB: *The English title makes it seem as if the film is about escapes and freedom, when it's actually about boundaries and limits.*

JR: Aren't they the great themes, the great facts, of our time?

Q & A: Jean Renoir

DIGBY DIEHL/1972

Jean Renoir, the famed director of 37 French and American films, was born in Paris on September 15, 1894. His life and experience reach back into an era of personal artistic vision and humanistic expression personified by his father, the great French Impressionist painter, Pierre Auguste Renoir. And it is the richness of this philosophical outlook which has made Renoir a seminal influence for contemporary film makers and students of the cinema.

In his films, even more than in his book *Renoir, My Father*, Renoir pays filial tribute to the artistic heritage which has made him, too, a painter in light. After early starts as a ceramicist and a journalist, he found himself convalescing from a World War I leg wound by constantly going to the movies. His growing fascination with film culminated with a first effort in 1924, *La fille de l'eau*. But it was his adaptation of Emile Zola's classic novel, *Nana*, which established his unquestionable talent as a director. French historian Georges Sadoul has described this as ". . . one of the best French films of the later '20s, rich in its combination of the pictorial inheritance of Impressionism and the realism of Zola's naturalist tradition."

Throughout the '30s Renoir's sense of visual poetry embodying humanistic themes set the pace for French film making. *La Chienne* (1931), *La Nuit du Carrefour* (1932), *Madame Bovary* (1933), *Boudu Sauvé Des Eaux* (1933), *Toni* (1935), *Le Crime De M. Lange* (1936), *La Marseillaise* (1938), *La Bête Humaine* (1938), and *La Règle du Jeu* (1939) dramatically

From *Los Angeles Times West Magazine*, 16 April 1972, pp. 32–38. Reprinted by permission of Digby Diehl.

captured social and cultural movements in France during that period, despite the historical settings and fictional plots of most of these works.

In *La Grande Illusion* (1937), Renoir focused all of his accumulated cinematic power upon the theme of men at war. Within the confines of a prisoner of war camp where French and English of all classes learn to confront themselves and their German captors, we are confronted with Renoir's continuing fascination with the themes of liberty and freedom as well as the futility of war. It was the first unheroic war film without violence and glory—it shows the pathos of men caught up in that grand illusion of the War to End All Wars.

With the German occupation of France in 1940, Renoir fled to the United States and has resided here since. He was one of the few European directors who seemed to be adaptable enough to survive in the unfamiliar atmosphere of Hollywood. Here he directed *Swamp Water* (1941), *This Land is Mine* (1943), *The Southerner* (1945), *Diary of a Chambermaid* (1946), *Woman on the Beach* (1946), and for the Theatre Guild he directed *The River* on the banks of the Ganges in India in 1951. More recently, Renoir has made several fine films, such as *Picnic on the Grass* (1960), which was derived from the famous painting by Manet that outraged art critics in 1863, and *The Elusive Corporal* (1962), which might be considered a World War II remake of *La Grande Illusion*.

Despite a recent illness, Renoir and his charming wife Dido sparkled with French hospitality and conversation rich with philosophy, cinematic observations, and reminiscences when I spent several evenings with them in their Beverly Hills home, which is decorated, appropriately enough, with a wall-to-wall, one-man show of his father's vivid visions of life.

Q: *You have said that Hollywood is destroying creativity in film directors and that they no longer have rapport with the audiences. Why?*
RENOIR: The film industry wants perfection. Perfection is really extremely boring. But they sacrifice anything for perfection; they sacrifice the meaning of the story. They sacrifice even the performance of the actors for technical perfection. It would be better to start with directors who have something to say. But today most directors have

nothing to say. It doesn't matter if you say nothing as long as you say it perfectly. A production which is the work of a crew, or a gang, is very difficult. And when it is a gang that's good, that picture will be tied together. But usually a production is the work of people who don't know each other.

The author of the book doesn't know the author of the screenplay. The author of the screenplay doesn't know the director. The most that will happen is that they meet in a club in an evening for a drink. But it's not a collaboration. It should be a real collaboration, from the beginning to the end. Many directors don't cut their own pictures. In Europe we had—we still have—more personal films. A film had the feeling, the expression of a director, and he had invested most of the money. Now, with many people putting up money, that many more people "own" the film and have a say in production.

Q: *I know you are against "message films," but how do you distinguish between a message film and one of personal commitment?*
RENOIR: In what I would call a director's film the actor is the most important element in fulfilling the director's personal vision. But a film that doesn't reflect a personal vision is a producer's film, one in which the producer chooses the film, director, style and actors. The best kind of film is one authored by the director. That's the way I work.

Q: *You've always believed a director should control every element of the film. Would you explain this auteur theory of film making?*
RENOIR: Creativity is a meeting, a conversation. When you listen to a symphony by Mozart, that is a conversation with Mozart. If you kill this spirit of conversation, you kill the picture, you kill the music, you kill everything. This has been a problem for a long time in Hollywood. They ignore creativity by giving you a script which has to be approved by 20 people. But what interests me is what a director has to say. In this conversation, this dialogue between director and viewer, there is so much that is intuitive and not spoken. And the public must be coauthor. It must have the feeling that it made the picture. And the picture must be shown only to people who agree. It must be shown to people who know your language.

Q: *But aren't you negating the concept of art as a medium for persuading audiences, changing points of view?*
RENOIR: No, because the artist must be patient. If he's a real artist, in the beginning he will be followed by a half a dozen people, and eventually he will earn international acclaim. Many people now understand my language, my style. Now, I think the *auteur* concept of film making is pretty much taken for granted all over the world as a necessity.

Q: *One time you spoke of* Grand Illusion *as a "structured documentary" and, of course, since then you've done many documentaries.*
RENOIR: To me, when you say a documentary, that means you're working on documents. That means an absolute way of life. For instance—do you know my picture *The Human Beast?* Well, part of my picture is a documentary of the railroad. The documentary helped the romance.

Q: *Where did you get the idea for* Grand Illusion?
RENOIR: I was in the First Cavalry and the Air Force during World War I. My experience covered a big field. In the Air Force I piloted a plane with a photographer taking pictures of the German lines. We were often attacked by the Germans, who weren't very happy that we were taking pictures, and we were saved three or four times by a French pilot named Adjutant Pinsard who belonged to a squadron nearby. He had the typical image of the handsome noncom of the Hussars—a beautiful moustache, hair with *cosmetique.*

Many years later I was shooting a picture called *Toni* in southern France. We were disturbed by a pilot from a big air base who was diving to see us shoot the picture. I decided to pay a visit to the base commander. When the door opened, it was my friend Pinsard. He had become a general. Of course, he told me I would no longer be disturbed by his airplane. And while I wasn't shooting, we would have dinner together and he would tell me stories of his war adventures. He was shot down by the Germans seven times and escaped seven times. I wrote a short outline, so as not to forget the stories. However, I was shooting something else at the time. My first script was completed with the help of Charles Spaak.

Q: *How long was it in the planning stage?*

RENOIR: I got in touch with every producer in Europe and in America; no one wanted it. I tried to find a producer for two years. I had hoped to use Jean Gabin. He'd been very successful in one of my films, *The Lower Depths,* taken from Gorky, and he had the influence of a star. So Gabin became a producer with me. He was very devoted.

Q: *Were the producers afraid of it because of the subject matter?*

RENOIR: It was that the conception of the war didn't fit in with their own conceptions. There was a controversy over the numerous war pictures with heroes and heroes. But I thought there could be heroes without singing about it. And also, they didn't like my refusal to use the spectacular side of the war. My heroes were very close to the models. I knew a Gabin, another Gabin, who was a colonel; that became the character for Gabin. The script was expressing a certain sense of reality that terrified producers.

Q: *I thought the scene in which you showed the emotions of finding the women's clothing expressed genuine aspects of war that weren't shown in that period.*

RENOIR: No, I don't believe that it existed in any other picture. It was one of the stories the general told me. In the beginning, the picture was for me just an escape story. While I was working on the script, and shooting it, I discovered more about it. I learned that a prison is a wonderful place to make men work together on characters. It was an occasion to show people in the army as they were. And I did it very much like a documentary picture. For instance, we open on the commissary. The set was a duplicate of the commissary of my own squadron. The military uniform that Gabin was wearing was my own.

Q: *What was the approximate budget for* Grand Illusion?

RENOIR: I've forgotten, really. The picture helped the actors in the picture to become stars. Erich Von Stroheim became a star in Europe. He wasn't known before. Also, the picture was shot before directors were asking high salaries. If I translated it into modern terms, I could say that it cost a half a million dollars.

Q: *It's amazing the production values you got—*

RENOIR: We took advantage of many things, for instance the second prison. The old castle. The castle was not really old. It was built as a copy of a medieval castle. And we shot everything there. The location was Alsace because it is very German, and it was the start of the war. Alsace is a state, a province, which was constantly caught between France and Germany. In a certain part you are in Germany and in another part you are in France. Some of the people in Alsace speak German. We used the inhabitants of the village who had served in the German army, and they were very good German soldiers, and very good bit players. They were paid only a few pennies.

Q: *When you work with that sort of thing, using available materials, you get a certain flavor.*

RENOIR: Yes. When I wanted to film a dog fight, the producer told me, "That's too expensive, you cannot afford it." So I was forced to describe the fight in three words. It came out in a far more interesting manner than an actual fight.

Q: *Yes, and then, of course, that segment where all of the men are in the window looking down at the marching band. It's effective to see their faces, their reactions.*

RENOIR: I think it's a way to have audiences participate in the making of the picture. You know, something which was very difficult to me came out quite nicely. It was the character of the cavalry officer. You know, even in France, certain accents are unnatural. Certain accents mean, "I'm superior to the rest of the world."

Q: *I meant to ask you why they were speaking English.*

RENOIR: It's sort of an aristocratic tradition, probably coming from the horse races. The first horse races were an English affair, and of course, the French aristocrats would come to them.

Q: *Boeldieu is not empathetic until he and Von Stroheim have that conversation about the days before they were officers. That scene is remarkably warm.*

RENOIR: I treated it the same as I would have treated a love scene. I felt that this friendship between this German and the Frenchman was a kind of love affair.

Q: *I have the same feeling when Von Stroheim comes back and says, "I beg you to come back, I'm going to have to shoot you."*
RENOIR: I asked him to give it the feeling of a lover begging his mistress not to leave him.

Q: *I gather that getting on with some fairly sensitive actors like Von Stroheim is a testament to the fact that you were very generous and easy to work with; otherwise, I can imagine how explosive that kind of relationship could have been.*
RENOIR: He was a nuisance in the beginning. After two or three days, I took him aside, and said, "Erich, I have such great admiration for you, but I don't want to fight with you. If you don't follow my ideas concerning this picture, which is my story, a story you don't know anything about, I'll just quit." He changed and became the most devoted actor I ever had.

Q: *I think you mentioned that it was his idea to do that funny puffing cigarette, the thing that Arte Johnson does as a symbol of Prussian aristocracy. Was it his idea to have the collar and brace also?*
RENOIR: It was in the directions of the script, but not exactly as it turned out. What was good about Von Stroheim was that he understood that he should act in contrast with Fresnais. A big part of the picture deals with the contrast between the two men. The story is many things, but most of it is the story of Von Stroheim and Fresnais.

Q: *Especially that scene in which they are sitting in the window, talking about the old days before the war.*
RENOIR: Don't you think their time is over? Von Stroheim says, "Don't you think it's too bad?" and Fresnais says, "Perhaps."

Q: *You were talking about how the film is shaped by the actors that you have, playing those roles.*
RENOIR: Yes. Each time I see the picture, I'm impressed by one idea. It is that you don't do anything with bad actors. Now, everyone considers *Grand Illusion* as good, so that's all right, but I know that I owe so much to the actors.

Q: *You have said that your ideal picture would be one long take.*
RENOIR: That's what the new director Andy Warhol does. I don't
believe very much in the improvement given a picture in the cutting
room. The film industry makes cutting room pictures. The trick is
to shoot more or to cut a different picture in the cutting room. But
I believe that an actor gives me a much more moving progression if
the progression comes from his own feeling and not from the
cutting room.

Q: *Nowadays, that fast cut with the constantly changing point of view—*
RENOIR: I did it 40 years ago.

Q: *But you think it's better to catch the actor from one space than from different angles. One scene that's a good example is one in which you're really
tight on a group of actors, then you pull back a little so two people walk by
carrying bottles of wine, then you move in again and there's a different conversation going on.*
RENOIR: That's the way it should be. The way it happens is one; ideally,
the picture in the cinema should be one long take. I'm trying not to cut.

Q: *But isn't there a cinematic vitality that can be generated by rapidly shift-
ing scenes?*
RENOIR: Perhaps so, but it is my feeling that the extended dramatic
interplay between the actors and the building up of emotional relationships that are sustained on camera make a film great. The actors have to
express themselves. They must bring to their roles a reality of emotional feeling that cannot be built up by jumping from scene to scene
in a series of short takes. This is why I feel so strongly that a director
must have good actors and give them freedom.

Q: *And that theory fits in well with your theories of spontaneity and
improvisation in working with the actors in your films.*
RENOIR: Yes. It's the same thing with any project. The project begins
and you start believing that this project is your whole life. You begin
changing things spontaneously because things don't work out as you
thought they would. What is dangerous to our civilization is the blueprint. Too many people mindlessly follow that blueprint and they fail

to realize that the world is changing around them. When the potter was making dishes by hand, each dish was a work of art. Each dish was an expression of the soul of the potter. Now we work with computers and dishes come out of a machine. I may change something 10 times in my films because I'm confounded by something with which I've never been confronted. People think I like to improvise. I don't like to improvise; I like to have things terribly precise. But I am forced to change elements of a film as I'm working.

In movie making sometimes the thing that is unexpected is better than the thing that was planned. The scene on the mountain in the snow in *Grand Illusion* is much better than what I had planned. I had written 30 pages which I thought were beautiful. But when we arrived on the mountain, it started snowing. The actors were freezing that day and men who are freezing don't act like men who are comfortable in the studio. The whole scene had a new life-improvised feeling.

Q: *As you mentioned, most directors who make their films with personal commitments—such as Bergman, Fellini and Truffaut—are European. Do you respect any American directors?*

RENOIR: To me one of the best directors in the world is John Ford. He is amazing. He worked all the time, and I don't know how he did it. But, of course, John Ford is the triumph of the Hollywood system. He has made it work for him. I couldn't work in it; I don't know how it works.

Q: *What do you think of Ingmar Bergman's films?*

RENOIR: Bergman is a great man, but he is more than a great man to me. He is the only film organizer who works logically. He is not the victim of an economic situation because his films don't cost money. He has a contract with the Royal Theater. Thus, his actors are also stage actors so they have enough money on which to live. They don't make a fortune, but they can make films without things being too difficult. To be able to make a film is a terrible fight, because you have to convince so many people and you quickly become tired of convincing people.

Q: *Apparently, half the job is the fund-raising when you make a film.*

RENOIR: Yes. I admire Bergman because he can be successful commercially and yet make a film to which he can sign his own name.

Q: *But I think Bergman has said many times that his first love was really the stage. How do you feel about the theater?*

RENOIR: Well, in the beginning of my career, I hated the stage. I couldn't bear the artificial way the actors were working. It went against my imagination. The older I get, the more I understand the possible greatness of stylization. And because of that I came back to the stage with enthusiasm. Now I love it.

Q: *Mainly because of a feeling for stylization, rather than a feeling that you can accept the artifice?*

RENOIR: Yes. I began to enjoy theater more when I understood that any artist builds his own inner world. When Chaplin made *Monsieur Verdoux,* critics said to me, "Oh, it's no good. It's supposed to be set in France; France is not like that." My answer was, "It isn't supposed to be set in France; it's set in the Chaplin world. That's a kingdom, very special. With special rules and special ways." For Bergman, there is also a Bergman world. But I believe that the tools that the theater gives you are easier to build this inner world with than the tools that the cinema gives you. The cinema always has its eye on the realistic photograph of everything. Outside reality is almost non-existent on the stage. No attempt at realism. On the stage, the world is never real.

Q: *But you have said that you think reality is magical.*

RENOIR: Yes, it is. But on one condition: you must translate it. Reality may be very interesting, but a work of art must be a creation. If you copy nature without adding the influence of your own personality, it is not a work of art. A work of art becomes even more important when it is finished, when the artist is added to the reality, which often disappears entirely. Reality is merely a springboard for the artist.

Q: *I'm not sure I understand. For example, on the stage, you don't use reality at all. It is a cardboard world, an imitation of reality.*

RENOIR: Which to me would be real.

Q: *Because you accept the fact that everything is an artifice?*

RENOIR: I don't accept anything. I'm here as a witness to an action which takes place in a world, which is not the real world. And to me, it is a real action. The artifice makes the action more pure, more naked. In the movies it would be foolish to neglect what we call mere reality. We must start a film by studying the reality of the actors and the surroundings. But the final result must not be reality. It must only be what the actors and the director or author of the film selected of reality to reveal.

Q: *What, in your view, is the purpose of film? Some people say that it is to entertain. Others say it is to educate.*
RENOIR: I believe that film and books and paintings are necessities because they are representations of life. When people were living in caves they started to represent the life around them by drawing on the walls. Later they took these representations onto the stage. So it seems to me that cinema is just the latest form of the need of human beings to present the reality around them.

Q: *And to take that reality and transform it into a kind of human vision?*
RENOIR: It is necessary for the propagation of the world because it is the film which is influenced by the surroundings, but also the world which is influenced by the movies or by any form of art.

Q: *Are you saying that the films being made today actually influence the world in ways that we can see?*
RENOIR: Yes. The influence of any art on the surroundings is evident to me. I think the influence of *Bonnie and Clyde* was only in the way to wear a certain dress. That's true, but a certain dress influences the body and the mind. You know that is why armies give uniforms to the soldiers.

Q: *You mean it influences the way they think about themselves, the way they operate?*
RENOIR: Yes. You give a uniform and a flag to a man, and perhaps he'll be a hero. But I don't think that the influence of films brings about violence. The world was violent before the movies were violent. And I even believe that film violence could act like medicine. If you see violence on the screen, it could stop violence in the streets.

Q: *Are you suggesting that there isn't any particular danger in showing violence or sex on the screen?*

RENOIR: I believe that there might be a danger, but not the kind which changes the habits of the entire world.

Q: *You have never really had much sex or violence in your films.*

RENOIR: No, it is evident that the murders that I have had in my movies have been forgotten. I don't see violent films because they bore me. I hate violence, and I don't think I should pay to see violence. It would be terrible. I have a theory about the use of violence in a film and violence in life. It is just the natural movement of balance. The world is in balance. And we are constantly trying to keep the two sides of the balance equal. But we cannot. If we put something on one side, somebody puts something else on the other side. For two centuries, the United States experienced a period of very severe puritanism. Now, to balance, we have the opposite.

Q: *But is either extreme particularly good? Can't you find a middle way?*

RENOIR: True. But the middle way is not often found. The middle was easier to find before all of our technical improvements. When the body of the artist was playing a bigger part, his hands, for instance. I'll give you a simple example. If you love music, and you get a Gramophone and a record, you can get a most beautiful piece by Mozart, conducted by the most wonderful conductor—and you enjoy Mozart completely. In the old days, if you liked music, you couldn't hear Mozart. You had to buy a flute, a two-penny flute, and play for yourself. Now, which is the best way to enjoy music: to be a witness to the masterpiece, or to be a participant in the creation of the music? That is the question.

Q: *What would you choose?*

RENOIR: I would choose the flute. And in the days of the flute, the balance was easier to find. Because probabilities of chance would bring about an evolution of human beings—in our brains, our bodies, our hands. But it was difficult to absorb, in only half a century, all the art which was produced over thousands and thousands of years, which is exactly what we try to do now. In other words, I believe that the way to be happy is to create. When you do something, especially with your hands, you are happy. And the beauty of civilization was giving to human beings so many possibilities to achieve something. Something humble, but something. Now, we are deprived of the joy of creating. If we love good cooking, we open a can. If we love travel, we have TV or movies. We don't have to travel.

Q: *It's all provided for us by technology.*
RENOIR: Yes. The Africa shown in the paintings of Henri Rousseau is more real than the real Africa. The personal vision of Rousseau's Africa interests me more than a beautiful photograph of a beautiful spot in Africa.

Q: *Having worked in French television, did you find it different from working in film?*
RENOIR: Yes, there is one difference—that you must be fast in your work. You cannot sleep on the job. Most people think TV shows are bad. I don't agree. Many of them, especially the westerns, are very good. They are as good as were the films of the "film noir" period, the '30s. The only thing bad about them is that they have to tell the same stories 100 times. A machine can be renewed, but the human brain cannot. In 100 years, 50 years, there should be a revolution in telling the same story in a different way.

Q: *But now aren't they telling them in the same way that films told them 30 years ago?*
RENOIR: But I am amazed. Several years ago, there was a TV show here, *The Untouchables*. It was as good as *Scarface* or *Little Caesar.*

Q: *Then why does it appear that films are being made better than television shows?*
RENOIR: There is a kind of optimism in the television show. A kind of life, which to me is very pleasant. When I say they're good, I'm exaggerating. They are possibly good with the sense of a movement of life, a moment of gaiety—which to me is the beauty of television.

Q: *Your father once said that each painter just painted for other painters. Do you think that directors create for other directors?*

RENOIR: Yes, that's very much what people do in a film. Every profession is in its own world. When you talk the language of the theater, you address the people of the theater world, because only they can see the nuances.

Q: *But film has become a mass art.*

RENOIR: The essential artist takes a narrow little world and makes it an enormous world. The artistic questions are just life questions. Everything interrelates—I try to point that out in my art. I believe very much in my "theory of the mandarin." When I was a small child I was told that by pushing a button I could kill a mandarin far on the other side of the world in China. Although you probably don't know any mandarins in China, you must realize that your killing him will matter greatly, because he is a human being, a part of the whole, who will be missed by the world. And in the ultimate sense, you who pushed the button will miss him, too. I sometimes think that in my whole career as a director I have made only one film—one film with 37 stories. And the theme of that life work is: everything interrelates—the world is one.

Renoir at 80

S C O T T   E Y M A N / 1 9 7 5

"All men who have created something of value did so not as inventors, but as catalyzers of existing forces as yet unknown to the common man among mortals. Great men are simply those who know how to comprehend."

—from Jean Renoir's *Renoir, My Father*

Inside Jean Renoir's unostentatious pink stucco house in Beverly Hills there are many paintings, most by Renoir's father, Auguste, and all revealing a taste for pastels that are almost fragrant in the lyric intensity of their colour. But, out of them all, there is only one that manipulates its space and controls its own seemingly massive environment—the abiding hallmark of all great art.

It is a large work, about three by five feet, and done mostly in shades of Royal Blue—a dark, luminous colour scheme that contrasts and accentuates the youthful freshness of the face it explores. The subject of the painting is a boy of perhaps fifteen years; he is standing, holding a rifle in one hand with the other hand poised delicately on his hip in what could be the conventional mannerism of the subtly arrogant but is more likely the common adolescent inability to control the body in an unobvious manner.

The eyes of the boy—mellow, tranquil and with a tangible glint of humour—stare back at you with the unashamed curiosity and frankness of the natural aristocrat. The boy's bearing embraces sophistication; his

From *Focus on Film*, 22 (Autumn 1975), pp. 36–37. Reprinted by permission of Scott Eyman.

eyes deny it. It is a warm portrait of a would-be bourgeois, done with diffused elegance and incomparable style; as with most of Auguste Renoir's work, the painting is a quietly orchestrated display of contemplative ecstasy. He adored his subjects and the love seeps through the canvas to rest inside us.

The portrait is called (with a tangible hint of irony) *The Huntsman*, and it is, indisputably, a portrait of Jean Renoir. So great was the father's insight into the son's character and personality that, despite the ravages of time and the passing of sixty-five years, it is instantly recognisable; Renoir's face still retains that air of inquisitive sensitivity and his eyes, those surpassingly gentle eyes, their lucidity and wit.

It is in this atmosphere of quiet laughter, dark woods, delicate nuances and serenely shaded sunlight that Renoir—eighty years old and very frail—has agreed to discuss his adventures in America and the underrated splendours of his American films, works whose circumstances of creation he discusses in selective detail in his new book *My Life and My Films*, works that constitute much-maligned, invaluable fragments in the enduring mosaic created by the greatest Grand Maître of the Cinema.

"I came to America because I had never been there before; I came to 20th Century-Fox because Darryl Zanuck was most persuasive and generous.

"Hollywood was more organised than what I was used to, but not a great deal. It was not the film-making system itself that was bad, anyway. In my opinion, it was the whole machine. What was wrong was that the aim of an industry is to make money. I always felt that there was something more, something which I always struggled to achieve: the desire for planned perfection.

"I believe in spontaneity, in the personality of the artist; not the final product, but the heart of the artist. Perfection comes before money, at least I always thought so. I feel that the studios were ruined looking for the impossible perfection of the perfect money-making machine.

"The difference is that in Hollywood it is an assembly line, and if an artist is twenty people, it is finished, individual creativity is gone. Nothing truly great can be created by committee."

When discussing Hollywood and how he found it, Renoir is by turn ruefully humorous and courteously proud. What he isn't—ever—is defensive, despite the vilifications heaped on him by the formerly kind

European critics of the day, who regarded his American work as a denial of the principles he espoused in Europe, and the inability of the American critics, who dismissed his films as "simple" and "naïve", to comprehend the translucent emotional expansiveness of his work.

"I know the critics—Georges Sadoul especially—felt that the war hurt me, disrupted my development as an artist. I respect their opinions, but I disagree. First of all, I don't think you can put a label of quality on a film as you can on a ham or a can of biscuits. I don't feel the war influenced my work one way or the other.

"No, I don't blame Sadoul or any other critic for feeling like that; at least, not any critic who cares. They do what they do out of love for the cinema and that should never be stifled.

"You see, my reputation hurt me everywhere and every time. If you are fortunate enough to make what people feel to be a great film, then each succeeding film is compared to it, even if they have nothing in common; people said that each film wasn't as good as the one that preceded it.

"People misinterpret. They think a man should do the same thing. They even misinterpret individual films. When *Rules of the Game* came out, people thought of it as an attack on the bourgeoisie. That's not true at all. Those people are indeed bourgeois, but they are elegant, they have style. That is their saving grace. I thought it might be interesting to do a film about poor people who also have style—that is how I came to make *Swamp Water*.

"Zanuck at first wanted me to shoot it entirely in the studio, but I convinced him to let me go on location for the exteriors—all the way to Georgia. Since, at that time, I couldn't speak very good English, Zanuck helped me with the casting and gave me an interpreter. That, and pidgin English, got me by. With some of the actors, it worked out better than with others. Walter Huston was wonderful, for instance. He knew instinctively what I wanted.

"Zanuck was mostly quite helpful. He gave me trouble about one thing only. I was working in long sequences, without a cut. This was not liked. They wanted what they called "protection" for the cutting room, so it would be easier for them to re-edit the way they wanted to. They did not understand that I did what I did out of style, not out of a desire to sabotage their editing. I simply felt that this was the most harmonious way of exploring the characters."

Perhaps Renoir's finest, most ignored film of this era is the shamefully unexplored *This Land Is Mine*, in which he fearlessly took on the Four Horsemen of the Forties: Death, Tyranny, Hitler and the redoubtable Charles Laughton.

This lovely humanist paean was castigated by critics of both left and right, the former because he dared make the heretofore Beastly Nazi into a more or less likeable, cultured man (this was ten years before Hathaway's *Desert Fox* with a Rommel out of a disillusioned college professor), the latter because he dared make a deeply felt, civilised tract which insisted, in the most direct terms imaginable, on the mutual humanity of man.

Specifically, James Agee's objections to the de-physicalisation of the totalitarian threat are certainly reasonable enough in the face of both the Fascist Ogre and our own matchless hindsight. What Agee didn't realise is there are many means of thought and people control and the continuing use of brute force is the least effective in the long term. Renoir, using a Smiler with a Knife like Walter Slezak, a continental actor of easy smiles and seldom-utilised intimations of depravity, was merely anticipating the smarmy mind manipulators of the masses that are now a regrettable daily fact of life. Being twenty-five years ahead of your time isn't at all bad.

"The spirit of man is a fragile set-up, you know. The collaborationists, about whom everybody seems so interested nowadays, collaborated mostly for only two reasons: those who did so because it was more convenient to do so than not; and those who thought of collaborating as heroic, as an outgrowth of their sophistication and elegance. That was the kind I used in the film, the lackadaisical effete like George Sanders. Men like that can kill themselves out of boredom.

"Laughton and I had small quarrels but only one large one. He was quite unreasonable about it, so I was too. He was supposed to be looking out of his prison cell and see a close friend shot by a firing squad. He complained that he couldn't do the scene because, when he looked out of the iron bars, all he could see was the back of another set!

"Laughton's character, the meek schoolteacher, fights against tyranny and for freedom in the only way he knows how. As a result, he dies—a hero, at least to me. To die for freedom is heroic, don't you think?"

In Jean Renoir's small universe (and this is his great talent: as a miniaturist of the soul), seemingly petty victories signal large triumphs. In *The Southerner*, along with *Swamp Water* Renoir's most popular American film, parity with nature is finally achieved only when a legendary and spectacularly pesky catfish is vanquished. The land giveth and the land taketh away; the crushing realism of the situations and the uninsistent lyricism that Renoir accords his characters, seemingly contradictory, are in reality the yin and the yang of Renoir's art. Neither could function successfully without the other.

"One thing I've learned about people—they are crazy for clichés. In *The Southerner*, I had a scene where a mother cries for her dead son. I wanted it restrained and quiet. Nobody liked it. If you try to be as true as possible, nobody will ever like it. If, on the other hand, you use clichés—tears pouring down her face, ruining her make-up, etc.—they will like it.

"But then everybody wears a mask anyway. Perhaps people see films to see how they would like to react, not how they actually do. Even children wear other people's masks until they develop one of their own.

"I always tried to do one thing when I was directing and that was to avoid typical movie situations. I analysed the situations the characters were in and tried to make as accurate and realistic a reaction as I could. Life is different from the movies, you know."

INDEX

CONVERSATIONS WITH FILMMAKERS SERIES
PETER BRUNETTE, GENERAL EDITOR

The collected interviews with notable modern directors, including

Robert Aldrich • Pedro Almodóvar • Robert Altman • Theo Angelopolous • Bernardo Bertolucci • Tim Burton • Jane Campion • Frank Capra • Charlie Chaplin • Francis Ford Coppola • George Cukor • Brian De Palma • Clint Eastwood • John Ford • Terry Gilliam • Jean-Luc Godard • Peter Greenaway • Alfred Hitchcock • John Huston • Jim Jarmusch • Elia Kazan • Stanley Kubrick • Fritz Lang • Spike Lee • Mike Leigh • George Lucas • Michael Powell • Martin Ritt • Carlos Saura • John Sayles • Martin Scorsese • Ridley Scott • Steven Soderbergh • Steven Spielberg • George Stevens • Oliver Stone • Quentin Tarantino • Lars von Trier • Orson Welles • Billy Wilder • Zhang Yimou • Fred Zinnemann